Michael Brown has written an impor
that one would have thought would
and the revulsion it produced agains
returned and found a home in the p
Michael Brown's book is a welcome
abandoned their faith to further this hateful cause.

—David Horowitz
Author, *Mortality and Faith*

Dr. Brown's book doesn't make for easy or pleasant reading, but his message is urgent and true. As the depravity of our materialistic culture deepens and the concrete results of rejecting faith and reason become more painfully obvious, the lazy will search for scapegoats. Instead of carefully analyzing the intellectual heritage of contemporary heresies, some will blindly lay blame on whole tribes or nations. The Jews make an easy target.

Left-wing Jew haters blame Jewish people for capitalism and the failure of Arab states. Right-wing Jew haters blame Jewish people for every facet of modernity that offends them. They will cherry-pick lists of genuine villains throughout history and trot out the Jews who took part in mostly Gentile movements. They'll skip the Marquis de Sade and talk about Al Goldstein. They'll skip over Margaret Sanger and Alfred Kinsey, then rant about Gloria Steinem.

Brown rightly calls out among Catholics E. Michael Jones and his disciples for engaging in this kind of slothful, ad hominem argument. I'm mortified to see legitimate revulsion against the evils of modern life hijacked by ignorant tribalism. Surely the abortion and pornography industries and the totalitarian LGBT movement are delighted to see criticisms of their profound internal evils associated with primitive racial hatred. That serves their power and profit. And Christians who scapegoat Jews play right into their hands.

—John Zmirak, PhD
Author, *The Politically Incorrect Guide to Catholicism*
Coauthor, *The Race to Save Our Century*

In his book *Christian Antisemitism,* Dr. Michael Brown reveals in print what he is in person—one of the most vocal, ardent, and courageous opponents of modern-day antisemitism. A must-read.

—Dexter Van Zile
Christian Media Analyst, Committee for Accuracy in Middle East Reporting and Analysis

CHRISTIAN ANTISEMITISM

To Rob,
Rom 9:1-5

CHRISTIAN ANTISEMITISM

MICHAEL L. BROWN, PHD

CHARISMA HOUSE

Most Charisma House Book Group products are available at special quantity discounts for bulk purchase for sales promotions, premiums, fund-raising, and educational needs. For details, call us at (407) 333-0600 or visit our website at www.charismahouse.com.

Christian Antisemitism by Michael L. Brown, PhD
Published by Charisma House
Charisma Media/Charisma House Book Group
600 Rinehart Road, Lake Mary, Florida 32746

Visit the author's website at https://askdrbrown.org/, booksbydrbrown.com.

Library of Congress Cataloging-in-Publication Data:
An application to register this book for cataloging has been submitted to the Library of Congress.
International Standard Book Number: 978-1-62999-760-5
E-book ISBN: 978-1-62999-761-2

21 22 23 24 25 — 987654321
Printed in the United States of America

TABLE OF CONTENTS

PREFACE

THIS IS A book I wish I did not have to write, a book that I wish was not urgent and relevant. But it had to be written, and it certainly is urgent and relevant. Antisemitism is raising its ugly head again right within the church, including the evangelical church. Something that I rarely encountered in almost fifty years of walking with the Lord as a Jewish believer in Jesus is becoming increasingly common. How can this be?

It was one thing to document the ugly history of "Christian" antisemitism, an oxymoron if ever there was one. (Please note that, after the first reference to *"Christian" antisemitism* in the main text of the book, the quotation marks around the word "Christian" have been removed. But I trust our point is clear: you cannot be truly and consistently Christian while at the same time being an antisemite.) I have been documenting that history for years, most prominently in my book *Our Hands Are Stained With Blood*, first published in 1992.

Yes, it was one thing to talk about how early church leaders demonized the Jewish people, or to talk about Crusader armies marching through Europe who turned on their Jewish neighbors, or to talk about Martin Luther's blatantly antisemitic writings. All that was in the past, so disconnected from today. All that was so different from what I experienced in congregation after congregation around the world for decades, where I encountered special love for Israel and the Jewish people. The "Christian" antisemites were rare, their sentiments quite fringe. But things have changed in recent years, and with what feels like ever-increasing intensity, the old lies are being spread and the standard libels are being embraced *right within the church*. "It's those evil Jews who are destroying the world!"

How jarring it is to watch an evangelical Christian broadcast where the host talks about wanting to see Jewish people come to faith in Jesus and claims deep loyalty to the Lord, only to hear him spread vicious lies about the Jewish people in the next breath. I ask again: How can this be?

The purpose of this book, then, is to focus on contemporary "Christian" antisemitism, starting with a short, painful journey into the past and ending with a shocking arrival into the present. From there, we will define the term *antisemitism,* demonstrate how widespread this is in the church today, look at some of the major issues and key players, examine the key scriptures that are being misused, understand the role of modern-day Israel, and look ahead to the return of the King.

The fact that you are holding this book in your hand (or reading it in digital form or listening to it as an audiobook) is a good sign already. You want to know the truth. You are interested in the subject matter. You do not want to turn a blind eye. That is very positive. Now brace yourself for what is coming. Not a word is exaggerated and not a syllable is taken out of context.

May truth triumph over lies, may love triumph over hate, and may God fulfill His purposes for the people of Israel!

I express my appreciation once again to Stephen Strang and the entire Charisma Media team for their solidarity and support in tackling such a volatile subject, and to my editor, Adrienne Gaines, and her team, who, as always, painstakingly reviewed every sentence and scrutinized every endnote. I am also deeply grateful to my team at AskDrBrown, who work sacrificially to glorify God and to serve you. I must also thank our Torchbearers and Patreon patrons, who help undergird our work financially, and the army of prayer warriors, some known to me personally but so many who are nameless and faceless—but not to God! To each of you, from my heart, I say thank you.

Let us then get on with the journey. It deserves your urgent attention.

—MICHAEL L. BROWN
OCTOBER 16, 2020

CHAPTER 1

A TRAIL OF BLOOD AND TEARS

The year was 387, the location the ancient city of Antioch. There, one of the most famous preachers of his day stood to deliver the first of eight sermons against the Jews. Full of passion, he began to denounce the Jewish people as a whole, calling them "the slayers of Christ"![1]

The preacher was named John, but after his death, because of his eloquence, he was given the name Chrysostom, meaning "golden mouth." And that is how he is known today: Saint John Chrysostom, a man hailed for his Christian virtues and uncompromising message. But those Christian virtues came to a screeching halt when it came to his homilies against the Jewish people.[2]

Over the course of these powerful sermons, Chrysostom said things like this about the Jews:

> They live for their bellies, they gape for the things of this world, their condition is not better than that of pigs or goats because of their wanton ways and excessive gluttony. They know but one thing: to fill their bellies and be drunk, to get all cut and bruised, to be hurt and wounded while fighting for their favorite charioteers....
>
> ...Indeed the synagogue is less deserving of honor than any inn. It is not merely a lodging place for robbers and cheats but also for demons. This is true not only of the synagogues but also of the souls of the Jews....
>
> Do you see that demons dwell in their souls and that these demons are more dangerous than the ones of old? And this is very reasonable. In the old days the Jews acted impiously toward the prophets; now they outrage the Master of the prophets. Tell me this. Do you not shudder to come into the same place with men possessed, who have so many unclean spirits, who have been reared amid slaughter and bloodshed? Must you share a greeting with them and exchange a bare word?[3]

Yes, this powerful preacher said, "I hate the synagogue and abhor it. They have the prophets but not believe them; they read the sacred writings but reject their witness—and this is a mark of men guilty of the greatest outrage."[4]

According to Chrysostom, the Jewish people as a whole were guilty of killing Christ, making them guilty of deicide, killing God. What should be done to a people such as this? What should be done to such evil transgressors? He says:

> When brute animals feed from a full manger, they grow plump and become more obstinate and hard to hold in check; they endure neither the yoke, the reins, nor the hand of the charioteer. Just so the Jewish people were driven by their drunkenness and plumpness to the ultimate evil; they kicked about, they failed to accept the yoke of Christ, nor did they pull the plow of his teaching....
>
> Although such beasts are unfit for work, they are fit for killing. And this is what happened to the Jews: while they were making themselves unfit for work, they grew fit for slaughter. This is why Christ said: "But as for these my enemies, who did not want me to be king over them, bring them here and slay them."[5]

The blood of countless thousands of Jewish martyrs testifies to what happens when rhetoric like this—*the Jewish people, the killers of Christ, are fit for slaughter*—is taken literally. Is it any surprise that the Nazis reprinted Chrysostom's sermons to justify their murderous cause?[6]

Fast forward to the year 1096. Crusader armies had begun to march through Europe en route to the Holy Land, where they would seek to dislodge the Muslims who had taken control of the region. But as they began their long and arduous march, they realized the Muslims were not their only enemies. Within their very own communities were the assassins of Christ!

Author Susan Jacoby tells the story:

> Pope Urban II did not tell crusaders to murder Jews, but that is what happened when at least 100,000 knights, vassals and serfs, unmoored from ordinary social restraints but bearing the standard of the cross, set off to crush what they considered a perfidious Muslim enemy in a faraway land. Why not practice on that older group accused of perfidy—the Jews?[7]

And what exactly happened to these European Jews? What did they suffer at the hands of the Crusaders, who marched under the standard of the cross?

> Albert of Aix, a Christian born in the late 11th century, describes atrocities in Mainz—another stop on the crusaders' rampage through the Rhineland—by a band headed by one Count Emico. Again, there is a bishop who initially promises the Jews protection for what Albert describes as an "incredible amount of money." But Emico and his Christian soldiers broke into the hall where the Jews were held.
>
> "Breaking the bolts and doors, they killed the Jews, about seven hundred in number, who in vain resisted the force and attack of so many thousands. They killed the women, also, and with their swords pierced tender children of whatever age and sex."[8]

And this was done in the name of Jesus, supposedly for the glory of God.

Fast forward now to 1523. A German monk named Martin Luther is so grieved over the Catholic Church's treatment of the Jews that he writes an essay titled "That Jesus Christ Was Born a Jew." In it, he reaches out with humility to the Jewish community in Germany, telling them that if he had been Jewish and seen the ways the popes and bishops ran the church, he would rather have been a pig than a Christian. And he honors them as the older brothers, hoping to soften their heart to the gospel.[9]

Twenty years later, in 1543, an old and sick Luther struck a very different tone. He had not seen the mass conversion of Jewish people for which he hoped. And he had been exposed to Jewish literature that blasphemed Jesus. He even thought the Jewish people cursed Christians every day in their synagogue prayers. And some of his own parishioners had taken an interest in Jewish customs and beliefs.

So he took his pen in hand and wrote his infamous treatise *On the Jews and Their Lies*. In it, he counseled the German nobles on how they could be free of this "unbearable, devilish burden of the Jews":

> First, to set fire to their synagogues or schools...
>
> Second, I advise that their houses also be razed and destroyed...Instead they might be lodged under a roof or in a barn, like the gypsies...
>
> Third, I advise that all their prayer books and Talmudic writings, in which such idolatry, lies, cursing, and blasphemy are taught, be taken from them.
>
> Fourth, I advise that their rabbis be forbidden to teach henceforth on pain of loss of life and limb...
>
> Fifth, I advise that safe-conduct on the highways be abolished completely for the Jews...
>
> Sixth, I advise that usury [charging interest] be prohibited to them, and that all cash and treasure of silver and gold be taken from them and put aside for safekeeping...

> Seventh, I recommend putting a flail, an ax, a hoe, a spade, a distaff, or a spindle into the hands of young, strong Jews and Jewesses and letting them earn their bread in the sweat of their brow.[10]

All this from the pen of Martin Luther!

Fast forward to Wednesday evening, November 9, 1938. This is the date most historians mark as the beginning of the Holocaust, as Nazi troops destroyed or set fire to Jewish homes and synagogues, looted and smashed the windows of Jewish places of business, and killed or wounded scores of Jewish residents. This was Kristallnacht, the Night of Broken Glass, when the Nazis carried out Luther's recommendations to a tee, starting with the burning of the synagogues and the destroying of Jewish places of business.

To the delight of some German pastors, the fires were still burning on November 10, the birthday of Martin Luther, the father of the Protestant Reformation, who was born in 1483. Political scientist Daniel Jonah Goldhagen notes:

> One leading Protestant churchman, Bishop Martin Sasse of Thuringia, published a compendium of Martin Luther's antisemitic vitriol shortly after *Kristallnacht*'s orgy of anti-Jewish violence. In the foreword to the volume, he applauded the burning of the synagogues and the coincidence of the day: "On November 10, 1938, on Luther's birthday, the synagogues are burning in Germany." The German people, he urged, ought to heed these words "of the greatest antisemite of his time, the warner of his people against the Jews."[11]

During the post–World War II Nuremberg trials for war criminals, Julius Streicher, one of Hitler's top henchmen and publisher of the antisemitic *Der Stürmer*, was asked if there were "any other publications in Germany which treated the Jewish question in an anti-Semitic way." Streicher stated:

> Dr. Martin Luther would very probably sit in my place in the defendants' dock today, if this book had been taken into consideration by the Prosecution. In the book *The Jews and Their Lies*, Dr. Martin Luther writes that the Jews are a serpent's brood and one should burn down their synagogues and destroy them.[12]

REPEATING HISTORY

Fast-forward to October 2014. Texe Marrs, a best-selling evangelical author and Christian radio show host, reprints Luther's anti-Jewish book, which is released with this enthusiastic description: "Martin Luther, one of the greatest champions of the Christian faith ever to live, wrote this amazing book to warn Christians of the darkness of the Jewish religion."[13] Indeed, *On the Jews and Their Lies* is said to be "Luther's magnificent defense of Jesus the Messiah and his exposé of the unfounded lies and accusations of the rabbis." Yes, an evangelical Christian leader reprinted Luther's violence-inducing screed against the Jews.

As of March 2020, a 2017 reprint of Luther's infamous work, translated by Martin Bertram, had a four-star rating from readers on Amazon.[14] As one appreciative reader wrote, "Very interesting information (forbidden knowledge). Martin Luther was a smart man and Christian thinker. He stood up not only to the Catholic Church hierarchy but to Jews as well. God bless him."[15] Another wrote:

> Martin Luther has been labeled an anti-Semite because of this work and when you read it it becomes obvious why. In it he exposes Jewish lying, cheating, parasitism and stealing from the German people. All condoned and encouraged in the Jewish holy book "Talmud" which Luther was able to obtain and read in the Hebrew language. From the same "work" he exposes the Jews immense hate and slander of Jesus Christ and all of Christianity. Luther uses many scriptures to present his views which any Christian would have to agree.[16]

Move ahead to April 27, 2019. John T. Earnest, just nineteen years old, marches into an Orthodox Jewish synagogue in Poway, California, and opens fire, killing one and wounding three before his gun locks up. Among the injured are an eight-year-old girl and the rabbi, who lost a finger on one hand. According to a court affidavit, Earnest told a 911 emergency line dispatcher, "I just shot up a synagogue. I'm just trying to defend my nation from the Jewish people... They're destroying our people... I opened fire at a synagogue... because Jewish people are destroying the white race."[17]

But that's not all he said. In a manifesto written prior to the shooting, he gives an in-depth explanation of why he tried to murder as many as Jewish people as possible, and it was not simply a matter of the Jewish people allegedly "destroying the white race." Earnest, you see, professed to be a devout Christian, was raised in a Christian home, and attended a local Presbyterian church.[18]

In his manifesto, he explains, "I did not choose to be a Christian. The Father chose me. The Son saved me. And the Spirit keeps me. Why me? I do not know." But he says that as a Christian, he has a responsibility: "There is no love without hatred. You cannot love God if you do not hate Satan. You cannot love righteousness if you do not also hate sin. You cannot love your own race if you do not hate those who wish to destroy it. Love and hate are two sides of the same coin."[19]

Earnest continues, "It is unlawful and cowardly to stand on the sidelines as the European people are genocided [*sic*] around you. I did not want to have to kill Jews. But they have given us no other option." Indeed, he claims, "My God does not take kindly to the destruction of His creation. Especially one of the most beautiful, intelligent, and innovative races that He has created. Least of all at the hands of one of the most ugly, sinful, deceitful, cursed, and corrupt,"[20] by which he means the Jewish people allegedly destroying white Americans of European origin. This, he believes, is his Christian duty!

To support his ideas, he marshals a number of New Testament texts that antisemites have quoted and misused throughout the ages, including Matthew 27:25 (where a Jewish crowd called for Jesus' crucifixion and shouted, "His blood be on us and on our children"); John 8:37–45 (which includes Jesus' word to nonbelieving Jews that they are of their father, the devil); 1 Thessalonians 2:14–16 (where Paul speaks of the Jews who killed Jesus and the prophets and now persecute the Jewish apostles); and Revelation 2:9 and 3:9 (where Jesus spoke of the "synagogue of Satan").[21]

Earnest then gives a list of sixteen reasons the Jewish people must be killed, repeating some of the standard, ugly, antisemitic libels, and concluding with this: "And finally, for their role in the murder of the Son of Man—that is the Christ. Every Jew young and old has contributed to these." Shades of the words of John Chrysostom. The Jewish people as a whole are guilty of killing Christ. Yes, "every Jew young and old has contributed" to the murder of the Messiah. "For these crimes," he concludes this section, "they [the Jewish people] deserve nothing but hell. I will send them there."[22]

Jump ahead to September 29, 2019. A man named Robert posts this comment on my YouTube channel with reference to the Poway synagogue shooting: "It is so shocking that your people pulled another false flag shooting and made sure the 'perp' was a violent 'Christian'. We know how evil you are Brown."[23]

What? My people—the Jewish people—pulled a false-flag operation with the synagogue shooting? We set it up for a woman to be killed in cold blood and for the rabbi to lose one of his fingers? And we "made sure" the shooter was a "violent 'Christian'"? Robert's sick comment ends with, "We know how evil you are Brown." But of course. I am Jewish myself.

This is beyond sick. This is demonic.

Finally, jump ahead a few days to October 2, 2019. A woman named Maria posted this comment on our ASKDrBrown YouTube channel: "Dr. Brown, I hope you are humble enough to hear this video to the end because I think you really need it." Her comment was linked to a six-and-a-quarter-hour video compilation containing the narration of all of John Chrysostom's sermons against the Jews.[24]

Yes, antisemitism is alive and well, and it is not only spreading among professing Christians; it is being propagated by professing Christians. What's worse, hate is being passed off as the gospel, and those who would dare challenge the misinformation and outright lies being told about the Jewish people are vilified.

Now you know why I have written this book. What you are about to read is painful and very distressing. Do you have the courage to continue?

CHAPTER 2

THE MATTER IS URGENT, AND I AM NOT EXAGGERATING

SHORTLY AFTER I came to faith in late 1971, at my father's request, I met with the local rabbi. By God's grace, my life had been radically transformed, and I went from a heroin-shooting, LSD-using, rebellious, hippie rock drummer to a Jesus-loving, clean-living child of God. And this happened virtually overnight. What a miracle!

But as much as my dad was thrilled to see me off drugs, he wasn't thrilled to see me believing in Jesus. After all, as he said to me, "Michael, we're Jews. We don't believe this."

So it was that I met with the local rabbi, who quickly befriended me and took a genuine interest in my well-being. He would challenge my beliefs, examine my understanding of the Scriptures, and force me to dig deeper. In many ways I'm indebted to him, as he provoked me to learn Hebrew and work through the Jewish objections to Yeshua (Jesus) being the Messiah of Israel.

He also challenged me to look at the record of church history, which was a total shock for me. What? Christians hated, persecuted, and even killed the Jewish people? He gave me a book to read, accompanied by a poignant letter, which I still have today, enclosed in the pages of that book. This is what he wrote, which I am publishing with his permission:

> Dear Mike,
>
> I'm lending you this book so that as you read its pages you can share in the thousands of years of agony your people have undergone for the sake of the Almighty G-d of Israel and His absolute unity. Perhaps it will touch a note in your heart which will help you realize what your destiny on earth is to be. As you read it, please keep these verses in

mind [the verses were written in Hebrew, which I could not really read at that time]:

> "My Lord G-D will wipe the tears away from all faces and will put an end to the reproach of His people over all the earth" (Isaiah 25:8).
>
> "And the LORD shall be king over all the earth; in that day there shall be one LORD with one name" (Zechariah 14:9).
>
> And finally, together with millions of your martyred brethren, "Hear O Israel, the LORD your God, the LORD is one" (Deuteronomy 6:4).

I pray our G-d give you the inner strength to face the truth no matter what the consequences.

What a moving letter this was to receive, and what a shocking book this was to read.[1] But to be perfectly candid, the book didn't affect me that much, even though it was filled with painful stories of the mistreatment of Jews at the hands of Christians. Growing up, I had been unaware of this history, and in the church where I came to faith as a sixteen-year-old in 1971, I was met with great love, not hatred. These dear Christians seemed to have a tremendous heart for the Jewish people, including those who rejected the gospel. They showed nothing but grace, and their hearts were also joined with the modern state of Israel, recognizing that it was God who brought the Jewish people back to their land out of the ashes of the Holocaust, as if He gave them life from the dead.

In the decades that followed, as I traveled around America and overseas (now with roughly two hundred ministry trips outside the United States), I also met believers with profound love for Israel and the Jewish people. And over the years, when I shared with these precious believers the history of "Christian" antisemitism (an oxymoron, as I explained in the preface, but a term I will use throughout this book to describe this trend, without the quotes from this point forward), they were absolutely shocked. As an Iranian Christian once said to me, "It is impossible to be a Christian and hate the Jews!"

That had been my experience for forty-seven years, with rare exception, and I could count on two hands the number of Christian antisemites I had met—until 2019. Frankly, I encountered more Christian antisemitism that year than in the previous forty-seven years combined. I am not exaggerating.

It's as if an ancient plague has been revived, spreading from person to person until millions are affected. It's like watching a nightmare unfold in front of your eyes as professing Christians from all branches of the church experience some kind of mass deception, coming to the "recognition" that the Jewish people are the cause of all the world's troubles. Those evil Jews! And to say it again: it is often professing Christians who are believing and spreading these lies. I can illustrate this for you in clear, statistical form.

At present, we have more than two thousand videos on the ASKDrBrown YouTube channel, covering a wide range of subjects: biblical, theological, cultural, historical, linguistic, and political. Many of the videos touch on highly controversial subjects, but on average they receive high ratings from viewers.[2]

For example, looking at the latest videos we posted, the "likes" average about 95 percent, with some videos receiving more than sixty thumbs-ups for every thumbs-down (better than a 98 percent rating). Videos that are more controversial still receive about 85 percent positive responses, which is no surprise, seeing that most of the people coming to my channel are fans of my material.

But things change dramatically when I begin to confront Christian antisemitism or expose false conspiracy theories involving Israel. For example, my videos addressing the Noahide Law hysteria (which I address in chapter 5) received ratings as low as 50 percent, meaning the dislikes were identical to the likes.[3] And all I did was explain the truth about these rabbinic laws. Yet for telling the truth, some viewers claimed I was not a real follower of Jesus. How dare I rebut the latest theory about those terrible Jews!

No Laughing Matter

When I confronted conservative comedian and professing Christian Owen Benjamin for his tirades that allege the Jews control everything and own everything—a classic antisemitic libel—the response was so ugly that, for one of the only times in our history, we had to disable comments on a video.[4] They were so vulgar, so venomous, so vile, so vicious that it was simply not appropriate for us to allow them to be posted on our channel. (As a result, some of the comments you will read in this book are no longer accessible online; we removed them after taking screenshots.) Yet many of the comments came from people who claimed to be believers in Jesus. How can this be?

Subsequent to posting the Owen Benjamin video, I had as my guest on the *Line of Fire* broadcast E. Michael Jones, PhD, a Catholic scholar whose views are widely considered antisemitic.[5] (Dr. Jones has greatly influenced Benjamin's thinking about the Jewish people as well. For more on Jones, see chapter 4.) Although my interview with Dr. Jones was cordial, he took issue with my labeling his views as antisemitic, posting his own video, in which he falsely accused me of editing a follow-up video of our dialogue in a misleading way. In response, I posted a fact-filled video titled "Are Dr. E. Michael Jones and Owen Benjamin Telling the Truth?"[6] As of October 11, 2020, this video had received 353 thumbs-ups, compared with 637 thumbs-downs, for a rating of just 36 percent. What a contrast from my other videos!

But this is what happens whenever I confront antisemitism, especially Christian antisemitism. Those who hate the Jewish people come out of the woodwork, repeating the standard (and/or latest) antisemitic tropes. I'm seeing it happen again and again.

On two occasions, I posted videos exposing the antisemitic claims of Rick Wiles and TruNews, an evangelical online news network. (Yes, I said *evangelical*; see chapter 4.) The first video, in which I took issue with ridiculous statements like, "The sexual revolution was a Zionist operation to break down American culture," received 672 thumbs-ups, compared with 1,000 thumbs-downs as of October 11, 2020, for a rating of just 39 percent.[7] The second video, in which I confronted horrific lies such as that Israel, not ISIS, was behind the attacks in Aleppo, Syria, received 991 thumbs-ups, compared with 1,700 thumbs-downs as of October 11, 2020, for an even lower rating of 37 percent.[8] (Wiles actually said, "I'm not so sure there was an ISIS."[9]) The pattern is undeniable, and it is a very disturbing pattern.

What do some of the hostile viewers have to say? Here's a tiny sampling of comments to the two videos that exposed TruNews:

- "When you have more dislikes than likes on YouTube, it proves more people are with Rick Wiles and have awoken to the truth of the Zionist occupation of America and I'm agnostic. If you read the Talmud it is Jewish supremacist literature! BDS"[10]
- "Brown is going IN THE PIT!"
- "You're a traitor to this country and if convicted should be hung from the tallest oak tree in the US."
- "Do you rape children too? Is that why you are protecting the Satanist Talmud worshipping fake jews?"
- "Well said Rick, time these bloodsuckers were seen for what they really are, the synagogue of Satan."
- "Pastor Wiles is a man of God who exposed you Mr. Jew Zionist.... You're destroying America with your Synagogue of Satan agenda.... American people leave this Brown Blackened and Join the TruNews church. The Killers Chabad Lubavitch[11] are in Control of our government.... All

of the conspiracies you mentioned is true. Your disobedience to god led to the nations to kicked out you out of their countries. You didn't repent to god so you don't deserve the land..."

- "Look at the ratio of thumbs down. Look at all the negative comments. You've exposed yourself as a Talmudic, Kabbalistic, Zionist son of Satan...poor idiot! ASKDrBrown You are one lost, Talmudic, Zionist, fool."
- "Look at this Jew infiltrator working so hard to do damage control with zio-Xtians. Would be such an easier life spreading the truth."
- "BROWN, YOU ARE NOT CHRISTIAN...!!! YOU ARE A BED BUG CRIMINAL JEW....!!!!"

Did I say I was not exaggerating? And to repeat: this is just a tiny sampling of the ugly comments that poured in from viewers of these videos, many of them quoting Scripture, many of them attacking my faith in Jesus, many of them propagating lies that foment hatred of the Jewish people, and many of them professing to be Christians.

How do we explain this phenomenon? I'm sure there are plenty of trolls who flood particular websites, blog posts, and videos, being drawn to certain controversial subjects like a shark is drawn to the scent of blood. But in the case of Christian antisemitism, I believe it's more than just trolls. Some sincere Christians are getting affected as well, almost as if they drank some kind of antisemitic elixir. Their thinking becomes unclear, their reasoning powers defective. And no matter how outlandish the lie or far-fetched the theory, if it indicts the Jewish people, they believe it.

In the pages that follow, we'll seek to understand the nature of this spiritual malady, first confronting the lies and misinformation head-on, then searching for the theological errors (and even demonic forces) that contribute to these wrongheaded and dangerous ideas, then pointing to the solution to this serious condition.

Let's start by getting some definitions in place, beginning with this: What, exactly, is antisemitism?

CHAPTER 3

WHAT IS ANTISEMITISM?

IT MAY SURPRISE you, but there is not only debate about the meaning of the term *antisemitism*, but also debate about how to spell it. Should we use the traditional form, *anti-Semitism*? If so, what is *Semitism*, and what does it mean to be "anti" this thing called *Semitism*? Or should we use the newer spelling, *antisemitism*, as is done throughout this book?[1]

According to an article in the *Encyclopaedia Britannica*, the word *anti-Semitism* refers to "hostility toward or discrimination against Jews as a religious or racial group." The article continues:

> The term *anti-Semitism* was coined in 1879 by the German agitator Wilhelm Marr to designate the anti-Jewish campaigns under way in central Europe at that time. Although the term now has wide currency, it is a misnomer, since it implies a discrimination against all Semites. Arabs and other peoples are also Semites, and yet they are not the targets of anti-Semitism as it is usually understood.[2]

So while the term was coined with reference to the Jewish community alone and still refers to Jews alone, it is a misleading term.[3] The Arab people are Semites. The ancient Babylonians and Assyrians were Semites. Yet when we speak of being "anti-Semitic," we don't mean anti-Arab, and we certainly don't mean anti-Babylonian or anti-Assyrian. Obviously!

Unfortunately, antisemites are quick to jump on the term in its traditional spelling, saying "Arabs are Semites too!" As Fred Maroun notes in a 2015 article in the *Times of Israel*:

> When I raise the issue of Arab antisemitism, I invariably get anti-Zionists riled up, and they invariably make the argument that "Arabs can't be antisemites since they are Semites too". I find it difficult not to pause

> at the idiocy of this response, but when examined further, this response provides useful insight into the core of the Israel/Arab conflict.
>
> The response that "Arabs are Semites too" is a fallacy of course, as anyone who can use a dictionary can tell. Oxford, Merriam-Webster, and Cambridge all give slight variations of the same definition, which is that "antisemitism" means hatred of Jewish people. Therefore whether Arabs are Semites or not is totally irrelevant to the issue of Arab antisemitism.[4]

So Arabs, who are Semites, can be anti-Semitic, since antisemitism refers to hatred of Jewish people, not hatred of Semitic people in general. As for the word *Semitism*, it can have a racial connotation or a linguistic connotation. As defined by the *Merriam-Webster* online dictionary, *Semitism* refers to "Semitic character or qualities" or "a characteristic feature of a Semitic language occurring in another language."[5] I encountered this second use of the word *Semitism* while doing my master's and doctoral studies in Near Eastern languages and literatures at New York University, where a scholar would identify a certain linguistic form as a "Semitism." We were certainly not "anti" that kind of "Semitism"!

That's why throughout this book I have adopted the more modern spelling of *antisemitism*. It is not hyphenated. It does not mean being against something Semitic. It means hatred and demonizing of the Jewish people, plain and simple.

But why, exactly, should hatred of Jewish people have its own category? And is it true that the term *antisemitism* can be used as a weapon to deflect valid criticism of the Jewish people and the nation of Israel? Is it true that charging someone with antisemitism is an effective way to silence them?

According to the Catholic scholar E. Michael Jones (whose rhetoric, I would argue, presents a classic example of Christian antisemitism), "Anti-Semitism now has an entirely different meaning. An anti-Semite used to be someone who didn't like Jews. Now it is someone whom the Jews don't like."[6]

So in Jones' opinion, *antisemitism* is a convenient term used by the Jewish community to demonize their opponents. To paraphrase, "If Jewish people don't like you, they brand you an antisemite." But this is not just a gross exaggeration on the part of Dr. Jones. It is also his way of making the term meaningless, since if you use it against him, that just proves his point: you're the bigot, not him. As noted by antisemitism expert Simon Plosker, and with specific reference to criticism of Israel, "The charge that accusations of antisemitism are made in bad faith to smear opponents of Israel and shut down legitimate debate over Israeli policies is a well-worn method of dismissing antisemitism and portraying those who attack Jews and Israel as the real victims."[7]

Thankfully, Jones has made his sentiments perfectly clear, writing, "No Christian can in good conscience be an anti-Semite, but every Christian, insofar as he is a Christian, must be anti-Jewish. In contemporary parlance the two terms are practically synonymous but their meanings are very different, and the distinction is deliberately obscured for political purposes." For Jones, "The Church is not and cannot possibly be anti-Semitic, because the term refers primarily to race and racial hatred."[8]

But is this true? When I interviewed Dr. Jones on my *Line of Fire* broadcast in April 2019, he stated that antisemitism "is a racial term," explaining that when it was coined by Wilhelm Marr in the 1870s in Germany, "This was a time when racial thinking was at a high point. Biological determinism was on the rise at this point. Darwin was a big topic of discussion. And basically he said that Jewish behavior was a function of Jewish biology, Jewish DNA, if you want to put it that way." But Jones then said, "I categorically reject that position. That's why I am not an antisemite."[9]

He continued, "Now, over the period of time since then, it has taken on the meaning which it has today, which is basically an antisemite used to be someone who…didn't like Jews and now it's someone Jews don't like." (You can see he's been using that line for a number of years.) Indeed, he added that today, "anyone who criticizes Jews is an antisemite."[10] And this would hold true, Jones argued, if a Gentile criticized someone who is Jewish using the exact same criticism the Jewish person used. If the Gentile lodged that same criticism against a Jewish person, the Gentile would be labeled an antisemite.

I responded to Dr. Jones by disputing his notion that for antisemitism to be genuine it has to be racial, saying:

> To me, if you demonize a people as a whole, if you can speak about "the Jews," and "the Jews," whether it's by nature or by religion or by a freak of historical development, "the Jews" as a whole are kind of demonized and spoken of in a certain way, there is a "Jewish problem"—then that to me becomes antisemitic. Now there are stereotypes. Now there are exaggerations. Now you're painting with too broad a brush.[11]

You might say, "It looks like you both have your opinions, and there's obviously no real way to define what antisemitism is."

With all respect, I beg to differ. Words do have meanings, and when it comes to *antisemitism*, though there is dispute about how to spell the word, the definition is not up for debate.

- According to Oxford's Lexico.com website, antisemitism is "hostility to or prejudice against Jews."[12]

- According to HolocaustRemembrance.com, citing the official definition of the International Holocaust Remembrance Alliance, "Antisemitism is a certain perception of Jews, which may be expressed as hatred toward Jews."[13] This definition was also adopted by the government of the United States.[14]
- According to *Merriam-Webster*, the term refers to "hostility toward or discrimination against Jews as a religious, ethnic, or racial group."[15]
- According to Dictionary.com, *antisemitism* is "discrimination against or prejudice or hostility toward Jews."[16]
- According to Wikipedia, *antisemitism* is "hostility to, prejudice, or discrimination against Jews."[17]
- According to the online *Macmillan Dictionary*, "anti-Semitic people, opinions, writings, etc. show hatred or prejudice toward Jewish people."[18]

Enough said? I think so.

In short, it is false to claim that antisemitism must be racial and therefore your views can only be antisemitic if there is a biological basis for them. Rather, if you demonize the Jewish people as a whole, you are antisemitic. If you believe lies about the people as a people, you are antisemitic. If you falsely stereotype the Jewish people *as Jewish people*, you are antisemitic. Why deny it? It would be better to own the description and say, "Yes, I'm an antisemite, and that's because the Jews *are* evil," rather than to play semantic games.

Unfortunately, as you will see throughout the pages that follow, very few Christians who fit the definition of an antisemite are willing to own the term. To repeat: it would be far better if they accepted the description and said, "That's who I am." After all, they constantly try to justify their position by pointing out how bad the Jewish people are, as if to say, "I'm just telling the truth about some very wicked people. You can't call me an antisemite."

In his full-length study *The Definition of Anti-Semitism*, Kenneth L. Marcus explains that

> Anti-Semitism consists of negative attitudes toward the Jewish people, individually or collectively; conduct that reflects these attitudes; and ideologies that sustain them. In other words, it means hostility toward Jews, including thoughts that are not acted upon and actions that are not fully thought out. As a set of attitudes, it ranges from mild disdain to virulent loathing. As a form of conduct, it embraces hostility toward individual Jews, Jewish institutions, and Jewish collectivity. As

> an ideology, it provides a way to make sense of the entire world and all of history, not just the relatively small territory occupied by the descendants of Jacob.[19]

Did you catch that? Antisemites think a key to making sense of world history and contemporary politics is to understand "the Jews." They are somehow pulling the strings behind the major events taking place on the globe, in particular the bad ones. "It's those miserable Jews! They're behind it all!" And so, whether it is world wars or world banks, whether it is the 9/11 terrorist attacks or ISIS, it is "the Jews" who are somehow controlling the outcome and directing the course of the world. It's always "the Jews"!

Marcus continues:

> The ideology of anti-Semitism can be articulated in various ways. Sometimes it is conceived in opposition to the perceived Jewish "religion" and at other times against an imagined Jewish "race." In the end, anti-Semitism is not about race or religion. Rather, it is a process of working up Jews into a distorted image of "the *Jews*." Whether this image borrows from racial or religious ideas is ultimately immaterial. Nevertheless, it bears mentioning that anti-Semitism characteristically constructs a figure of "the *Jews*" that is commonly characterized, at least in its extreme forms, by the related phenomena of demonization and bestialization.[20]

So there is a world of difference between fair and honest criticism of Jewish individuals (or groups) and antisemitism, just as there is a world of difference between, say, fair and honest criticism of African American individuals (or groups) and racism against African Americans. So when it comes to Jewish Americans, it is fair to ask, "Why do so many Jewish Americans support abortion and same-sex 'marriage' when the Torah is part of their heritage?" There is nothing antisemitic about that, any more than it is racist to ask, "Why do so many African American Christians vote for Democrats when the Democrats embrace so many unbiblical values?" But it *is* antisemitic to say, "The Jews don't care about biblical morality," just as it would be racist to say, "African Americans don't care about biblical morality."

I would also emphasize that it is not antisemitic to state that some of the historic suffering of the Jewish people is the result of divine judgment, as unpopular as that notion might be. From an Old Testament perspective, the destruction of the first temple and the exile of the Jewish people to Babylon was the result of our people rejecting the Law and the Prophets. From a New Testament perspective, the destruction of the second temple and the exile that followed was the result of our national rejection of Jesus the Messiah.

Surely if we Jews had been in complete obedience to God and enjoying His covenantal blessings in full, we would not have been scattered around the world and we would not have endured so much pain and heartache. It is not antisemitic to say that. At the same time, from a biblical perspective, the nations of the world consistently go far beyond Israel's allotted punishment, seeking to wipe the people off the map. It is clear that Satan wants to destroy the Jewish people because of their important role in God's plan of redemption. Once again, the issue is being fair, balanced, and accurate in raising criticisms and concerns. Antisemites are none of the above.

What about the charge that Jewish groups sometimes use the word *antisemitism* as a weapon against all criticism? Is this true? Yes, in certain cases, I believe that is true. The moment a criticism is lodged against Jewish Americans or Israeli Jewish communities, some will cry, "Antisemitism!" But just because some people use the word too much (just like the term *racism* can be overused), that does not minimize or negate the very real presence of antisemitism in the world today. It is a presence that is growing and that cannot be denied, a presence that is not just in words but in deeds, with hate crimes against Jewish people in America and the nations rising to alarming rates—including the cold-blooded murder of Jewish people in Europe, America, and the Middle East.[21]

A Jewish Professor Shares Her Concerns

Deborah E. Lipstadt is a professor of modern Jewish history and Holocaust studies at Emory University in Atlanta and the author of several books confronting Holocaust deniers.[22] But her name is known outside of academic circles because of the movie *Denial,* which told the story of her victory in a British court over Holocaust denier David Irving.[23]

In her newest book, *Antisemitism: Here and Now,* Professor Lipstadt says this:

> As horrific as the Holocaust was, it is firmly in the past. When I write about it, I am writing about what was. Though I remain horrified by what happened, it is history. Contemporary antisemitism is not. It is about the present. It is what many people are doing, saying, and facing *now.* That gave this subject an immediacy that no historical act possesses.[24]

Yes, what has happened in history is terrible. But what is happening before our eyes today—not yesterday, but today—is terribly concerning. She continues:

> What should alarm us is that human beings continue to believe in a conspiracy that demonizes Jews and sees them as responsible for evil. Antisemites continue to give life to this particular brand of age-old hatred. They justify it and the acts committed in its name. The historical consequences of this nefarious passion have been so disastrous that to ignore its contemporary manifestations would be irresponsible.[25]

But it is not just antisemites in general who are spreading conspiracy theories, demonizing Jewish people, and making them responsible for virtually all evil on the planet. Professing Christians are embracing and spreading these lies. And they are using the Bible to justify their viewpoints. How dangerous is that?

Lipstadt also makes this important observation:

> Like a fire set by an arsonist, passionate hatred and conspiratorial worldviews reach well beyond their intended target. They are not rationally contained. But even if the antisemites were to confine their venom to Jews, the existence of Jew-hatred within a society is an indication that something about the entire society is amiss. No healthy society harbors extensive antisemitism—or any other form of hatred.[26]

And no healthy church—or healthy Christian—can harbor antisemitism.

A Perspective From England

Having spent her entire life in England, Jewish author Julia Neuberger has noted with great concern the ominous rise of antisemitism in Europe. In years past, she was actually more concerned about anti-Islamic attitudes than antisemitic ones. But that is not the case today. She writes:

> I have been deeply disturbed by the rise of antisemitism in Europe over the last fifteen years or so, with its attendant violent attacks on Jewish targets in some places. Verbal antisemitism is also on the rise, with an acceptability in many circles of what would hitherto have been condemned as outrageous antisemitic discourse.[27]

She then explains how widespread this hatred of Jewish people has become:

> The far-right remains the most antisemitic demographic, but the far-left, by the force of numbers and its new-found influence over British politics, was found to be roughly on an even keel with reactionaries when it comes to harbouring anti-Jewish feelings. These figures are alarming. But, though these are important groupings, the most worrying evidence

> is that antisemitism—or signs of its influence in populations where it never existed—has become quite widespread in British society.[28]

That's how I feel as I look at the spread of antisemitism among professing Christians. It is taking root in places where it had previously been uprooted. Worse still, it is taking root in places where it never took root before. Dare we ignore it or minimize it? Or, God forbid, dare we justify it?

And so Neuberger writes:

> Like the canary singing in the mine, I want to call out the antisemitism that exists now, not because, as yet, it encompasses violent incidents—here in the UK it largely does not—but because violent name-calling has a habit of morphing into violence perpetrated against people or buildings, with desecration of what is regarded as holy or sacrosanct, and the engendering of fear. The appalling shooting, as I was writing this book, at the Etz Chayyim synagogue in Pittsburgh, in the middle of Sabbath services, by a man who believed Jews were responsible for bringing Muslims to America, shouting out 'All Jews must die', is a case in point.[29]

And lest you think Neuberger or Lipstadt are being alarmist or that I am either, I remind you that only months after the Pittsburgh synagogue shooting by a white supremacist, there was a synagogue shooting in Poway, California. But this time, the shooter was not only a white supremacist. He was also a churchgoing Christian, as we noted in chapter 1, and in his eyes the Jewish people had to die because they were children of the devil, guilty of killing Jesus. While I was writing this book, there was yet another shooting, this time at a kosher grocery in Jersey City, New Jersey. The shooters allegedly held to Black Hebrew Israelite theology that claimed that today's Jews are "fake Jews."[30] Dangerously violent antisemitism is on the rise!

How, then, do we define *antisemitism*? It is *not* antisemitic to criticize Jews or the state of Israel in a fair, objective manner. Neither the Jewish people nor the Jewish state is immune from criticism. And both the people and the country are as flawed as any other people or country. That's because Jews are human beings, and human beings are flawed.

And so Neuberger explains:

> Nobody sensible thinks that 'reasonable' criticism of Israel (more on this shortly) is antisemitic; but there is real concern about questioning its right to exist or using explicitly antisemitic language about it, using Zionist, or Zio for short, as a term of abuse, or using vitriolic and vile language about Israel in a way that one would not do about another state.[31]

This was underscored in a letter to *The Times* of London on November 6, 2017, penned by Simon Schama, Simon Sebag Montefiore, and Howard Jacobson. They write:

> We do not object to fair criticism of Israel governments, but this has grown to be indistinguishable from a demonisation of Zionism itself—the right of the Jewish people to a homeland, and the very existence of a Jewish state. Although anti-Zionists claim innocence of any antisemitic intent, anti-Zionism frequently borrows the libels of classical Jew-hating. Accusations of international Jewish conspiracy and control of the media have resurfaced to support false equations of Zionism with colonialism and imperialism, and the promotion of vicious, fictitious parallels with genocide and Nazism. How, in such instances, is anti-Zionism distinguishable from antisemitism?[32]

That is where the criticism of Israel crosses a line. That is where it becomes antisemitic. And when Christians seek to justify this criticism by use of Scripture, it becomes a manifestation of Christian antisemitism. In the same way, when the Jewish people are demonized as a group, when Jewish people are lied about and falsely blamed, when Judaism is grossly mischaracterized, that is antisemitism. And when it is done in the name of Jesus and with the alleged support of Scripture, that is Christian antisemitism.

Let's confront it and expose it here and now.

CHAPTER 4

BUYING INTO THE ANTISEMITIC LIES

It's a scary thing to see, but once people start to believe lies about the Jewish people, it's as if they'll believe anything, no matter how absurd. There's even a Wikipedia article titled "Israel-Related Animal Conspiracy Theories," which says:

> Zoological conspiracy theories involving Israel are occasionally found in the media or on the Internet, typically in Muslim-majority countries, alleging use of animals by Israel to attack civilians or to conduct espionage. These conspiracies are often reported as evidence of a Zionist or Israeli plot.
>
> Examples include the December 2010 shark attacks in Egypt, Hezbollah claims of capturing Israeli spying eagles, and the 2011 capture in Saudi Arabia of a griffon vulture carrying an Israeli-labeled satellite tracking device.[1]

Listed under the heading "Birds carrying Israeli tracking devices and tags" are the following: griffon vulture, bee-eater, vulture, kestrel, Bonelli's eagle, and Gamla eagle. Listed under "Mammals" are: boars and pigs, hyenas, rats, and dolphin. There's even a section on reptiles, meaning reptiles the Israelis allegedly used for spying.

Yes:

> In February 2018, Hassan Firouzabadi, a military advisor to Iranian supreme leader Ali Khamenei, accused Western countries, including Israel, of spying on Iranian nuclear sites using lizards and chameleons, which according to him attract "atomic waves." "We found out that their skin attracts atomic waves and that they were nuclear spies who wanted to find out where inside the Islamic Republic of Iran we have uranium mines and where we are engaged in atomic activities," he said.[2]

There you have it! I guess you can never really trust a lizard or chameleon. Who knew?[3]

Over the centuries, the church has also believed wild and crazy things about the Jewish people. Something happens when you buy into the antisemitic lies. As I noted in *Our Hands Are Stained With Blood*, the Black Death devastated Europe from 1348 to 1349, wiping out a third of the population. Of course, the blame was placed squarely on the Jewish people, despite the fact that the plague decimated Jewish communities as well. How did the Jewish people manage such far-reaching destruction? They contaminated the wells with a poisonous mixture of lizards, spiders, and hearts of Christians, mixed with the elements of the Lord's Supper.

What's worse than the lie itself is the fact that *hundreds of thousands of Christians believed it*! And as a result, angry mobs killed thousands of Jewish people, and "Jewish children under the age of seven were then baptized and reared as Christians after their families were murdered."[4] As "proof" that the Jewish people were guilty, Christians pointed to "confessions" given under severe torture. Beyond that, there was no evidence.[5]

Unfortunately, that is not an isolated incident. To this day, professing Christians believe insane lies about the Jewish people.

Take, for example, the writings of evangelical author Texe Marrs, who passed away November 23, 2019 (during the very week I was writing this chapter). Marrs was an evangelical minister and radio host. But he is best known for being an extreme conspiracy theorist—and I mean extreme. As reported by *U.S. News and World Report* on December 19, 1999:

> David Icke, a former British television sportscaster turned prophet of doom, and Texe Marrs, a retired U.S. Air Force officer turned pastor, have issued Web site warnings that, come millennium eve, former President George Bush and fellow members of a cult known as the Illuminati will summon oppressive evil forces at a black mass in a burial chamber deep inside the great Cheops pyramid.[6]

I bet you never heard that before!

Not surprisingly, "the Jews" and Judaism were a major focus of Marrs' writing, with titles like these, all published between 2011 and 2018:

- *Conspiracy of the Six-Pointed Star: Eye-Opening Revelations and Forbidden Knowledge About Israel, the Jews, Zionism, and the Rothschilds*[7]
- *DNA Science and the Jewish Bloodline*[8]

- *Holy Serpent of the Jews: The Rabbis' Secret Plan for Satan to Crush Their Enemies and Vault the Jews to Global Dominion*[9]
- *Blood Covenant With Destiny: The Babylonian Talmud, the Jewish Kabbalah, and the Power of Prophecy*[10]

Marrs even reprinted two of the most notorious antisemitic works ever penned, *The Protocols of the Learned Elders of Zion* (which is a complete fabrication, originally published by the Russian secret police to make the Jews look bad)[11] and Martin Luther's infamous *On the Jews and Their Lies* (which called for rabbis to be forbidden to teach under penalty of death and for synagogues to be set on fire, as we saw in the first chapter).

The description of Marrs' edition of Luther's book exclaims, "Martin Luther, one of the greatest champions of the Christian faith ever to live, wrote this amazing book to warn Christians of the darkness of the Jewish religion."[12] Not only so, but in the catalog of books on his website, the words *Jew* or *Jews* or *Jewish* appear sixty-one times while *Israel* appears fifteen times.[13] Talk about being obsessed with the "evil Jews."

Again, Marrs' book *Holy Serpent of the Jews* is described this way:

> Today, we are on the threshold of a horrifying new epoch of Jewish history. Now, comes the Holy Serpent, slithering from his fiery abode in hell to wreak havoc upon humanity. Jesus once declared, "Ye serpents, ye generation of vipers. How can ye escape the damnation of hell?"
>
> Amazingly, the Jews have proven to be exactly what Jesus prophesied. They are the People of the Serpent, unregenerated hypocrites whose religion is unparalleled in its treachery, its wickedness, and its unbounded filth. The Kabbalah and the Talmud, authored by the rabbis, are the very code of hell, the doctrines of devils.
>
> On the surface, the Jews appear to be pious, humanitarian, charitable, and good. The very picture of saintly human beings, they are said to be exalted and true, God's Chosen.
>
> But appearances are deceiving. The evil spirits of those who once worshiped Moloch, who fashioned a golden calf in the desert, and who tortured and tormented Jesus Christ are back, and the whole world is in jeopardy.[14]

This is what happens when you buy into the antisemitic lies. In his article "All the Master Race," Marrs puts these words on the lips of the Jews:

> Our race is the Master Race. We are divine gods on this planet. We are as different from the inferior races as they are from insects. In fact, compared to our race, other races are beasts and animals, cattle at best. Other races are considered as human excrement. Our destiny is to rule

> over the inferior races. Our earthly kingdom will be ruled by our leader with a rod of iron. The masses will lick our feet and serve us as our slaves.[15]

But Marrs is convinced. He writes:

> Of all the diseased schools of racial supremacism, I am convinced that the Jewish specimen is the most evil and most threatening to the lives, bodies, and eternal destinies of humankind.... Zionism has existed as a satanic ideological force in opposition to all things good and even to life itself for three thousand years.... Zionism and its accompanying religious disease, Judaism, are the champions of all time in terms of the total number of innocent men, women, and children being imprisoned in concentration camps, beaten, bludgeoned, raped, robbed, humiliated, and unmercifully slaughtered.[16]

Yes, he writes, "So satanized is the House of Israel (World Jewry), it is simply not feasible that this high vision [of their turning to the Lord for salvation] could ever be realized." [17]

He continues:

> The Jews are on the fast track to their occult fate. They have made an agreement with hell, a covenant with death, and payments on their debt to Satan must be made in accordance with that contractual agreement.... The ultimate goal of the Jews is the annihilation of almost every Gentile man, woman, and child and the establishment of a satanic Jewish-led global dictatorship (the Jewish Utopia) encompassing the planet. This goal is expressed by the Jews in their most sacred books, the Babylonian Talmud and the Kabbalah.[18]

In sum, according to Marrs, "The Jewish majority hates humanity, they despise life, they hate God. Therefore, they are psychopaths and love death.... The plan of the Jews is to employ the tools of chaos magic—to use deception, lies, money, craft and magic—to obtain their ultimate goal. That goal is the conquest of the Gentile world by Jews and the establishment of a Holy Serpent Kingdom on earth."[19]

Marrs once even claimed to know who the Antichrist would be, as explained in the online blurb for his book *The Feast of the Beast*:

> This is the first book written for both Gentiles and Jews which fully explains the doctrines of kabbalistic Judaism pertaining to the events of the Last Days. Kabbalistic Judaism teaches that when the Messiah of the Jews comes, the Jews will universally celebrate the Feast of the Beast. This will be a time of great joy as their Messiah promotes the

> Jews to godhood. He will make the Jews to reign over the whole earth as wise rulers and kings.
>
> But the wretched Gentiles will be demoted. Their wealth will be taken from them and be given to the Jews. What's more, all Gentiles will be given a choice. Either they will agree to become the slaves of their Jewish Masters or they will be killed. The Earth and its riches shall be the sole heritage of the divine Jewish race.
>
> And exactly who is this Messiah who will promote the Jews to godhood and elevate them to global power while smiting the Gentiles? The Jewish Kabbalah tells us his name. You will be both shocked and dismayed to discover his identity.[20]

And remember: Marrs was an evangelical minister who preached salvation through the blood of Jesus and who warned against the dangers of sin. Yet he himself was deeply deceived when it came to Israel (among other subjects).

After Marrs' passing, an announcement was posted on his website that began with these words: "Texe Marrs passed to his heavenly home Saturday evening, November 23, to be with his Saviour whom he loves with all his heart."[21] Assuming that he was a true (but deceived) believer, I'm glad he is enjoying God's presence, and I'm thrilled that his deception is over. It's just a shame that he can't come back and undo the damage that he did with his antisemitic words.

Not-True News About the Jewish People

Or consider the reporting of Rick Wiles and TruNews, an evangelical, professionally produced online news broadcast that had almost 200,000 YouTube subscribers before it was banned from that platform in February 2020. Although Wiles is often described as a conspiracy theorist, he has ministered with mainstream Charismatic leaders and has only recently become known for his antisemitic views. It looks like he's making up for lost time.

To be sure, Wiles had already damaged his credibility with his 1998 book that focused on Y2K. (Do you remember that?) It was titled *Judgment Day 2000: How the Coming Worldwide Computer Crash Will Radically Change Your Life*. The back cover proclaims:

> America's darkest hour is ahead. A worldwide computer crash beginning in 1999 will plunge the global economy into a depression. Governments will declare bank holidays when panic spreads throughout society. The biggest meteor storm in 33 years will destroy several vital satellites. Violent solar storms will disrupt telecommunications and the electric power grid. Families will shiver in the winter of 2000 when electric utilities shut down. An oil shortage and severe drought will devastate

> America's food supply. Drinking water will be rationed by National Guard troops. Terrorists will launch a coordinated attack in America's 100 biggest cities.
>
> Is this science fiction or America's future?
>
> In this explosive book, author Rick Wiles will stun you with unheard facts about Y2K. To your shock and dismay, you'll discover the startling news that the media isn't reporting![22]

So much for accurate predictions! But all this is relatively harmless, especially when compared with his recent attacks on Israel and the Jewish people.

Media analyst Dexter Van Zile, who focuses on antisemitism and anti-Zionism, notes that in one TruNews video, Wiles toyed with the idea that President Trump had secretly converted to Judaism in 2017. In another, Wiles declared that the Antichrist "will be a homosexual Jew."[23] Yet Wiles' views are becoming more popular, as incomprehensible as that may sound.[24] (See some of the YouTube data and comments cited in chapter 2.)

I first met Wiles in Bethlehem in 2018 at the Christ at the Checkpoint conference, a biannual Palestinian Christian conference often accused of propagating an extremely hostile position, if not a downright antisemitic position, toward Israel. The leaders generally invite at least one pro-Israel speaker to join each conference, and in 2018 that was me.[25] (For the record, I was graciously received and made new friends in the midst of our deep differences.) TruNews was filming the conference in its entirety, which didn't catch my attention until later. This was fuel for their growing anti-Israel fire.

Based on comments Wiles made after the trip, it seems this was Wiles' first time in the region, and he bought into the anti-Israel narrative hook, line, and sinker, quickly fashioning himself an expert on the Middle East and sharing more and more about the evil Israeli regime. But it didn't stop there. He was soon speaking against "the Jews" in the strongest of terms. In the year 2019 alone, he claimed that "Donald Trump is owned by the Jews"; that American evangelical Christian leaders connected to Trump will look the other way concerning sin because they don't want to jeopardize their ability to push Israel's agenda; that pastor John Hagee has been Judaized and espouses kabbalistic Judaism; and that "the sexual revolution was a Zionist operation to break down American culture" (among other charges).[26]

According to Wiles:

> The power of the Israeli lobby in America is the most detrimental force in America. Our culture has been decimated through abortion; pornography; the sexual liberation movement; filthy, raunchy movies [and] television shows; vile, violent rap music and hip-hop, and all of it owned by the synagogue of Satan. And I cannot be a preacher of the gospel

> and not confront the synagogue of Satan, even if it costs me my life. A day is coming [when] Christians are going to lose their lives as they confront the synagogue of Satan. You cannot stand for Jesus Christ and righteousness in this world without confronting the synagogue of Satan.[27]

What extraordinarily dangerous rhetoric, especially from an evangelical Christian news network.

Although Wiles claims to be anti-Zionist but not anti-Jew, that is clearly not true, as many of his attacks are launched against "the Jews" in general.[28] On Holocaust Remembrance Day (May 1, 2019), the TruNews panel, led by Rick Wiles, had this discussion:

> Rick Wiles: The Soviet Communist party was founded and run by Bolshevik Jews...and they killed tens of millions of Christians in Russia.
>
> Matt Skow: ...When they scream, 'We want Moshiach now,'...their Messiah, to come back as a political leader, they believe that these *goyim* will be their slaves....
>
> Rick Wiles: ...They are teaching the future soldier, the future military officers Messianic values, which means that they are instilling in these Israeli military officers a view that the Jewish Messiah will be a military conqueror.
>
> Edward Szall: That's what Judas wanted.
>
> Matt Skow: That's why they rejected Jesus....
>
> Rick Wiles: They wanted to kill Romans, and so they're looking for a military leader. Ben Shapiro said he's looking for a military Messiah....
>
> Matt Skow: It's time to wake up, people.[29]

Those dangerous, evil Jews! Christians, you had better wake up! And remember: this discussion took place on Holocaust Remembrance Day.

As soon as I saw some of this rhetoric coming from TruNews, I reached out to them. They invited me to join them on their show, and I immediately said yes. But for fairness, I asked Rick to come on my show as well. We waited for weeks for an answer, then reached out again, only to be told that no, he would not join me on my show. I offered to have a formal, moderated debate. Again, the answer was no. Then I offered to come on his show without him coming on my show, as long as I was guaranteed equal time in my responses and the video would air without being edited. But their door was closed. They would not interact with me at all, nor would they allow me to challenge their views in a fair and neutral setting.

Not surprisingly, their views have gotten even more extreme, with Wiles making these claims on November 22, 2019, in the midst of the impeachment hearings:

> That's the way the Jews work. They are deceivers. They plot. They lie. They do whatever they have to do to accomplish their political agenda. This "Impeach Trump" movement is a Jew coup, and the American people better wake up to it really fast because this thing is moving now towards a vote in the House and then a trial in the Senate. We could have a trial before Christmas. This country could be in civil war at Christmastime. Members of the US military are going to have to take a stand, just like they did in the 1860s with the Civil War. They are going to have to decide: Are you fighting for the North or the South?...Instead of North/South, it's going to be Left or Right.[30]

Yes, "the Jews"—as a people—"are deceivers. They plot. They lie. They do whatever they have to do to accomplish their political agenda." So "the Jews" wanted to oust Donald Trump, leading to a literal, bloody civil war. And Wiles wanted you to stand up against the evil Jews!

Ironically, just a few months earlier, Wiles told us that "the Jews" owned the White House and Donald Trump. In fact, some conspiracy theorists claimed that it was really Jared Kushner, Trump's Jewish son-in-law, who was calling the shots. Why, then, would "the Jews" seek to remove the man they own and control? Not only so, but Trump has been a true friend of Israel. And to confuse matters even more, a religious Jewish website, shocked by Wiles' claims that Trump's impeachment was a "Jew coup," posted an article saying someone should remind Wiles that "Orthodox Jews just donated millions to Trump's reelection campaign in an event attended by hundreds of Yarmulka-wearing Jews."[31]

It looks like "the Jews" need to get their act together, since they can't decide whether to support Trump or oust him. (Here's a quick reality check: there are millions of Jewish Americans, with millions of different viewpoints among them, and they do *not* act as a unit.)

But there's more still. On the same broadcast, Wiles said:

> People are going to be forced, possibly by this Christmas, to take a stand because of this Jew coup in the United States....This is a coup led by Jews to overthrow the constitutionally elected president of the United States, and it's beyond removing Donald Trump—it's removing you and me. That's what's at the heart of it....
>
> You have been taken over by a Jewish cabal....The church of Jesus Christ, you're next. Get it through your head! They're coming for you. There will be a purge. That's the next thing that happens when Jews take over a country—they kill millions of Christians.[32]

This is incredibly irresponsible, incendiary rhetoric, the kind of rhetoric that can lead to Jewish bloodshed, as unstable people hear the words of Rick Wiles and decide to take matters into their own hands. To say it again, this is what happens when you buy into the antisemitic lies: you lose touch with reality.

As for Jews taking over a country and killing millions of Christians, there's one country in the world that is run by the Jewish people, namely Israel, and Christians there have more religious liberty than in any other country in the Middle East. Not only so, but throughout history, millions of Jewish people have been killed in Christian, Muslim, and atheistic countries—not the reverse.

But people who embrace antisemitic views don't care about the truth. Instead, because Jewish activists were involved in the Communist Revolution in Russia, that means "the Jews" took over and killed millions of Christians. And, we are told, they will do the same thing in America when they take over here.

It's Time to Expose the Lies

My friend, we must expose this fearmongering, we must reject these hateful lies, and as followers of Jesus, we must shout from the rooftops, "We will not allow antisemitism to triumph, and we will not allow the Lord's name to be tarnished by Christians who demonize the Jewish people!" Together, we can help push back this evil tide.

On May 17, 2019, Doc Burkhart, the vice president and general manager of TruNews, gave a passionate on-air appeal to Christian viewers, urging them to renounce their support for Israel and to recognize that they have been duped by people who use Israel to line their own pockets. He then exhorted his Christian viewers to confess, "Jesus, You are my Promised Land." So much for the Jewish people having a place to live, let alone a place promised by God. (See chapters 8 and 11 for more on this.) And Burkhart made this call like an evangelist, instructing those watching to write to the address on their screen if they had prayed with him. Talk about a perversion of the altar call.[33]

Tragically, even though TruNews and Texe Marrs have gone to new extremes, these views have been propagated by other evangelical leaders in recent decades. As I pointed out in the first edition of *Our Hands Are Stained With Blood*, published in 1992, Rev. Ted Pike, who leads an evangelical prayer ministry to this day, quoted "Does Israel Have a Future?" author Ray Sutton saying this about Israel back in 1984:

> The representative view can therefore advocate love for the Jew, while being able to reject his anti-Christian nation that persecutes Christians and butchers other people who need Christ just as much as they. It can work for the conversion of Israel without becoming the pawn of a maniacal nationalism, a racial supremacy as ugly and potentially oppressive as its twentieth century arch enemy, Aryanism [i.e., Nazism].[34]

Pike went on to say:

> We have unearthed irrefutable evidence that Israel is a dominant and moving force behind the present and coming evils of our day. To our amazement we find that Israel is not that trusted, familiar friend we thought we had known. Rather she is a misshapen facsimile of everything we had so fondly bid godspeed to.... We are at last confronted with a monstrous system of evil which, if unresisted, will destroy us and our children and bring the entire world into such darkness, oppression, and satanic dominion that only the coming of Jesus Christ can make it right again.[35]

When Reverend Pike joined me on the air on May 13, 2019, he still held to these views. He also pointed to the allegedly evil nature of the Talmud, claiming he had documented it all on his website.[36] How tragic and how pathetic. When I asked him if he could read the Talmud in its original Hebrew and Aramaic, his answer was no. Yet somehow he was an expert on its contents.

On the Catholic side, perhaps the most prominent voice making antisemitic claims is that of Dr. E. Michael Jones. Among Jones' anti-Jewish books (and mini-books) are:

- *The Jews and Moral Subversion*
- *The Catholic Church and the Jews*
- *Catholics and the Jew Taboo*
- *Jewish Fables: Darwinism, Materialism, and other Jewish Fables*
- *Jewish Privilege*
- *Shylock's Ewes and Rams: Economics and Morality*
- *The Jewish Revolutionary Spirit: And Its Impact on World History* (this is his magnum opus, amounting to twelve hundred pages)

It certainly looks like Jones is obsessed with "the Jews." The Anti-Defamation League (ADL) summarizes Jones this way:

> E. Michael Jones is an anti-Semitic Catholic writer who promotes the view that Jews are dedicated to propagating and perpetrating attacks on the Catholic Church and moral standards, social stability, and political order throughout the world. He portrays the Jewish religion as inherently treacherous and belligerent towards Christianity. He describes Jews as "outlaws and subversives [who use] religion as a cover for social revolution," and claims that Judaism possesses "a particularly malignant spirit." Jones also imagines the contemporary world, with its social ills, as having been cast in the imprint of Judaism, characterizing 21st-century civilization as "a Jewish world run on commercial principles." He also identifies this "Jewish modernity" as representing "blood, the law, calculation, and hate."[37]

The ADL goes on to say:

> In the tradition of conspiracy theorists, Jones credits Jews with orchestrating occurrences as varied and disconnected from the Jewish experience as the Protestant Reformation and the French Revolution. He also blames Jews for Bolshevism, Freemasonry, and an alleged contemporary "Jewish takeover of American culture."...Jones argues that mass killings of Jews throughout history have been understandable reactions to Jewish beliefs and behavior. He goes so far as to justify Eastern European pogroms and even the Nazi Holocaust on these grounds. As he wrote in a 2003 *Culture Wars* article, "[T]he Nazi attempt to exterminate the Jews was a reaction to Jewish Messianism (in the form of Bolshevism) every bit as much as the Chmielnicki pogroms flowed from the excesses of the Jewish tax farmers in the Ukraine."[38]

Those "evil Jews" are always guilty, even when they're getting massacred. Somehow they provoked it. As Jones explained in an interview with Alex Jones of InfoWars, "One of the books that Hitler burned were [*sic*] the books of Magnus Hirschfeld," who was a Jewish-German sexologist who advocated for homosexual and transgender rights. Dr. Jones continued:

> If [Hirschfeld] didn't exist, Hitler would have to create him.... Suddenly these people [meaning the Jewish people] are let loose, people like Magnus Hirschfeld are let loose, and suddenly the people [meaning the German people] are resentful, they don't want the corruption of their morals, and they turn to somebody like Hitler because he said he would straighten them out.... This could have been stopped earlier.... The great uncle of Pope Benedict wrote a book *Jüdisches Erwerbsleben*, Georg

> Ratzinger. And he said if the church doesn't step in and defend the people by enforcing the laws that protect the moral order, the German people are going to look for a leader. Well guess what the German word for *leader* is? It's *Führer*!...They found their leader. This is the type of reaction we want to prevent here in America. And the way we prevent this is by open dialogue...where we are able to criticize the people who have subjected us to this reign of pornographic terror![39]

Jones has frequently claimed "the Jews" have used pornography as a weapon to destabilize societies and take over American culture.[40] So when Jones says he must be able to call out "the people who have subjected us to this reign of pornographic terror," he means to blame "the Jews" for the rise of pornography. Otherwise, Jones alleges, failure to have the freedom to demonize the Jewish people will mean that society will react against their immorality, potentially leading to another Holocaust.

What utterly twisted logic. And need I mention that the man known as the father of the sexual revolution in America was Alfred Kinsey, who was anything but Jewish? Or that the man most responsible for the rise of pornography in America was Hugh Hefner, who was also anything but Jewish? The same could be said of porn king Larry Flynt of *Hustler* infamy, among other non-Jewish porn pioneers.

But as the ADL notes:

> Jones' views are not limited to religious Jews. He applies his theory of Jewish subversiveness to Jews of all ideological and religious stripes, from traditional rabbis and political conservatives to militant atheists and Marxists. For Jones, any Jew who does not embrace Christianity rejects God and the natural order of the universe. Jones therefore concludes unambiguously that "every Christian, insofar as he is a Christian, must be anti-Jewish."[41]

In short, Jones believes that since Jesus is identified in John's Gospel as God's Logos[42]—which for Jones includes God's wisdom, morality, and self-revelation—and since every Jewish person (who is not a Christian) *consciously rejects Jesus*, then everyone who is Jewish has consciously rejected God's wisdom, morality, and truth. And so by rejecting Logos, the Jewish people *as a whole* have set themselves on the path of moral subversion.[43] In another context, Jones writes, "Ethnos [meaning every people group] needs Logos, especially if it aspires, as every ethnic group does, to become a nation."[44] Israel's rejection of Logos, then, dooms it on a national level. This explains the titles of some of Jones' books, such as *The Jews and Moral Subversion*. This is simply who they are.

In reality, the vast majority of the global Jewish community does not consciously reject Jesus any more than the vast majority of Christians worldwide make a conscious decision to reject Buddha. Neither group really thinks about these figures outside of their own group, other than to know, "We don't follow that religion." This would be true of religious Jews, in particular, who are inundated with the claims of Judaism from their earliest days. Yet Jones tries to make one and the same case against both secular and religious Jews, as if their moral base or view of God or sexual ethic were identical. And so Jones can blame the Jewish people for pornography and the sexual revolution, knowing full well that religious Jews view pornography as a terrible plague and stand categorically against the sexual revolution.

This means, in reality, "the Jews" are not to blame. Rather, *some* Jewish people played a major role in the rise of pornography and in the sexual revolution, while *the great majority* did not (in particular, those who are religious). But why quibble over facts when your whole case is based on demonizing "the Jews"?

Dexter Van Zile, Christian media analyst for the Committee for Accuracy in Middle East Reporting and Analysis (CAMERA), notes:

> Jones regularly portrays Jews and Israel as interfering with and controlling American foreign policy. In one interview he declared that... Israel shared responsibility for the assassination of U.S. President John F. Kennedy with the CIA and Lyndon Johnson. In this same interview he boasted of traveling to Iran where he told audiences that there are three reasons why Iran no longer has a nuclear agreement with the United States—Sheldon Adelson, Bernard Marcus and Paul Singer.
>
> "Three rich Jews determine American foreign policy," he said. In another trip, which was paid for by the mullahs, Jones told his audience that Iran, a country whose elites hang gays and orchestrate mob violence against women to keep them in the hijab "is the leader of the free world."[45]

Somehow, though, the Iranian Muslims are not the bad guys. It's "the Jews" who are sabotaging things. Van Zile continues:

> "If it weren't for Jews, we would not have abortion in this country," [Jones] said in an interview late last year posted on the internet in the aftermath of the murder of 11 Jews at the Tree of Life Synagogue in Pittsburgh.
>
> The Pittsburgh shooter, Jones said, was acting out the lessons taught by Jews both conservative and liberal. Liberal Jews promote and invite their murder with their support for abortion. Conservative Jews promote and invite their murder by supporting Israel despite the violence

> the Jewish state has inflicted on the Palestinians, particularly at the Gaza Strip, which he deceptively reduced to a confrontation between Israeli snipers and unarmed Palestinians—as if Hamas operatives haven't promised to murder Israelis and haven't tried to cut their way into Israel with explosives.
>
> "They've been undermining the moral law in the name of liberation," he said. "That's what abortion is. That's what pornography is. That's what gay rights is. And now, that's what Zionism is."[46]

But there's more, and it's the perfect illustration of what happens when you buy into the antisemitic lies:

> Jones portrays the priest abuse scandal that is rocking the Catholic church as a Judeo-Protestant conspiracy designed to destroy the church and its ability to stand up against the excesses of capitalism. In 2010, Jones told a group of Catholics in Ireland that, "the current scandals are being orchestrated by the church's traditional enemies—Protestants and Jews—in order to destroy traditional cultures and make the world safe for capitalism and the universal rule of mammon."[47]

Yes, the Jews are responsible for the Catholic priest sex scandals! For good reason, Van Zile concludes by saying, "No matter how much he and his followers want to deny it, Jones's mystical Jew-hatred represents a real threat to the safety and welfare of American Jews, just as the writings of antisemites in Russia and Europe in the late 1800s and early 1900s set the stage for violence against Jews in the 1930s and 40s."[48]

And when African Americans committed a series of violent antisemitic attacks in greater New York in late 2019—including a deadly shooting and a vicious machete attack—Jones tweeted:

> Black people are attacking Jews in record numbers. Abe Greenwald says "there's nothing that self-pitying 'victims' find easier than blaming Jews for their misery."
>
> Who does Abe think taught the blacks to play the victim card in the first place?[49]

So everything is the fault of the Jewish people!

And as antisemitism rises in America and the nations, who is to blame for that? Obviously, the Jewish people! As Jones posted on Twitter on January 5, 2020, in response to an article by the *Christian Science Monitor* titled "Why Anti-Semitism Is Surging Across the Political Spectrum," "The Christian Science Monitor doesn't really tell us why. To learn why, read my book Jewish Privilege."[50]

After Iran responded to President Trump's decision to kill arch-terrorist Gen. Qasem Soleimani in early 2020 by drone attack in Iraq, Jones appeared on Iranian-run Press TV to say this:

> You don't want to play into the hands of your enemies. And I'm talking about the Israelis. I mean the whole point of this is to get America to fight Israel's wars. That's been going on for twenty years now. That was the whole point of the neoconservative takeover. Do you want to do that?...I'm talking about you, the Revolutionary Guard now. Do you want to propel America into another war in the favor of Israel?[51]

Commenting on this, Van Zile said, "It's time to call Jones what he is: The Ayatollah's man in South Bend."[52]

When I interviewed Dr. Jones on my radio broadcast (it was an interview, not a debate), I warned him that his rhetoric could lead to violence against American Jews. This is a charge that he rejects categorically, emphasizing that he holds to the Catholic doctrine of *Sicut Judaeis Non*, meaning that no one has the right to harm the Jewish people.[53] Nonetheless, as Van Zile rightly notes, "Boiled down to its basics, Jones's message is 'Don't attack the Jews (*no matter how badly they deserve it!*)' but after a few iterations and echoes, Jones's message is reduced to 'They deserve it!'"[54]

After the Poway synagogue shooting, I made clear that the shooter, John Earnest (rather than Dr. Jones), was responsible for the murderous act. And I stated that we did not have any proof that Earnest was familiar with Jones' material. But I emphasized that Earnest's ideology was in harmony with that of Jones (in terms of the guilt of the Jewish people) and that the Poway shooting underscored the warnings I had given regarding the danger of such rhetoric.

Jones responded by writing a mini-book titled *Is Christian Anti-Semitism Responsible for the Poway Synagogue Shooting?* It functions primarily as an attack against me (my name occurs forty-five times in just twenty-four pages) while answering the larger question posed by the title. In short, according to Jones, the issue was white nationalism rather than Christian antisemitism, and had Earnest been a good Catholic with sound theology, he would not have carried out such acts.

My only response is this: If the good Catholic theology of E. Michael Jones has produced this level of antisemitism, not to mention the Catholic Church's historic sins against the Jewish people, this is like a black pot—a very black pot—calling the kettle black. In sum, if Dr. Jones believes he is protecting the Jewish people from violence with his accusations against them, then the old saying applies quite well here: *With friends like these, who needs enemies?*

CHAPTER 5

WILL JEWS BEHEAD CHRISTIANS UNDER THE NOAHIDE LAWS?

THE HEADLINE IS stark and dire: "The Noahide Laws and Planned Guillotine Genocide of All Christians and Non Jews Worldwide."[1] Christians, beware! The "evil Jews" are about to pass laws that will take effect worldwide, and soon you will be beheaded as idolaters!

Other warnings are just as horrifying:

- "When it comes to the Noahide Laws or the seven laws of Noah, seriously you should be terrified."[2]
- "Most people in the World have no knowledge of the Noahide Laws. These laws will cause the death of many. The question is, are you prepared?"[3]
- "Let's be blunt. This blog post is a complete denunciation of the Noahide Laws—these are anathema to the followers of the truth in MASHIACH—who is the way, the truth, and the life."[4]

There are even websites devoted entirely to warning followers of Jesus about the dangers of these Noahide Laws.[5] One such site announces, "The Goyim Evangelicals Seek to be Raped on Yom Kippur and Palestinian Noahide Enforcement."[6]

Why all the fearmongering? Why the hysteria? This is just the latest conspiratorial, antisemitic lie, the most recent version of "The evil Jews will take over the world and kill all their enemies, starting with the Christians."

Someone might say, "But I've seen presentations about these Noahide Laws, and it's really quite scary. There's nothing manufactured or made up.

I've seen the quotes from the rabbis. I've read the relevant texts. This stuff is really dangerous!"

Are you sure? One-hundred-percent sure? I'm quite happy to separate fact from fiction, and in a moment we'll review the relevant texts. But first, let me show you what happens when I post videos on YouTube challenging this hysteria. I get responses like these, which alone should tell you that something is amiss (and notice the rampant character assassination, coupled with accusations of lying, much of this coming from professing Christians):

- "Wow, Dr Brown—you are an absolute liar. You claim the noahide laws are related to Scripture (Acts 15)? I always knew something was wrong about you: you always seems proud of your intellectual knowledge calling yourself doctor but you also always lack zeal passion. We worship God thru Lord Jesus Christ spiritually, not by knowledge as God is spirit and we keep faith in Lord Jesus Christ thru out faith and walk with Jesus thru His Holy Spirit. why are you deceiving christians? what is your true agenda?"
- "Dr Brown—Why would you lie & deliberately deceive christians??? You have explaining to do to christians. How can you lie to bodies of Lord Jesus Christ?"
- "If you are such a christian, why do you support the noahide laws? you are not a christian, you are a talmudic jew just like any pharisee that JESUS rebuked. wolf in sheep's clothing."
- "It's refreshing to see an honourable Jew but does he dare speak about the Jewish agenda, the dark, demonic vision of the world as pushed by the Zionists? Does he dare talk about the filth in Talmud? And yes, I know not all Jews are the same, but Israel is supposedly a democracy, people have the power to remove the psychotic, murderous, lying thug Netanyahu and they don't, so they're complicit in crimes against humanity and will be held accountable sooner or later, as they have been held accountable before in history but then we were merciful and naively believed they can change."
- "Jew worshiping Dr. Brown. Dr Brown is an ignorant man and has not enough information to defend his position. Stop worshipping Jews. He is a foolish man."
- "The Lord rebuke you Satan."

- "Dr Jack—for sure. Silliness for utter fools."
- "But you're full of it promoting nohaide laws. Why not tell the christens they are about to be beheaded for believing in Jesus tell your fellow Jews to love one another. You're a Zionist in sheeps clothing Over five million Palestinians have been murderd since 1948 tell the people about the [old yidden] plan. Tell america what going to HAPPEN."
- "You are leading the flock to Hell Dr. Michael Brown so we know that Jews are allowed to lie about their ancestry etc. You had better expose the truth about the 7 Noahide Laws for Hell awaits you and the Lake of Fire."
- "Mr Brown, who controls the media? Who controls Congress? Why do we have a majority of people in our government who have dual citizenship? Who controls Hollywood? Who controls what we can and cannot say about Israel with the anti-semitic trick? Who are the banksters? Who created Israel? And no God, would never create a racist, cruel occupation of ethnic cleansers. So why, should we not be concerned? We aren't blind to the Zionist agenda, and Zionists are not friends to Christians. Shame on you Brown. Dr Brown is laughing at Christians who have legitimate concern. His hubris is nauseating. He is a Zionist gatekeeper. Beware of his koolaid. Mikeal Brown. The Zionist gate keeper. Beware of his lies."
- "Dr Brown is lying to his audience about the Noahide Laws and Judaism. He will never bring up the evidence."
- "You're in bed with the deep STATE because you flip flopped on Noahide Laws that are NOT Torah their plan is to kill all Christians!"
- "Why are you so evil? Noahide.com is not a theory. sub laws Courts of justice #16 IS the EVIDENCE! "That the court is to administer the death penalty by the sword" [i.e., decapitation]. Why do you ignore this by Rabbi Cohen and UN that means UNIVERSAL NOAHIDE? YOU ARGUE ABOUT REALITY."
- "Brown your a kaballist that's easy to spot by the [expletive] that comes out of your filthy lying mouth.... Wipe that

> [expletive] eating grin off your face Brown, you're a shill [expletive] gate keeper."

To repeat: much of this rhetoric comes from professing Christians, some of whom claim to have enjoyed my teachings before this. But now that they have bought into the Noahide lies, I have become a dangerous liar and deceiver, in bed with the deep state—and more.

In reality, though, this is not about me. Not in the least. Rather, as I have done throughout this book, I cite these quotes to point to a larger problem. Why would people react so irrationally? Why would they get so worked up over something so far-fetched? Why would they impugn the motives of a fellow believer (and leader in the body of Christ) rather than question the evidence they've seen?

In my opinion, there are two primary reasons. First, in these days of viral internet conspiracy theories, once something catches fire, it's hard to stop the flames from spreading. The momentum grows by the minute, and before you know it there are tens of thousands of related links, giving the theory an air of credibility. Second, this particular conspiracy theory is about the Jewish people, in particular the Jewish rabbis. Surely these men are capable of doing anything![7]

What, then, are the simple facts about the so-called Noahide Laws? And what is the basis for the hysteria?

According to rabbinic tradition, God gave Adam six laws in the garden, supplementing them with a seventh law given to Noah after the flood, hence the so-called Seven Noahide Laws,[8] and Judaism believes that these seven laws are incumbent on the entire human race.[9] In contrast, Judaism believes God gave the Torah to Israel alone, with its 613 commandments, supplemented and expanded by rabbinic tradition. The relevant Wikipedia article presents an accurate summary: "The Seven Laws of Noah include prohibitions against worshipping idols, cursing God, murder, adultery and sexual immorality, theft, eating flesh torn from a living animal, as well as the obligation to establish courts of justice."[10]

Can these laws be derived from Old Testament texts? Overall, yes, but not exclusively from the texts used by the ancient rabbis, namely Genesis 2:16 and 9:4–6. They can only be derived from these specific verses by means of a forced, rabbinic reading of the texts.

But are the laws themselves good? Would followers of Christianity, Judaism, and Islam agree that we should not worship idols, curse God, or commit murder, sexual immorality, or theft? Would we agree that we should not eat flesh torn from a living animal and that we should establish courts of justice? Certainly, we would.

Where, then, is the basis for such hysteria and fear among Christians? The line of reasoning goes like this: 1) according to rabbinic teaching, Christians are guilty of idolatry because of their belief in the Trinity, in particular their belief in the deity of Jesus; 2) under the Noahide Laws, the penalty for idolatry is death by beheading; and 3) because these laws seem innocent, the world will embrace them, leading to the beheading of millions of Christians.

As a viewer commented on our YouTube channel:

> According to Rabbi Tovia Singer, Christianity is idolatry. Tovia Singer supports the Noahide Laws. The Noahide Laws require death to all those who practice 'idolatry.' This is supported by the Talmud. The Vatican supports the Noahide Laws. The United Nations support the Noahide Laws. President Donald Trump supports the Noahide Laws. Where will you stand, Dr. Brown?? For Jesus Christ or the 'harmless' Noahide Laws?

So, the argument goes, you either follow Jesus, or you support the Noahide Laws. You either warn the Christian world about this nefarious Jewish plot, or you deny the Lord. There is no in-between.

As for me, I support the preaching of the gospel of Jesus to every human being on the planet. I support presenting Yeshua, the Messiah and Lord, to my Jewish people, calling them to repent and turn to Him and be saved. I support taking the message of the cross to the ends of the earth until every last people group on the planet has heard the word of the Lord.

I do not support a worldwide movement that seeks to improve human beings without converting them. I do not support an ecumenical effort where the religions of the world work as one to bring about moral reformation. But I also do not support spreading lies and sparking unneeded fears, and that's why I have spoken against the Noahide Law hysteria.

Looking at the Sources in Greater Depth

Is this latest conspiratorial theory, then, made up out of whole cloth? Certainly not. Rather, like many other conspiratorial theories, it mixes fact with fiction, creating a very toxic potion.

Let's start by asking if the concept of the Noahide Laws is gaining more and more support around the world. It certainly is, as the AskNoah.org website is proud to announce:

> The universality of these principles and global import was recognized in 1982 by President Ronald Reagan when he spoke of "the eternal validity of the Seven Noahide Laws [as] a moral code for all of us regardless

> of religious faith" (Proclamation on the National Day of Reflection, April 4, 1982).
>
> Seven years later, in 1989, President George H. W. Bush not only proclaimed that these "Biblical [Bush actually said, "Ethical"] values are the foundation for civilized society," but he also recognized that "A society that fails to recognize or adhere to them cannot endure."[11]

Even more importantly, AskNoah.org points to

> House Joint Resolution H.J.RES.104.ENR, Designating March 26, 1991, as Education Day, U.S.A. The Seven Noahide Laws: "Congress recognizes the historical tradition of ethical values and principles which are the basis of civilized society and upon which our great Nation was founded...these ethical values and principles that have been the bedrock of society from the dawn of civilization, when they were known as the Seven Noahide Laws."[12]

More recently, the Stop Noahide Law blog noted that every year since President Trump entered office, he has signed the Education Day USA proclamation but with no mention of the Noahide Laws, speaking only of "the importance of 'education'" and honoring Rabbi Schneerson, who was a strong proponent of the Noahide Laws.[13]

And the blog is quick to point out, "Jewish Noahide Law calls for the death of anyone practicing idolatry, blasphemy or sexual morality; it also obligates non-Jews to set up courts to carry out these executions."[14]

The Vatican, too, has spoken favorably of the Noahide Laws, leading to this response from the same blog:

> If the Jews have made it clear that the Noahide Laws are not Biblical but Talmudic and that Christians are most certainly idolaters why is the Vatican using obvious deception to mislead Catholics into believing the Noahide Laws will not negatively effect [*sic*] Christians who are supposed to submit to these laws which override their "individual freedoms"?[15]

In keeping with this, the Seven Laws of Noah website asks, "Is Christianity compatible with being a Noahide and observing the Seven Laws of Noah?" The answer is categorical and clear. It is absolutely impossible for a Christian to be a true Noahide, since "Christianity is a despicable form of idol worship." It brands Christianity a cult, claiming that it "has led to the deaths and tortures of tens of millions of Jews at the very least." The website even alleges that Christianity is a "form of psychological warfare against Jews," which is why there is no possible way a Christian can be an observer of the seven laws of Noah.[16]

The obvious question, then, is this: Why would American presidents and the pope affirm these laws if it meant the death penalty for Christians? The answer is simple: according to the prevailing rabbinic view in recent centuries, Christianity is not idolatrous (at least not for Gentile Christians). As the My Jewish Learning website explains:

> The prohibition against idolatry refers specifically to idolatrous worship, and not to beliefs. In later generations, Jews had to determine whether the prevailing religious cultures in which they lived were idolatrous. Since Islam is strictly monotheistic, Muslims have always been considered Noahides. Since the later Middle Ages, Jews have acknowledged that the Christian doctrine of the Trinity was not the same as idolatry, and they were also recognized as Noahides.[17]

As noted by Rabbi Louis Jacobs, who was one of the most respected conservative Jewish scholars of the last century, although the earlier rabbis viewed Christianity as idolatrous,

> eventually, a distinction was made, unknown in the talmudic sources, according to which Christianity did constitute idolatry for Jews but not "for them" (i.e. Christians). A Christian did not offend against the Noahide Laws...since the Torah allows a Gentile, but not a Jew, to worship another being in addition to God.[18]

That's why an organization like the Jewish Institute for Global Awareness can teach the following:

> By understanding, internalizing and following a set of Divinely-ordained moral imperatives and universal ethics known as the Seven Noahide Laws, the world can produce more just societies, which are better able to receive and retain G-d's Presence. We seek to inspire our fellow human beings, because we are all descendants of Noah who, together with his family, is described in the Hebrew Bible as the survivor of The Flood and who thus became the ancestor of all of humanity. However, not only do we seek to inspire everyone who follows the Abrahamic religions (Jews, Christians, and Muslims) to follow these Noahide Laws but also those of every race, color, or creed.[19]

As professor David Novak explains, the result of the progressive development of rabbinic law on this subject "was to consider pure idolatry to be, at least in the Christian West, a thing of the past....Theological grounding for this was made by emphasizing the historical connection between Judaism and Christianity, especially the explicit Christian acceptance of the Hebrew Bible and the doctrine of *creatio ex nihilo*."[20]

To be sure, there is ongoing discussion about the question of Christianity and idolatry, as explained on the Wikinoah website, which states, "Within Judaism it is a matter of debate whether all Christians should be considered Noahides." Then, after outlining the issues, it concludes with, "In summary, classical idolatry has been clearly defined by Jewish Law. Christianity, however, has been defined as something less. The problem is defining how much less, and for what purposes."[21]

Interestingly, the article on this site devoted to Christianity and Noahide Law ends with entries on Christian opposition to the laws and Christian support of the laws. Regarding Christian opposition, the article notes:

> Some Christians believe that their existence implies that Jews may set up a legal system that would effectively outlaw Christianity. Based on the out-of-context claims that…"all Christians are idolators," and "punishment for idolatry is the death penalty," and that "the Rabbis have absolute control and authority over Noahides," some Christian groups [have] generated a lot of noise against the Noahide community.[22]

Yes, "a lot of noise" would certainly describe this Christian opposition, as illustrated in some of the angry quotes I cited previously. In response to these concerns, the Jewish community has explained that 1) Noahide Law can be compared to Catholic social teachings, which seek to establish a "minimal threshold of morality"; 2) Judaism "does not set up governments to force Jewish beliefs on non-Jews"; 3) Jewish law does *not* treat Christians as idolaters; 4) the Jewish people do *not* carry out the death penalty, even within their own religious communities; 5) the rabbis have no control of any kind over the Noahides. Indeed, "Even in theory, the Rabbis cannot enforce their decisions on non-Jews anywhere outside of the Land of Israel."[23]

As for Christian support of the Noahide Laws, the article is not accurate here, referring primarily to groups that have left traditional Christianity in favor of becoming Noahides. Personally, I don't know any Bible-based Christian groups that support preaching the Noahide Laws rather than preaching Jesus. But the important takeaway here is simple: the idea that Jewish leaders are trying to get the Noahide Laws passed worldwide in order to put Christians to death is a myth, plain and simple—and it is a dangerous myth at that.

Why do I say it is dangerous? Simply because it fuels an irrational fear of the Jewish community, especially the rabbinic leaders. It creates the idea that these men are secretly plotting our destruction, that they come to us as sheep, speaking of harmony and peace, when this is all a setup for the beheading of Christians as idolaters.

So a leading twentieth-century rabbi can say this:

> A particular task is to educate and to encourage the observance of the Seven Laws among all people. The religious tolerance of today and the trend towards greater freedom gives us the unique opportunity to enhance widespread observance of these laws. For it is by adherence to these laws, which are in and of themselves an expression of Divine goodness, that all humankind is united and bound by a common moral responsibility to our Creator. This unity promotes peace and harmony among all people, thereby achieving the ultimate good. As the Psalmist said: "How good and how pleasant it is for brothers to dwell together in unity."[24]

But a skeptic will hear this:

> We are seeking to catch you unawares, to lull you to sleep, to lure you into our trap. Then, once we have the cooperation of the Vatican and the Islamic nations and the major governments of the world, we will implement our nefarious agenda. Death to the Christians! Death to the idolaters! Off with their heads!

How does one argue with this kind of thinking?

I have done my level best to explain the truth about the Noahide Laws, pointing out why they are no danger to Christians. In response, I'm told, "You are not a christian you are Shabbatian zhevi follower...Which basically makes you worse." (Shabbatai Zevi was the most famous false Messiah in Jewish history, gaining a massive following in the late seventeenth century. Yet somehow, because I reject conspiracy theories about the Noahide Laws, I'm one of his followers!)[25]

So there you have it. The Jewish people, true to their colors, are using the deception of the Noahide Laws to carry out their ultimate plan of world domination. And since these "evil Jews" hate the Christians most of all, the culmination of their plan will result in the slaughter of hundreds of millions of Christians. Anyone who denies this is complicit with the plot! Anyone who denies this is secretly working for the Mossad (or the rabbinic community)! Anyone who denies this has blood on his or her hands!

Now, take a moment and reread the outrageous comments I quoted previously—quotes accusing me of being a liar, of being a wolf in sheep's clothing, of being a worshipper of Jews, of being Satan, of being on my way to hell. Is their ire starting to make sense to you—if you can call it sense at all? And yet,

I repeat: many of those who are the most upset about the Noahide Laws are professing Christians. How can this be?

Are the Noahide Laws Really Dangerous?

Let's dig in a little deeper to see if there's any possible support for the idea that the Noahide Laws are really dangerous, especially for Christians. Let's assume that the rabbis *do* consider Christians to be idol worshippers and that the views I previously cited are not accurate. Even if this were the case, we would have to imagine the following scenario.

First, Jewish rabbis, who are despised and rejected in so many nations, would have to gain enough power and influence to get these laws passed worldwide but without letting anyone know that Christians were idol worshippers, soon to be beheaded. Second, these rabbis would have to convince these world leaders to enforce their laws, including the death penalty. Third, once the various countries, like the United States, realized that they were duped into recognizing these laws, they would nonetheless carry out the death penalty against Christians.

To call this utterly absurd would be accurate, if not overly kind. Such theories are outlandish and ridiculous, and you can rest assured this will not happen. Yet the moment the facts are presented, we get responses like this one on Twitter: "You are a dumb, brainwashed idol worshipper who can't understand simple language."[26] Or, "Dr Brown is a Zionist Jew and Sophist calling people who seek the truth about the #NoahideLaws 'Conspiracy Theorists.'"[27] And to support this statement, the last commenter included a link to a video by a Christopher Jon Bjerknes, claiming to "expose" me.[28]

Who, exactly, is Bjerknes? Although claiming Jewish descent, he has been rightly described as antisemitic, as he refers to Hitler as a Zionist, devotes more than four hundred pages to "exposing" Albert Einstein as a plagiarist, and claims that the genocide of two million Armenian Christians was carried out by "crypto-Jews" (that is, Jewish people pretending to be Muslims or claiming some other non-Jewish identity).

An article by Dr. Steven Leonard Jacobs in *Armenian Weekly* details just how extreme Bjerknes' views are. Jacobs, who is a respected professor at the University of Alabama and whose specializations include the Holocaust and genocide studies, notes, "Without evidence, [Bjerknes] argues that there were six reasons why the Jews of Turkey were 'motivated' to murder Assyrians" (meaning Armenian Christians). Specifically:

1. Jews consider the Armenians to be the Amalekites of the Hebrew Bible, and in Jewish mythology, the Jewish God (sic) commands

the Jews to utterly exterminate the Amalekites down to the last man, woman and child.

2. The Hebrew Bible, Jewish Talmud and Jewish Cabalistic writings instruct Jews to murder Christians and to impose the "Noahide Laws" in the "End Times," which laws forbid Christianity on pain of death, because Jews consider Jesus to be an idol, and the Noahide Laws forbid idol worship.

3. Jews wanted to discredit and ruin the Turkish Empire and the religion of Islam in order to create a secure environment for the formation of a Jewish colony in the Land of Palestine.

4. Jews wanted to remove an ancient enemy from the region—an enemy which would oppose the anointment of a Jewish King in Jerusalem as the crowning of the Anti-Christ.

5. Jews wanted to eliminate a skilled business and political competitor.

6. Jewish [people] wanted to foment a war between Christians and Moslems, which would start in the Balkans and grow into a world war which would destroy many of the empires and monarchies, and which would artificially pit Moslems and Christians, Slavs and Teutons against one another and leave the Jews standing in Jerusalem.

(Needless to say, [Bjerknes] supplies no supporting evidence for any of these claims because there is no supporting evidence to be had!)[29]

And notice once again how the Noahide Laws reenter the picture. Are you seeing a pattern? Do you now understand why I reference this as just the latest in a long train of conspiratorial, world-domination lies about the Jewish people?

Some might say, "But what about that quote from the Seven Laws of Noah website? That was pretty direct." It certainly was, but it is a totally fringe position on a totally fringe website with a totally anonymous web host. Why? As explained at the bottom of the homepage, "This site was created by a Ben Noach who would rather remain anonymous than risk persecution. This is the Olam Ha-Sheker (world of falsehood) and those who choose the path of truth are hated and reviled by the vast majority of people."[30]

Ironically, even as I write these words, Christians are being slaughtered around the world—and not by the Jewish community. They are being burned to death and hacked to death and beheaded, tortured, and imprisoned, especially by radical Muslims, Hindus, and communists. And yet, rather than focusing on the very real suffering experienced by our brothers and sisters worldwide, an increasing number of Christians are getting worked into a frenzy over the allegedly impending danger of the Noahide Laws. This is shameful and tragic.

"But," some might say, "what about the relevant texts that *do* speak of Gentiles being put to death for violating the Noahide Laws? Why do you keep ignoring them?"

Actually, I'm not ignoring them. I'm simply telling the truth about them. For example, in the book *The Divine Code: The Guide to Observing the Noahide Code, Revealed From Mount Sinai in the Torah of Moses*, it is stated that "a Gentile is forbidden to commit murder or bloodshed, and would be liable to the death penalty for this in a court of law."[31]

But this is purely theoretical. There has never, at any time in the last three thousand years, been an attempt by the Jewish community to establish worldwide courts of justice based on the rabbinic interpretation of the Noahide Laws that would then carry out the death penalty against violators. Not a chance. As Rabbi Jacobs notes, "It has not been sufficiently appreciated that all the Talmudic discussions about the seven laws of the sons of Noah were purely theoretical."[32] Pop goes the balloon!

That's why this same book, *The Divine Code*, explains, "If a Gentile is determined to commit idolatry, eat a limb from a living animal, or steal money or the like, one may not prevent the person from sinning by injuring him. One should rather warn the would-be violator about the severity of his forbidden action, and if he still sins, he can be judged in a court of law."[33]

"But," still others might say, "haven't you heard about the reconstituting of the Sanhedrin in Israel? The Jewish rabbis are about to assume control again!" As author and attorney Stephen Pidgeon, PhD, argues, "The Noahide Laws are being proposed as the standard of morality worldwide, and they will be adjudicated by an impaneled Sanhedrin, a group of seventy Jewish elders who will be adjudicating the world's morality, predicated upon the Talmud."[34]

So according to this scenario, the entire world—Russia, China, India, America, and all the Muslim nations—will submit to a panel of seventy Jewish rabbis, who will enforce their moral code under penalty of death. Right! The rabbis can't agree among themselves within Israel, let alone impose their will as a whole on the nation, let alone on the entire world, let alone with the result being that hundreds of millions of Christians are beheaded as idolaters. That's *a lot* to swallow—unless, of course, you already have swallowed the lie that the Jewish people already control the world and that the end goal of rabbinic Judaism is the destruction of Christians and others.

"But what if the theoretical death penalties became real death penalties?" some would ask. "What then?" One Orthodox rabbi who is a proponent of the Noahide Laws explained it this way to me:

> A number of people have been asking me about it. I'm not sure why it has become such a major issue. As I think I already mentioned, there's no movement that I am aware of (in the Jewish community) that is moving towards establishing a court for the purpose of killing non-Jews who violate the 7 Noahide Laws.
>
> It is true that according to the Jewish understanding of these Laws, when Moshiach [Messiah] comes, those who violate these commandments will be put to death. But that would be true of those who violate Shabbos [Sabbath] with witnesses etc.[35]

So this rabbi has also seen this sudden, unexpected fear about the Noahide Laws, which surprised him as it surprised me. But, he explains, there's nothing to worry about. There's no movement in the Jewish community to establish courts of law that would put Gentiles to death. (And again, who would enforce this? The Gentiles?) Rather, when the Messiah comes, then the death penalty will be enforced, both for Jew and Gentile. So a Gentile who committed adultery would be put to death, just as a Jew who violated the Sabbath would be put to death, since the whole Torah was given only to Israel. So much for Christians being singled out for slaughter.

"But," some might say, "this could happen under a one-world government set up by the Antichrist. After all, the Book of Revelation speaks of believers who have been beheaded."

Yes, but according to Revelation, the Antichrist will demand that the whole world worship him! And those who refuse to worship him and bow down to his rule will be beheaded. That is the exact opposite of the Noahide prohibition against idolatry. Instead, this is a call *for* idolatry, and those who will be killed are the ones who refuse to worship the Antichrist—called the beast—and his image. (See Revelation 13:11–18.)

This is confirmed by Paul, who wrote that the Antichrist "will oppose and will exalt himself over everything that is called God or is worshiped, *so that he sets himself up in God's temple, proclaiming himself to be God*" (2 Thess. 2:4, NIV, emphasis added). How utterly ludicrous, then, to argue that this same wicked ruler who sets himself up as God and demands to be worshipped will then outlaw idolatry under penalty of death. The Antichrist will hardly be the one to call on the world to worship the one true God alone. And the bottom line is that when the Antichrist comes, the last of our concerns will be the Noahide Laws.[36]

But there's no need for all the speculation and fearmongering, especially since throughout history believers have been beheaded for every reason *other* than the Noahide Laws. Just ask Paul, who was beheaded for refusing to acknowledge Caesar as Lord. Or ask the courageous Ethiopian Christians who were beheaded by ISIS terrorists for refusing to deny Jesus as Lord. That's where our focus should be.

Do I believe that Messianic Jews in Israel will suffer persecution from the religious Jewish community there? They already have, and they will in the future as well. It wouldn't surprise me if a fanatical, ultra-Orthodox Jew one day tried to stop the spread of Messianic Judaism by actually killing a believer in Jesus for his faith. (This was actually attempted once already.)[37] But there is zero connection between the religious persecution of Messianic Jews in Israel and a purported scenario in which a reconstituted Sanhedrin will dictate morality and religious practice worldwide at the point of the sword. Not in the least.

In addition, as I have stressed repeatedly, the major Jewish proponents of the Noahide Laws today do *not* view Christians as idolaters, as is evident in a January 2017 article from Breaking Israel News titled "Sanhedrin Calls on President Trump to Uphold Seven Noahide Laws." (Note that this newly reconstituted Sanhedrin is hardly recognized within Israel, let alone by the worldwide Jewish community.) The article, written by Adam Eliyahu Berkowitz, explains:

> In an ancient and honored Jewish custom, the nascent Sanhedrin sent a letter to the new leader of the U.S., President Donald Trump, blessing him and calling on him to take the lead in restoring America and the world. The Sanhedrin also called on the new president to acknowledge and uphold the Seven Noahide laws.[38]

Then, quoting directly from the beginning of the Sanhedrin's letter, we read this: "We thank God that a suitable man was chosen to lead America, whose values in the past symbolized a belief in God, and educated its people in morals and family values."[39]

Do you see that? The Sanhedrin recognizes that America's Christian values derived from "a belief in God"—not in idols. And that's why Rabbi Shimon Cowen, one of the world's leading proponents of the Noahide Laws and himself an ultra-Orthodox Jew, has called on Jews, Christians, and Muslims to unite around these laws. In the words of a joint statement issued by Rabbi Cowen and an Islamic and Catholic leader:

> "The common values making up this shared ethic are found in the Abrahamic stem of the world religions, Judaism, Christianity and Islam." They suggest that although western societies were founded on what has become known as the Judeo-Christian ethic, "the interaction of Islamic culture with Judeo-Christian culture, both in Australia and

> globally, has now made it desirable to seek a deeper common denominator, which we have here called the Abrahamic values."[40]

Interestingly, Cowen is a Chabad rabbi, meaning he is a follower of the late Rabbi Menachem Mendel Schneerson (1902–1994), still hailed the Messiah by many of his devotees and known simply as the Rebbe.[41] Yet while critics of the Noahide Laws claim that Schneerson equated Gentiles with animals and advocated for the death penalty for Christians, when the Supreme Court removed prayer from schools in 1962, the Rebbe argued against it, stating that the children should be allowed to pray to God. He also stated that this was in keeping with the nation's origins, which put a premium on religious liberty.[42]

Not only so, but biographer Chaim Miller writes:

> While the notion of the Trinity is rejected by the absolute monotheism of Judaism, the Rebbe pointed to numerous *halachic* [legal] rulings that the Trinity is not idolatrous for a non-Jew and is an acceptable form of worship for him. According to this view, it would be a positive fulfilment of the Noahide Code when Christians embrace their faith, especially if the alternative is atheism.[43]

As for Rabbi Cowen, the best-known Chabad spokesman for the Noahide Laws, he recognizes Gentile Christians as non-idolaters. What do you know! And when you read Cowen's summary of idolatry according to the Noahide Code, you quickly see it has no reference to Christians whatsoever.[44] In point of fact, Christian belief in the Trinity exalts the one true God—and the one true God alone. There is nothing even remotely idolatrous about it when rightly understood.[45]

But that is really beside the point. It is more likely that Santa Claus will come down your chimney than that the Sanhedrin would make an appeal to President Trump to recognize these laws, then say to him, "But wait! You didn't read the fine print. Christians are idolaters, so you need to start beheading them immediately. In fact, you'll need to find someone to behead *you* as well, since you profess to be a Christian."

Right! And surely the president will say, "Whatever you say. After all, you're Jewish, and the Jewish people rule the world. And be sure to behead Vice President Pence and Secretary of State Pompeo and Secretary of Housing and Urban Development Carson, among many others, since all of them are Christians." This is beyond nonsensical.

So a Noahide website makes this appeal:

You can be a beacon of light to dispel the darkness in the world, by reaching out to others with acts of goodness and kindness.

These 7 Goals will uplift your life and the lives of those around you:

1. Knowledge of the One True G-d.
2. Respect G-d's Holy Name.
3. Respect the Sanctity of Human Life.
4. Respect the Classic Family.
5. Respect the Property of Others.
6. Respect All Creatures.
7. Uphold Righteousness in your Judicial System.[46]

And a conspiracy theorist reads it like this: "We're encouraging you to pass a dangerous set of laws to be enforced by a group of elderly Jewish rabbis in Israel that will result in the beheading of hundreds of millions of Christians worldwide."

That is the madness we face today. And for exposing this madness, I'm told that I'm a "supporter of Rabbi Schneerson, of Chabad Lubavitch the Talmudist Cult that controls worldwide organized crime and the racist, segregated criminal state of Israel."[47]

What of the fact that I recently wrote a book contrasting the (false) claims that Rabbi Schneerson was the Messiah with the (real and wonderful) claims that Jesus is the Messiah?[48] That just proves how deep I have gone undercover! As one YouTube critic claims, "This guy is a mossad funded psyop to convince evangelicals that they should be bestest goys for Zionists." There you have it! And as another urges, "Michael just admit that you're a fake Christian and nothing but a subversive Jew." My cover has been blown!

Crazier still, after appearing on an anti-Zionist YouTube channel to discuss the Noahide Laws (the host, Adam Green, was fair and gracious), some of the commenters implied I was a Mason.[49] Yes, a Mason! (Adam had asked me if I was a Mason, as I asked him, for fun. I know almost nothing about the Masons and don't have a single friend who is an ex-Mason, let alone a practicing Mason.)

Some of the comments have been removed, but they included:

- "Mason is squirming out like the viper he is."
- "'I don't know any Free Masons' (rubs his eye)"
- "Someone else pointed out that at 1:35:30 that when he says 'I don't know any Freemasons' he covers one of his eyes....could be coincidence, but that is one symbol of their

little cult. The all seeing eye of Lucifer. Just an interesting observation."

- "That guy is a total Freemason!!! Or at the very least, he was lying his [expletive] off when you asked him. I was a communications major, I've learned lots about how to spot a liar & am practically a human lie detector & that guys nonverbal communication was SCREAMING so much louder than his spoken words!"[50]

So they *really* found me out. I'm a secret Mossad agent *and* a Mason, and I use secret Luciferian eye signals to dupe my unwitting audience. And people actually believe this! Hatred of the Jewish community really does make people lose all reason.

In all seriousness, I pray that God would have mercy on these deluded souls and that they would be delivered from deception. And may He act quickly, before someone decides it's time to shed Jewish blood lest the "evil Jews" start decapitating Christians. God help us!

CHAPTER 6

THE TRUTH ABOUT THE TALMUD

I WANT TO MAKE something perfectly clear at the outset of this chapter. I am not a Talmudic Jew. I do not believe in the authority of the Talmud or the divine inspiration of the Talmud, and I do not submit to Talmudic authority. In fact, the fifth and final volume of my Answering Jewish Objections to Jesus series is largely devoted to rebutting the Talmudic claim that there is an unbroken chain of authoritative tradition that runs from Moses on Mount Sinai to the rabbis of the Talmud.[1] At the same time, when the Talmud is falsely represented, I will set the record straight, especially when those false representations are used to demonize the Jewish people.

Sadly, given today's heightened climate of Christian antisemitism, telling the truth about the Talmud is like committing a cardinal sin. You are instantly accused of being a Judaizer, of being disloyal to Jesus, of not being a true believer. How dare you defend the Talmud! As expressed by Anne W. on our YouTube channel (in response to a video where I rebutted lies about the Talmud), "You are a wolf in sheep's clothing and an anti-Christ."

So for *telling the truth*, I am now "a wolf in sheep's clothing and an anti-Christ." For *combating lies*, I am now a dangerous deceiver. Do you see how blinding this hatred is?

It would be one thing if Anne had said, "Dr. Brown, I believe you are misinformed here, and your arguments are not convincing." But that's not what she (and many others) said. In her eyes, there was only one choice: I was not a true follower of Jesus. Rather, I was a wolf in sheep's clothing and an antichrist.

Others expressed similar sentiments. David wrote, "Get behind me Satan. He is swimming in the vomit of Judaism. In the name of Christ protect the peoples from the lies of this false teacher."

Another opined:

> If I had one [meaning, a Talmud], I'd urinate on the satanic garbage then burn it. It's only good for the dung hill. Dr Brown, you should have the same attitude if you loved your Mashiach because of what it says about him....I believe you love your Jewish (i.e., edometic benjimites) deniers in Christ and what their opinion is of you more than you love Christ himself and his instruction and the instruction of the apostles.[2]

And on and on it goes, with commenter after commenter claiming that I'm a deceiver and a liar and not a genuine follower of Yeshua—all because I defended the Talmud against inflammatory lies. This, to these viewers, is proof positive that I love Jewishness more than Jesus and that I have secretly infiltrated the church (yes, some make this claim!) to lead Christians away from Jesus and into Judaism.

But this is not really about me at all, although to attack me in these ways is more than ironic since I have probably written more books focused on preaching Jesus to the Jewish people and engaged in more public debates with rabbis than any man on the planet. That's why, more than twenty-five years ago, an ultra-Orthodox rabbi branded me "Public Enemy Number One." That's why another ultra-Orthodox rabbi told a colleague of mine that my writings were the most serious missionary threat to his community. And that's why yet another ultra-Orthodox rabbi told me that my aforementioned volume challenging the Talmud was the most substantial book of its kind in decades. Yet the moment I refute a popular lie about the Talmud, I become an antichrist, a wolf in sheep's clothing, and a denier of Jesus. Can you see how deeply this anti-Jewish prejudice runs?

Is it true that the Talmud says terrible things about Jesus? Is it true that the Talmud claims that Jesus was conceived when His mother, Miriam (Mary), had sex with a Roman soldier named Pantera? That Jesus went to Egypt to learn magic arts and returned to Israel to deceive the nation? That He is presently burning in excrement in hell?

It is *possible* that it does, as we will discuss shortly. But the fact I only say *it is possible*, rather than saying, "We know for sure the Talmud says all this," makes me suspicious to some. How dare I lessen the guilt of the evil rabbis who compiled the Talmud!

To be sure, there is no doubt at all that in the centuries following the compilation of the Talmud (by which I refer to the Babylonian Talmud, which received its final editing around AD 600), a collection of blasphemous, anti-Jesus Jewish legends was compiled titled *Toledot Yeshu*, meaning "The Story (or History) of Jesus."[3] And this book contains every one of the atrocious lies I just listed, along with many more.

That's why there are ultra-Orthodox Jews who to this very day believe these horrific things about Jesus. I have talked to some of them myself and watched them spit on the ground after saying His name (which they also mispronounce in a mocking way). This is grievous and ugly, a massive deception of the devil. Tragically, however, the horrific, even murderous, treatment of Jewish people at the hands of professing Christians over the centuries has only confirmed to these religious Jews just how evil this "Jesus" really is.[4] And it was largely in response to church persecution that *Toledot Yeshu* was compiled.

That, of course, does not lessen the blasphemous, disgraceful nature of these writings. They are as inexcusable as they are ugly. But it does underscore how little these Jewish leaders knew about the real Jesus, since most of them had never read a page of the New Testament and the only Jesus they knew was the false Jesus found in some of their own traditions. And this Jesus appeared to be the same false Jesus displayed by hypocritical and corrupt Christians.

Either way, though, whatever the reason for such blasphemous writings, Paul's words in Romans 11 to Gentile Christians should dictate our attitude and response:

> As far as the gospel is concerned, *they are enemies for your sake*; but as far as election is concerned, they are loved on account of the patriarchs, for God's gifts and his call are irrevocable. Just as you who were at one time disobedient to God have now received mercy as a result of their disobedience, so they too have now become disobedient in order that they too may now receive mercy as a result of God's mercy to you. For God has bound everyone over to disobedience so that he may have mercy on them all.
>
> —Romans 11:28–32, niv, emphasis added

So even if some (or even many) Jewish people are enemies of the gospel, they are still loved by God "on account of the patriarchs," and His gifts and promises to Israel are irrevocable. Not only so, but Paul calls on the Gentile believers in Rome to have a merciful attitude toward the lost sheep of the house of Israel, since they, the people of the nations, have received mercy from God as a result of Israel's disobedience. Would to God that the Messiah's own people could know the truth about Him! And would to God that Christians worldwide would demonstrate to the Jewish community who Jesus really is—in word, in deed, in sacrificial love, and in the power of the Spirit.

As to whether the Talmud itself makes these false accusations against Jesus, there's a long-term, scholarly debate about the topic. One major reason is that in some texts, the chronology is way off. In other words, there are different men named Yeshu—that's the Talmudic way of saying Jesus[5]—who lived more than a century apart. How could both of them be Jesus of Nazareth? Perhaps one or both of these texts is speaking of someone else? It's also true that in some cases, Jesus is not spoken of directly but is allegedly referred to as Balaam or the like (since Balaam was a notorious false prophet in Israel's history). But was this really a backhanded slap against Yeshua, or was the text literally speaking of Balaam?

After reviewing the relevant passages in depth, Orthodox Jewish teacher Gil Student writes:

> The standard rabbinic understanding of these passages is that these passages refer to at least two different people.... The first lived in the first half of the first century BCE during the reign of Alexander Janneus. The second lived in the first half of the second century CE, during the time of the Roman persecution that led to Rabbi Akiva's tragic death.
>
> The first, Yeshu Ben Pandira, started his own sect and had many followers. His heretical and idolatrous teachings lasted centuries after his life but, like so many Jewish sects, slowly died out after the destruction of the Temple.
>
> The second, Ben Stada, was simply a public idolater from an illustrious family who was caught and punished.[6]

So even though these different people are called Yeshu, they didn't live when Jesus lived. One lived about one hundred years before Jesus; the other lived more than fifty years after Jesus. Student also claims that "Balaam is not a talmudic codeword for Jesus." Rather, "Balaam in rabbinic literature is one of the archetype villains."[7]

In support of his views, Student cites some highly respected Jewish and Christian scholars, including Louis Ginzberg and John Meier. According to Ginzberg, "One may therefore state with absolute certainty that the entire Talmudic-Midrashic literature does not know of any nicknames for Jesus or his disciples."[8] In other words, *Balaam* is not a code word for Jesus, nor are other coded names used to mock the disciples. According to Meier, with regard to "the Mishna and other early rabbinic material: no text cited from that period really refers to Jesus."[9] What a strong, categorical statement.

Student concludes:

> It seems clear by now that there is no consensus whether Jesus is mentioned at all in the Talmud. Most of the supposed "blasphemies" of Jesus and Mary in the Talmud do not refer to them at all. However, there can be no denying, and no rabbi would deny this, that the authors of the Talmud did not believe in Jesus' messiahship or his divinity. If you are looking for Christian fellowship then Jewish literature is not

> the place to look. However, there is no basis at all to state unequivocably [*sic*] that the Talmud calls Jesus a bastard or that Mary was a prostitute who had sex with many men. As has been shown, those passages definitely do not refer to Jesus.[10]

Again, it's possible that the Talmud *does* make these terrible statements about Jesus, although Rabbi Moshe Shulman, a "counter-missionary" who strongly opposes my views about Jesus being the Messiah, believes the Talmud says absolutely nothing about Him.[11] Either way, there are some anti-Christian polemics in the Talmud and in later rabbinic literature, along with some deeply anti-Christian sentiments expressed to this day, in particular in ultra-Orthodox writings. But even so, it is not terribly different for a traditional Jew to believe that Jesus is a false prophet burning in hell than it is for Christians to believe that Muhammad is a false prophet burning in hell. This is blasphemous to Muslims, for whom Muhammad is the perfect man and the model of piety. Yet Christians have no problem believing that Muhammad is a false prophet who is lost for eternity. (That is my own belief.)[12]

Remember, we're talking about religious beliefs, and from a Christian perspective, Hinduism is a false religion filled with idolatry. We believe that Hindus who don't know Jesus are lost. We feel the same way about atheists, Buddhists, and others who do not know the Lord. We see them as lost and hell-bound unless God intervenes. Why should it shock us that many traditional Jews feel that way about Jesus?

Many of the Christians who bash me for telling the truth about the Talmud have no problem affirming that the greatest of the Talmudic rabbis are presently in hell. They have no problem saying they are snakes or false teachers or deceivers, based on the Lord's seven woes against the Pharisees in Matthew 23. This, of course, is terribly offensive to traditional Jews, who believe the Talmudic rabbis were exceptionally godly men who lived careful lives in the Lord's sight and sought to follow His laws with scrupulous devotion. Yet these same Christians who have no problem vilifying the heroes of the Jewish faith want to burn the Talmud for alleged attacks on Jesus. Why not simply say, "It looks like each group has some passionate beliefs"?

What Does the Talmud Really Say?

Again, there is great debate as to what, if anything, the Talmud does say about Jesus. But even if all the negative statements were in fact directed at Him, that still gives a false impression of the Talmud, which is a massive collection of twenty large volumes containing almost two million words of main text and far more than that in the commentaries. The passages that might speak of Jesus and His disciples amount to perhaps a few hundred words. So much for the Talmud being a collection of anti-Christian writings.

If you don't believe me, here's a sampling of the Talmud from the beginning of the tractate (meaning book) called Shabbat, which deals with Sabbath laws. You might find the text boring, dense, confusing, and very legalistic sounding. But you will certainly not find it to be focused on Jesus or Christian beliefs. And that's what you will find throughout the rest of the Talmud.

We start with the text of the Mishnah, the first compilation of Jewish laws dating back to roughly AD 220, using the translation of Jacob Neusner, who presents the text in outline form. The Mishnah here is trying to decide what constitutes work on the Sabbath, since it was forbidden to carry a load on that sacred day. (See Jeremiah 17:19–29.) This is how Shabbat begins:

1:1

A. [Acts of] transporting objects from one domain to another [which violate] the Sabbath
(1) are two, which [indeed] are four [for one who is] inside,
(2) and two which are four [for one who is] outside.
B. How so?

I C. [If on the Sabbath] the beggar stands outside and the householder inside,
D. [and] the beggar stuck his hand inside and put [a beggar's bowl] into the hand of the householder,
E. or if he took [something] from inside it and brought it out,
F. the beggar is liable, the householder is exempt.

II G. [If] the householder stuck his hand outside and put [something] into the hand of the beggar,
H. or if he took [something] from it and brought it inside,
I. the householder is liable, and the beggar is exempt.

III J. [If] the beggar stuck his hand inside, and the householder took [something] from it,
K. or if [the householder] put something in it and he [the beggar] removed it,
L. both of them are exempt.

IV M. [If] the householder put his hand outside and the beggar took [something] from it,
N. or if [the beggar] put something into it and [the householder] brought it back inside,
O. both of them are exempt.[13]

Are you confused yet? Well, that was the easy part (and again, just the opening lines). Now we delve into what is called the Gemara, which makes up the heart and soul of the Talmud, as the rabbis comment on the text of the Mishnah. Here, we'll use the expanded Steinsaltz translation, where the actual words of the Talmud are in bold print and his explanatory words are in regular type:

> **GEMARA:** We learned in our mishna: The acts of carrying out on Shabbat are two that comprise four. Similarly, **we learned** in the mishna **there,** in tractate *Shevuot*: **Oaths** on a statement, which, when violated, render one liable to bring a sin-offering **are two that comprise four.** The first two cases, which are mentioned explicitly in the Torah, are: One who swore that he would perform a specific action in the future and one who swore to refrain from performing said action. Based on an amplification in the language of the Torah, two more cases are added: One who swore that he performed a specific action in the past and one who swore that he did not perform said action.
>
> Similarly, with regard to **awareness of ritual impurity,** there **are two** cases **that comprise four.** It is prohibited for one who is ritually impure to enter the Temple or to consume a consecrated item. However, one who unwittingly violates this serious prohibition is obligated to bring a sacrifice for his transgression only if he was clearly aware of his ritually impure status both before committing the transgression and thereafter. The two cases of unwitting transgression in this area are: One who was aware and then forgot that he is ritually impure, and then either ate consecrated meat or entered the Temple, and subsequently recalled that he was ritually impure. Two additional cases are: One who was aware of his ritually impure status but was unaware that the food he was about to eat was consecrated and ate it, or he was unaware that he was about to enter the Temple and entered it.[14]

Is your head spinning now? And note that in this translation, these two detailed paragraphs of Gemara are based on just a handful of words from the original text. But the meaning is so concise and written in such a coded way that it takes many lines to explain just a few words (yet the Talmud consists of about two million words of text just like this). Then notice that the Gemara begins not by discussing the text we just read from the Mishnah but by discussing another text from a different tractate in the Mishnah, one that is similar because it also speaks of subdivisions within Torah law. Are you getting this?

This goes on for hundreds of pages, with ever-deepening, complex legal discussion, which then gets tied back to relevant verses in the Hebrew Scriptures and is then interspersed with stories, teachings, and edifying sayings. I can assure you that this is all very difficult to understand for an outsider, and it is virtually impossible to understand when simply reading isolated sentences translated into English. I can also assure you that Jesus is not the focus of the Talmud, if He is mentioned at all, nor is Christianity a topic of major concern for the Talmudic rabbis.

Again, if the Talmudic rabbis did make ugly comments about Jesus, that is inexcusable. And to this day, there are traditional Jews who spit on the ground after speaking Yeshua's name—which is really just a form of the name, since they won't pronounce it—believing He should be damned. But I repeat: 1) there is no certainty that Jesus is mentioned at all in the Talmud; 2) the Talmudic rabbis may have been reacting to hostile attacks from Christian leaders, with little idea of who Jesus really was; 3) even at worst, these attacks would be similar to the way some Christians view Muhammad, as a false prophet and dangerous misleader.

But what about other charges about the Talmud? Does the Talmud sanction pedophilia? Does the Talmud teach that Gentiles are like animals, made only to serve the Jewish people? Does the Talmud teach that a Jewish person can steal from a Gentile, or even kill Gentiles, with impunity?

Some might say, "I've seen lots of quotes taken straight from the Talmud—they are readily available online[15]—and I don't need you to explain them to me. They are simple and clear, and there's no denying what they say."

Here is the way some of the most commonly cited texts on anti-Jewish websites are interpreted. (As you read this list, try to view it through the eyes of someone who is already very suspicious of the Jewish people and in some cases downright hostile to them.)

- "When a Jew murders a gentile ('Cuthean'), there will be no death penalty. What a Jew steals from a gentile he may keep" (Sanhedrin 57a).
- "Jews may use subterfuges [lies] to circumvent a 'goy' [Gentiles]" (Baba Kamma 113a).
- "All children of the 'goyim' (Gentiles) are animals" (Yebamoth 98a).
- "Girls born of the 'goyim' are in a state of 'niddah' (menstrual uncleanness!) from birth" (Abodah Zarah 36b).
- "Gentiles prefer sex with cows" (Abodah Zarah 22a–22b).
- "Whosoever disobeys the rabbis deserves death and will be punished by being boiled in hot excrement in hell" (Erubin 21b).

- "If a 'goy' (Gentile) hits a Jew he [the Gentile] must be killed" (Sanhedrin 58b).
- "If a Jew is tempted to do evil he should go to a city where he is not known and do the evil there" (Moed Kattan 17a).
- "If a Jew finds an object lost by a 'goy' [Gentile] it does not have to be returned" (Baba Mezia 24a).
- "God will not spare a Jew who 'marries his daughter to an old man or takes a wife for his infant son or returns a lost article to a Cuthean'" (Sanhedrin 76a).
- "Christians (minnim) and others who reject the Talmud will go to hell and be punished there for all generations" (Rosh Hashanah 17a).
- "Those who read the New Testament ('uncanonical books') will have no portion in the world to come" (Sanhedrin 90a).
- "Jews must destroy the books of the Christians, i.e. the New Testament" (Shabbath 116a).
- "A Jew may marry a three year old girl (specifically, three years 'and a day' old)" (Sanhedrin 55b).
- "A Jew may have sex with a child as long as the child is less than nine years old" (Sanhedrin 54b).
- "When a grown-up man has intercourse with a little girl it is nothing" (Kethuboth 11b).
- "States that no rabbi can ever go to hell" (Hagigah 27a).
- "A rabbi debates God and defeats Him. God admits the rabbi won the debate" (Baba Mezia 59b).
- "The Rabbis taught: 'On coming from a privy (outdoor toilet) a man should not have sexual intercourse till he has waited long enough to walk half a mile, because the demon of the privy is with him for that time; if he does, his children will be epileptic'" (Gittin 70a).
- "A Jewish man is obligated to say the following prayer every day: Thank you God for not making me a gentile, a woman or a slave" (Menachot 43b–44a).

- "The gentiles are outside the protection of the law and God has 'exposed their money to Israel'" (Baba Kamma 37b).[16]

If you were skeptical of the Jewish people, this would confirm your worst suspicions, would it not? But is this really what the Talmud says? Are the rabbis this evil?

Frankly, if this was an accurate representation of the contents of the Talmud, I would shout it from the rooftops. It would be further proof that the Jewish people are lost, that they cannot look to their religious traditions to save them, and that they desperately need Jesus. As I mentioned at the outset of this chapter, I have written extensively *against* the inspiration of the Talmud, and I have no problem differing with its contents. And I do not believe our traditions can save us—I write this speaking as a Jew—while, conversely, I believe the gospel is to the Jew first and also to the Gentile.

But once again, this list gives a very misleading impression for several reasons. First, as you just saw from a tiny sampling of tractate Shabbat, Talmudic language is very difficult to understand, often requiring extensive commentary. Second, the Talmud records thousands of legal opinions and ethical statements, some of which are affirmed, some of which are rebutted, and some of which receive no comment. And often the context is very specific, because of which a single line pulled out by itself can seem to mean something very different than what the Talmud intended. Third, within the Talmud itself, many issues are not settled, meaning that just because something is stated in the Talmud doesn't mean Judaism holds to that position. Instead, it is the later Law Codes (including the *Mishneh Torah* and *Shulchan Aruch*) and Responsa Literature (meaning literature from leading rabbis answering legal questions) that give definitive rulings, and traditional Jews feel beholden to follow these later rulings.

Putting this all together, we learn that every quote from a single tractate of the Talmud must be analyzed against the evidence of the whole Talmud, which in turn must be analyzed against the evidence of the later definitive legal rulings. Only then can we get a picture of what Jewish people have taught and believed for centuries. And even then, sometimes the texts cannot be fully understood without the use of detailed commentaries. That's why rabbis refer to *yam ha-talmud*, "the sea of the Talmud," because the literature is so vast.

Let me give you just a few examples, and then I'll refer you to some videos and written material that will help you evaluate these charges for yourself. We'll start with Menachot 43b–44a, which we have been told teaches that a Jewish man is obligated to say the following prayer every day: "Thank you God for not making me a gentile, a woman, or a slave."

The Talmud does essentially say this, but it doesn't mean what you might think. Instead, it has to do with responsibility to observe the Law, something that Jews regard as a gift. In other words, contrary to the common Christian viewpoint, which basically says, "Thank God I'm not under the Law," a traditional Jew says, "Thank God for the gift of the Torah!" (See Psalm 19 and 119 for a similar point of view.)

Now, if you were a Gentile, you would not be required to observe the entire Torah since it was given to Israel, not the nations. The same holds true if you were a Jewish woman. There are certain commandments you would be exempt from keeping due to uniquely female situations that would not allow you to observe certain laws.[17] Finally, if you were a slave, you would not be able to keep the entire Torah because of your lack of freedom. Only a free Jewish male is considered responsible to observe the Torah, and for this privilege he thanks God every morning—yes, the privilege of being required to keep all the laws and commandments. That is something positive to him!

Now, you might find the concept chauvinistic or biased. And you can certainly contrast it with the words of Paul that in the Lord, "There is neither Jew nor Gentile, neither slave nor free, nor is there male and female, for you are all one in Christ Jesus" (Gal. 3:28, NIV). But the prayer itself is not as offensive as it might seem, since a free Jewish male is expressing thankfulness to God for the privilege of being called to observe the entire Torah.

Let's look at a more controversial—and serious—question. Does the Talmud sanction pedophilia? We'll look first at Ketubot 11b, which is often paraphrased as saying, "When a grown-up man has intercourse with a little girl it is nothing." (Internet sources often quote Yevamot 11b, which allegedly teaches that "sexual intercourse with a little girl is permitted if she is three years of age." In fact, the text says nothing of the kind, and it is a bogus citation.)

Regarding the text in Ketubot 11b, Gil Student notes:

> The discussion here relates to the dowry for virgins and non-virgins. It has nothing to do with what acts are allowed, encouraged, forbidden, or discouraged....
>
> The Talmud relates that a virgin is entitled a higher dowry. While the tell-tale sign of virginity is the release of blood due to the breaking of the hymen on the wedding night, there are occasions when the hymen has already been broken such as when the woman suffered an injury. The Talmud here quotes Rav Yehuda in the name of Rav that a sexual act with a male minor is not considered to be a loss of virginity because one of the participants is not fully active. While the female's

hymen may have been broken, she has not engaged in what can be classified as a sexual act (although it is certainly child abuse).

The Talmud continues and quotes Rava as saying that a sexual act between a male adult and a female under the age of three is also not considered a loss of virginity (although it is child abuse). Since the girl is too young for her hymen to be broken, she is still considered a virgin.

Nowhere is the Talmud permitting such behavior. Sex outside of a marriage is strictly forbidden (Maimonides, *Mishneh Torah*, Hilchot Ishut 1:4, Hilchot Na'arah Betulah 2:17; *Shulchan Aruch*, Even HaEzer 26:1, 177:5) as is this obvious case of child abuse. The Talmud is only discussing ex post facto what would happen if such a case arose.[18]

So when the Talmud says that if a three-year-old girl was sexually violated by a man "it is nothing," it means that she should still be considered a virgin when she gets married. She did nothing wrong. She was sexually abused and should not be punished. That's it. As Student emphasizes, the discussion here has to do with dowries, not sexual immorality.

What about the charge that, according to Sanhedrin 55b, "A Jew may marry a three year-old girl (specifically, three years 'and a day' old)"[19]? If you read through that passage, you will see a detailed discussion about when a father can marry off his daughter, including that she will become married to the man to whom she is betrothed upon the act of sexual intercourse. And at first glance, you might think that she could be married off and be forced to have sex with her new husband at the age of three years and one day. How horrific!

But elsewhere, in a tractate dealing with marriage laws (Kiddushin 41a), the Talmud states this:

> The mishna teaches: **A man can betroth his daughter** to a man **when she is a young woman.** The Gemara infers: **When she is a young woman, yes,** he can betroth her; **when she is a minor, no,** he cannot betroth her. This statement **supports** the opinion of **Rav,** as **Rav Yehuda** says that **Rav says, and some say** it was said by **Rabbi Elazar: It is prohibited for a person to betroth his daughter** to a man **when she is a minor, until** such time **that she grows up and says: I want** to marry **so-and-so.** If a father betroths his daughter when she is a minor and incapable of forming an opinion of the husband, she may later find herself married to someone she does not like.[20]

This, in fact, is the official Talmudic ruling: A man may not betroth his minor daughter to be married. She must be old enough to give her consent. The passage in Sanhedrin must be understood in this light and would therefore be addressing a different issue.[21]

As to charges that the Talmud sanctions a Jewish person killing or stealing from a Gentile, Student says this: "Robbing gentiles is absolutely forbidden.... In no way does the Talmud permit or encourage killing gentiles. Rather, it strictly forbids killing anyone, Jew or gentile."[22] He adds:

> While it is understandable that Jewish literature has been relatively quiet about something as obvious as the prohibition against killing gentiles, the following sources are just some of those who say it explicitly: Tosafot, Avodah Zarah 26b sv. Velo; Maimonides, *Mishneh Torah*, Hilchot Rotze'ach 2:11, Hilchot Avodah Zarah 10:1; R. Yoel Sirkes, *Bayit Chadash*, Yoreah Deah 158; *Taz*, Yoreh Deah 158:1; *Beit Meir*, Even HaEzer 17:3; R. Yosef Babad, *Minchat Chinuch*, 93:2; R. Avraham Yishayahu Karelitz, *Chazon Ish*, Bava Kamma 10:16.[23]

More succinctly, Judaism scholar Maurice M. Mizrahi offers responses to ten common misrepresentations of the Talmud. For example, Mizrahi responds to the charge that "Jews may kill Gentiles at will" by citing this alleged proof: "The Talmud says: Rabbi Shim'on ben Yochai taught: [Even] the good among the Gentiles must be killed. [*Tov shebe goyyim harog*] [Sofrim 15:10]." [24]

In reality, what this means in context is that "in war, one must kill enemy soldiers, even if they are righteous people." In further support of this, Mizrahi cites these two well-known rabbinic teachings: "The righteous of all nations have a share in the World to Come" (Tosefta Sanhedrin 13) and "I call heaven and earth as witnesses: Any individual, whether gentile or Jew, man or woman, servant or maid, can bring the Divine Presence upon himself in accordance with his deeds" (Tanna Devei Eliahu Rabba 9).[25] These are hardly the sentiments of those who believe that even the best of Gentiles should be killed!

Again, if you're concerned about what the Talmud teaches, take the time to review the clear explanations provided by Student.[26] Then, if you want to dig even deeper into the relevant texts, you can check out the careful work of researchers Jan Irvin and Lloyd De Jongh, who point out that while Judaism is falsely accused of these various charges, radical Islam actually teaches and carries them out.[27] If you're truly concerned about what the Talmud teaches, do take the time to check out their research.

Without a doubt, there are many things in the Talmud to which I take strong exception. And as I have stated clearly and emphatically, I reject the claims of rabbinic authority as found in the Talmud. I also believe that many times rabbinic traditions stand in the way of God's Word. (See the Lord's words in Matthew 15:3–9; 23:13–28; and Mark 7:8–9.) And I acknowledge that there are some bizarre sayings and traditions preserved in the Talmud.

But I deny that the Talmud sanctions pedophilia or the killing of Gentiles, and it is uncertain whether the Talmud actually speaks of Jesus at all.

Does This Bother You?

If my saying these things causes you to respond with, "Well then, it's obvious you're not a real follower of Jesus! You're an antichrist and a Judaizer and on the payroll of religious Jews," then I encourage you to look in the mirror. Could it be that your negative attitude toward Jewish people is greater than your love for Jesus?

Let me also say this. There are many edifying teachings in the Talmud and rabbinic traditions—many wise sayings and beautiful traditions. There are moving prayers and heartfelt confessions, and for many religious Jews there is great delight in studying and applying God's Law. To them, nothing could be more sacred, even in its tiniest details.[28]

One rabbi who died in 2015 began his day by reciting the entire Book of Psalms, taking several hours to do it so as to focus on the words he was saying. And he would not begin reciting the traditional morning prayers until three in the afternoon, since it took him that long to prepare his heart to pray those prayers, which he finished by six in the evening, at which time he would have something to drink for the first time in the day.

He would then "accept visitors throughout the evening, stopping only to daven Maariv [pray the early evening prayers] and to finally eat his first meal of the day at midnight." After that, he "continued taking visitors throughout the night and as the morning broke, he would have some fruit before saying Birchos Hashachar [blessings over the dawn] and Kriyas Shema [the recitation beginning with Deuteronomy 6:4, 'Hear O Israel. The LORD our God, the LORD is one'], followed by a short 6 AM nap." Then, he would be up again by seven thirty to resume his spiritual activities.[29]

Most of his family was killed in the Holocaust, including his own father, yet his faith and devotion remained steady. And there are many other Jews like him, certainly not as extreme in their personal religious habits but just as committed to seeking to please God and obey His Torah. For them, the Talmud is a deeply spiritual set of books, a treasury of divine truth and a guide for life. They would be mortified to know that anyone would think the Talmud was filled with such evil.

And while I recognize that these same rabbis and religious Jews would look at me as a terribly lost soul, fervently opposing my efforts to reach our people with the good news of Yeshua, I don't doubt their sincerity and devotion. Just read stories of how Jews sought to observe the Sabbath and celebrate the feasts during the Holocaust—out of love for God—and you will realize that there is more to Judaism than you might realize.[30] As Paul said of the Jews of his day, "For I can testify about them that they are zealous for God, but their zeal is not based on knowledge" (Rom. 10:2, NIV). For a real Christian, that should produce sadness rather than anger. Let the truth be told.

There is a Jewish prayer called the Kaddish. It is recited in memory of the dead but is also included in the daily Jewish prayer cycle, so these words are repeated in prayer thousands of times in the life of a traditional Jew. Can you say amen as you read?

> Glorified and sanctified be God's great name throughout the world which He has created according to His will.
>
> May He establish His kingdom in your lifetime and during your days, and within the life of the entire House of Israel, speedily and soon; and say, Amen.
>
> May His great name be blessed forever and to all eternity.
>
> Blessed and praised, glorified and exalted, extolled and honored, adored and lauded be the name of the Holy One, blessed be He, beyond all the blessings and hymns, praises and consolations that are ever spoken in the world; and say, Amen.
>
> May there be abundant peace from heaven, and life, for us and for all Israel; and say, Amen.
>
> He who creates peace in His celestial heights, may He create peace for us and for all Israel; and say, Amen.[31]

May He bring His kingdom speedily—for the salvation of Israel and for the redemption of the world. And let everyone say amen!

CHAPTER 7

DO THE JEWISH PEOPLE WANT TO TAKE OVER THE WORLD?

HAVE YOU EVER wondered how something like the Holocaust could happen? How so many people from different ethnic backgrounds and different nations could be complicit in such a massive, inhuman crime? How they could all come together to slaughter millions of Jews?

There is certainly a spiritual answer to these questions, in that Satan wants to wipe out the Jewish people.[1] But there are natural answers as well, in that the Jewish people were blamed for many of the problems in Germany and beyond, and for centuries they had been scapegoated. When something bad happened, it was the fault of the Jewish people. Worse still, it was believed that those "evil Jews" wanted to take over the world and dominate the *goyyim*—the Gentiles.

We can gain further insights from the Facing History and Ourselves website, under the subject of "The Myth of the Jewish Conspiracy." We read that in 1919, in the aftermath of Germany's crushing defeat in World War I:

> Erich Ludendorff, one of Germany's top military leaders, announced that Jews were one of several groups responsible for the nation's defeat. By 1922, he was focusing almost entirely on Jews as "the enemy." He wrote, "The supreme government of the Jewish people was working hand in hand with France and England. Perhaps it was leading them both." As proof, he cited the *Protocols of the Elders of Zion*, a document supposedly containing the minutes of a secret meeting of Jewish leaders—the so-called "Elders of Zion"—held at the turn of the twentieth century. At that supposed meeting, the "Elders" allegedly plotted to take over the world.[2]

In reality, "In the 1920s, Germany's 500,000 Jews accounted for less than 1% of the total population of about 61 million. Yet by focusing on Jews as 'the enemy,' antisemites made it seem as if Jews were everywhere and were responsible for everything that went wrong in the nation."[3] Does this not sound familiar? Does this not sound just like some of the conspiracy theories and wild accusations cited earlier in this book? And is it any wonder that someone like evangelical author Texe Marrs, who spread antisemitism through his writings, would reprint the *Protocols*?

Regarding the composition of this infamous document, legal scholar Michael Fox said this in 2008:

> You read "The Protocols of the Elders of Zion" with mounting incredulity. The 24 Protocols document a Jewish plot to take over the world. They consist of a description given by a senior Elder to a new Elder on how the Jews, assisted by Freemasons, will achieve their goal. They will control the press, pervert financial systems, cause world wars, sponsor terrorism, destroy religion. Most significant of all—a telltale indication of the arch-reactionary source of the forgery—the conspiracy will undermine established society by spreading liberalism, freedom of the press, human rights and democracy. The sole speaker in "The Protocols," the senior Elder, says: "Do not suppose for a moment that these statements are empty words: Think carefully of the successes we arranged for Darwinism, Marxism, Nietzscheism. To us Jews, at any rate, it should be plain to see what a disintegrating importance these directives have had upon the minds of the goyim."[4]

In short, Fox claimed, "Only in 'The Da Vinci Code' could you encounter anything remotely as half-witted."[5] And yet millions of people have believed—and do believe—these lies, including government leaders, educational leaders, media leaders, and religious leaders (including Christian leaders).[6] Indeed, shortly after the English translation of the *Protocols* was published in 1920:

> The Times of London, then the most authoritative newspaper in the world, called it a "disturbing pamphlet," and called for an inquiry. And The Times was not alone. An article in The Illustrated Sunday Herald in February 1920 spoke about "the schemes of the International Jews" and a "world-wide conspiracy for the overthrow of civilization." The author had just been sent a copy of the new English translation of "The Protocols" and his name was Winston Churchill.[7]

(To be clear, Churchill did not believe that Jews worldwide were part of some conspiratorial plot to take over the world.)[8]

Fox does note, "To its credit it was The Times that produced and published conclusive proof that the pamphlet was not only a forgery, but a piece of blatant plagiarism as well."[9] But to the believers, specifically the antisemites, the *Protocols* confirmed their worst suspicions: the Jews do, indeed, plan to take over the world. Car inventor Henry Ford was so convinced of the *Protocols'* authenticity that he serialized the content in his own publication, calling it "The International Jew: The World's Foremost Problem." He later published the series in a book, distributing five hundred thousand copies in the process.[10]

As for the origin of the *Protocols*, it is likely they were written in Paris sometime between 1895 and 1899 by an operative in the Russian secret police. Though no one knows who actually wrote it, some claim it was "Pytor Ivanovich Rachovsky, who copied most of it from a French satire on Napoleon III that had nothing to do with Jewish people. The forgery was an attempt to destroy the Bolshevik-led political movement to modernize Russia by linking it to a Jewish plot to destroy western civilization."[11]

Initially, however, the book had little impact. But, as noted on the Facing History and Ourselves website, and with specific reference to Germany:

> After World War I, it became a worldwide sensation. Many believed that the *Protocols* explained seemingly "inexplicable" events—the war, the economic crises that followed the war, the revolutions in Russia and central Europe, even epidemics. Myths regarding a "Jewish conspiracy" had been around for centuries, but the *Protocols* gave them new life, even after the document was exposed as a hoax in 1921. For many people, the war and the earthshaking events that followed it confirmed the *Protocols'* authenticity, no matter what evidence was offered to the contrary.[12]

And that is how things remain to this day: no amount of evidence will dissuade someone who hates the Jewish people. They see it as evidence that the Jewish people are guilty indeed!

Look for a moment at these words, taken from introduction to the English translation of the *Protocols* published in *The Morning Post* in 1920: "The Jews are carrying it out with steadfast purpose, creating wars and revolutions . . . to destroy the white Gentile race, that the Jews may seize the power during the resulting chaos and rule with their claimed superior intelligence over the remaining races of the world, as kings over slaves."[13]

If you go back and read some of the quotes in chapter 4 from Texe Marrs, Ted Pike, Rick Wiles, and E. Michael Jones, you'll see there is nothing new under the sun. Even more chilling are the words of John Earnest, the Poway synagogue shooter, who explained to the 911 dispatcher that he shot up the synagogue because "Jewish people are destroying the white race."[14] (As we saw in chapter 1, he also referenced verses from the New Testament, taken out of context and completely misused, to justify his murderous acts.) The *Protocols* live on. (And does it matter to antisemites that most of the Jews they despise are themselves white?)

"But," a critic protests, "we don't need the *Protocols* to know that the Jews want to take over the world and subjugate the Gentiles. The rabbis tells us this themselves! It's written in the Talmud and Kabbalah, and contemporary Jewish scholars and teachers admit to it as well. In fact, some rabbis have written about it proudly, right here in the twenty-first century."

Is this so? Without a doubt, there are verses in the Hebrew Scriptures that could give the idea that in the Messianic era, the Jews will be serving God and the Gentiles will be serving the Jews (as one ultra-Orthodox rabbi once put it to me). And there are Talmudic and kabbalistic texts that speak of a glorious future age in which the Jews will function as the priestly nation, teaching the world about the God of Israel and being the head and not the tail. When some of these themes are put together, especially when viewed through hostile and suspicious eyes, it can give the impression that "the Jews" long to rule the world and enforce their laws on everyone.

But that is really a misreading of the texts in question, which is why I recently reached out to another ultra-Orthodox rabbi who is also a biblical scholar, asking him two questions: 1) What passages in the Tanakh would seem to support the idea that in the Messianic era, the Jews will be serving God and the Gentiles will be serving the Jews? (I also asked him if he would phrase the statement differently.) And 2) What, exactly, will this mean? Will the Gentiles be slaves of the Jews?

He responded:

> 1. I would word it differently: "In the Messianic era all of mankind will serve God alone in the sense of worship of the Divine (Zephaniah 3:9); in the sense of political structure, the nations of the world will serve the Jewish nation." Isaiah 14:2; 49:23; 61:5,6; 60:12; Daniel 7:27
>
> 2. The popular understanding is that the nations will maintain their identity, but the relationship will be like the priests to the Israelites, and/or like vassal states to a greater power—at the same time, individual gentiles will want to serve the Jews on a personal level. The closest parallel in the Bible is what happened in the days of Solomon, when the states around him brought tribute and the people came to hear his wisdom.[15]

So based on this understanding, when the Jewish people fulfill their destiny, exemplifying their calling as God's priestly nation on the earth, the

Gentiles will follow suit and also worship the one true God. And due to the Lord's exaltation of Israel, many Gentiles will honor and serve the Jews. This, in the end, would be the opposite of what the Jewish people have experienced for so many centuries. They would be ruling over those who for so long ruled over them—but all in a glorious era, dominated by righteousness and the manifest presence of God.

Now, this might sound offensive to many Gentile Christians, and it's quite possible that inherent in this scenario is a Jewish sense of pride or superiority. And to be candid, there are some rabbinic texts that indicate a Jewish soul is higher than the soul of a Gentile.[16] As you might imagine, these texts have been exploited (and often misrepresented) by antisemites such as David Duke. (See, in particular, his book *Jewish Supremacism: My Awakening on the Jewish Question.*)[17] Worse still, these rabbinic texts helped form the ideas of an outrageous book written by two Israeli rabbis in 2009 titled *Torat Hamelech* (The King's Torah).[18] It even contains statements like this:

> There are times in which we will want to harm the innocent from the outset. And their presence and their killing is actually beneficial and helpful to us. For example, harming the infants from the wicked king's family, who are currently innocent; their killing helps us to harm and pain the king so that he will stop fighting us.[19]

But that's not all. As noted on a Reform Judaism website in 2012, "This outrageous book received official rabbinic endorsement by prominent orthodox rabbis in Israel including Rabbi Dov Lior, who is employed by the State as the rabbi of Kiryat Arba."[20] Doesn't this, then, confirm the worst fears of those who believe the Jewish people see themselves as superior and want to take over the world, even using force to do so?

Actually, *Torat Hamelech* was widely condemned in the Jewish world, with one of Israel's leading ultra-Orthodox rabbis stating, "We should give considerable attention to the nations of the world and not assist in a writing that could be interpreted as racist. The Torah respects everyone since everyone was created in G-d's image."[21] Also, the book focused on "the theoretical attitude of Jewish Law toward killing a non-Jew in wartime," and so all of its statements must be understood in that context.[22]

The Israeli authorities arrested and questioned some of the rabbis who endorsed the book, and the authors themselves were brought to court for incitement to violence, with their case ultimately making it to the nation's Supreme Court. As the *Jerusalem Post* reported in 2015, "The High Court of Justice on Wednesday ruled in a split ruling that there is no basis to indict the authors of the book *Torat Hamelech* ("The King's Torah") for incitement."[23]

So even though the book was devoted to theoretical discussion of Torah law during times of war, the sentiments it expressed were considered so ugly that its publication produced a national outrage among Jews in Israel and an international outrage among the worldwide Jewish community, and it led to a major court case as well. Even after the case was closed, in 2017 one of the authors of the book, Rabbi Yosef Elitzur, "was indicted for incitement to violence," the news website Ynet reports, noting that the indictment was for "two opinion articles he wrote in which he allegedly justified civilians 'taking action against the enemy.'"[24]

Do I believe there are extremist rabbis who would use violence to advance their cause? I don't doubt that there are, just as there are extremists in every religion. But even then, books like *Torat Hamelech* do not call for general violence against Gentiles, nor they do support the idea of a Jewish (especially a secular Jewish!) takeover of the world. And as for the idea that a Jewish soul is superior to a Gentile soul, I've heard rabbis explain it like this: A Jew starts with his tank more filled, so to speak (or he starts life with a greater spiritual capacity by nature). But any righteous Gentile can pass that Jewish person spiritually. It's just a question of a Jewish person having a more advantageous starting point, due to divine calling and the gift of the Torah.

A TRADITIONAL JEWISH UNDERSTANDING

As for the idea that the Jewish people will one day be the lead nation, served by the Gentile nations, it's easy to see where a traditional Jew would get this idea. Consider some of these verses, and then ask yourself: How would I understand the following biblical texts if I were a traditional Jew?

> For the LORD will have compassion on Jacob and will again choose Israel, and will set them in their own land, and sojourners will join them and will attach themselves to the house of Jacob. And the peoples will take them and bring them to their place, and the house of Israel will possess them in the LORD's land as male and female slaves. They will take captive those who were their captors, and rule over those who oppressed them.
>
> —ISAIAH 14:1–2

> Thus says the Lord God: "Behold, I will lift up my hand to the nations, and raise my signal to the peoples; and they shall bring your sons in their arms, and your daughters shall be carried on their shoulders. Kings shall be your foster fathers, and their queens your nursing mothers. With their faces to the ground they shall bow down to you, and lick the dust of your feet. Then you will know that I am the Lord; those who wait for me shall not be put to shame."
>
> —ISAIAH 49:22–23

> Strangers shall stand and tend your flocks; foreigners shall be your plowmen and vinedressers; but you shall be called the priests of the Lord; they shall speak of you as the ministers of our God; you shall eat the wealth of the nations, and in their glory you shall boast.
>
> —Isaiah 61:5–6

> Thus says the Lord of hosts: In those days ten men from the nations of every tongue shall take hold of the robe of a Jew, saying, "Let us go with you, for we have heard that God is with you."
>
> —Zechariah 8:23

And what about the unrepentant enemies of Israel, those who are dead set on destroying the chosen nation? They will be judged by God, as Zechariah records:

> Then the Lord will go out and fight against those nations as when he fights on a day of battle. On that day his feet shall stand on the Mount of Olives that lies before Jerusalem on the east, and the Mount of Olives shall be split in two from east to west by a very wide valley, so that one half of the Mount shall move northward, and the other half southward. And you shall flee to the valley of my mountains, for the valley of the mountains shall reach to Azal. And you shall flee as you fled from the earthquake in the days of Uzziah king of Judah. Then the Lord my God will come, and all the holy ones with him.
>
> —Zechariah 14:3–5

It is no surprise, then, that if religious Jews took these verses seriously and literally, along with other verses like them, they would look forward to the day when the tables would be turned, when rather than being subjugated by the nations, they would be the lead nation. In reality, this would not be much different from the view held by many of us who are evangelical Christians, namely that when Jesus returns, He will destroy those who persecute us (2 Thess. 1:5–10) and then establish His kingdom on the earth, where He will rule for a thousand years. And we will rule with Him! (See Revelation 20:1–4.)

Why, then, is it so horrific that many religious Jews, based on promises in the Tanakh, have a similar view about their own future destiny? More to the point, just as Christians long for the day of the Lord's return but do not try to take over the world now and subjugate the nations, religious Jews wait for the Messiah's coming without trying to take over the world by violence and rule over the nations. And that's why all the fearmongering about Jews wanting to take over the world (again, as reflected in the quotes from

Christian leaders cited in chapter 4 and in the fears about the Noahide Laws) is so off base.

This future Messianic era longed for by traditional Jews is also one in which they, with the help of the Messiah, would be leading the whole world into the knowledge of the one true God. And in that role, as His worshippers, they would stand side by side with the Gentile nations, as Isaiah proclaims:

> In that day there will be an altar to the LORD in the midst of the land of Egypt, and a pillar to the LORD at its border. It will be a sign and a witness to the LORD of hosts in the land of Egypt. When they cry to the LORD because of oppressors, he will send them a savior and defender, and deliver them. And the LORD will make himself known to the Egyptians, and the Egyptians will know the LORD in that day and worship with sacrifice and offering, and they will make vows to the LORD and perform them. And the LORD will strike Egypt, striking and healing, and they will return to the LORD, and he will listen to their pleas for mercy and heal them.
>
> In that day there will be a highway from Egypt to Assyria, and Assyria will come into Egypt, and Egypt into Assyria, and the Egyptians will worship with the Assyrians.
>
> In that day Israel will be the third with Egypt and Assyria, a blessing in the midst of the earth, whom the LORD of hosts has blessed, saying, "Blessed be Egypt my people, and Assyria the work of my hands, and Israel my inheritance."
>
> —ISAIAH 19:19–25

They would not be trying to take over other nations by force or without the Messiah. They would not be part of a secret Jewish cabal, waiting for the moment to lead a "Jew coup" against their host nation. And as religious Jews, they would not be trying to destroy the ethics of the world through pornography and sexual sin. To the contrary, they would be opposing those vices as well.

You might say, "But you can't deny that Jewish Americans have a disproportionate amount of power when compared with their relatively small numbers."

Actually, I agree. At the same time, through much of American history, the Jewish people had very limited power and were often discriminated against. And throughout world history, especially the last two thousand years of exile, the Jewish people have often been herded into ghettos, barred from having good jobs, and forced to wander from country to country. So much for Jewish dominance of the world. And somehow, with all of this alleged Jewish control, the Jewish people seem unable to stop other nations from slaughtering them in large numbers.

As for Jewish influence in America, the vast majority of that influence is held by secular Jews, not religious Jews, meaning by Jews who are not that concerned with what the Bible, Talmud, or Kabbalah says about their destiny. And for the most part, they are not acting in a concerted way as a people trying to take over the nation. In fact, when I challenged the faulty logic of Rick Wiles, who accused the Jewish people of owning Trump and the White House while at the same time trying to remove Trump from the White House, Wiles replied:

> There's no conflict in my statements. By far, Donald Trump is the most pro-Zionist U.S. President in history.... Yes, Donald Trump is pro-Zionist and strongly influenced by the network of influential Jews around him. Mr. Trump, however, is aligned with religious Zionist Jews. He is opposed by secular political Jews. From the earliest days of Zionism, there has always been two factions of Zionist Jews fighting each other for control of world Zionism: political Zionists and religious Zionists. President Trump is aligned with religious Zionists, mostly Kabbalah-practicing Chabad Lubavitchers. George Soros, Adam Schiff, and the rest of the "Impeach Trump" crowd belong to secular political Zionists. We are witnessing is [*sic*] an internal war between two powerful Jewish factions for control of world Zionism.[25]

How extraordinary. The Jews are so powerful, they control Trump *and* the opposition to Trump. They control the Republicans *and* the Democrats. The massive divide in America today is actually a battle "between two powerful Jewish factions for control of world Zionism," between "political Zionists and religious Zionists." Those Jews are everywhere! The secular Jews want to take over one way, and the religious Jews want to take over another way. What a shame they can't get their act together and just rule the world as Jews. (Please forgive my sarcasm, but in this case, it is fully deserved.)

Of course, in the view of Catholic scholar E. Michael Jones (as noted in chapter 4), because the Jews rejected and continue to reject Logos in a conscious and active way, they live in continual rebellion to the ruling authority, having the end goal of moral and (ultimately) political subversion of the nations in which they live. From that viewpoint, both the secular Jew and the religious Jew are motivated by a similar destructive spirit.[26]

But as bizarre as that theory is, given the massive differences between secular and religious Jews ideologically, spiritually, morally, and politically, it still fails to explain why the Jewish people have so much influence in countries like America. It also fails to explain why over the centuries, despite being discriminated against and oppressed, the Jewish people have made such a powerful (and positive) impact on the world.

My answer is much simpler (and more biblically based). The Lord called the Jewish people to be a priestly nation and to turn the nations of the world toward Him, thus to be world changers. When we walk in harmony with His calling, we have massive positive influence. Think of Moses, David, Isaiah, John, Peter, and Paul, who like Yeshua the Messiah were all Jewish. When we walk in rebellion to God's purposes (or simply stray from His purposes), we have massive negative influence.

Now think of the destructive impact that Karl Marx has had with his *Communist Manifesto* or the strange theories that have been widely introduced by Sigmund Freud or even the corrosive influence of contemporary Jewish men like the porn jock Howard Stern or the ultraliberal financier George Soros. The Jewish people have been gifted in many ways by God, and those gifts can be used for good or for evil. Accordingly, an influential Jewish atheist like Peter Singer, once called "the most dangerous man in the world,"[27] holds to his extreme philosophical beliefs specifically because he *rejected* his Jewish heritage (which, in turn, was nominal at best).

But let's be realistic here. Friedrich Engels, who coauthored the *Communist Manifesto* with Marx, was not Jewish. Vladimir Lenin was not Jewish (his mother was half-Jewish, meaning that at most, he was one-quarter Jewish and three-quarters Gentile). Joseph Stalin was not Jewish. Adolf Hitler was not Jewish.[28] Mao Zedong was not Jewish. Yet these men are probably responsible for roughly one hundred million deaths.[29]

The major biblical scholars who popularized the destructive criticism of the Bible (so-called "higher criticism")—men like F. C. Baur and Julius Wellhausen—were not Jewish. Antichristian philosophers like Friedrich Nietzsche and Bertrand Russell were not Jewish. As I mentioned in chapter 5, leaders of the sexual revolution like Alfred Kinsey and Hugh Hefner were not Jewish. And more broadly, looking over the larger scope of history, Muhammad, with all his massive influence, was not Jewish, nor have terrorist leaders like Osama bin Laden, a founder of al Qaeda, or ISIS leader Abu Bakr al-Baghdadi been Jewish.

We also need to emphasize that with rare exception, the Jewish men and women who have had a destructive impact on the world have been those who most deeply rejected their own Jewishness. As journalist Daniel Greenfield noted in a December 24, 2019, article, "George Soros, like Karl Marx, was the product of two parents who loathed their Jewish ancestry and embraced hatred of Jews. Soros was nurtured on this same vileness and has spent much of his fortune putting it into play. He's not Jewish. He has a new faith. It calls for the destruction of Jews."[30] Had these men been traditional Jews, we would probably have never heard of either of them, as they likely would have been nurturing Judaism within their own communities.

Of course, if you are committed to an antisemitic reading of history, you'll find a way to blame the Jewish people for everything done by Lenin, Stalin, Hitler, and Mao. And you'll find a way to blame the Jewish people for the rise of Islam. (I kid you not! Check out the article on Dr. Jones' website titled "The Jewish Origins of Islam."[31]) In fact, if you're a Catholic who espouses antisemitic ideology, like Dr. Jones, you'll find a way to blame the Jewish people for Martin Luther and the Reformation. The ADL notes:

> In the tradition of conspiracy theorists, Jones credits Jews with orchestrating occurrences as varied and disconnected from the Jewish experience as the Protestant Reformation and the French Revolution. He also blames Jews for Bolshevism, Freemasonry, and an alleged contemporary "Jewish takeover of American culture." Jones reaches for tenuous connections to paint "the Jews" as inherently wicked and prone to colluding openly or secretly to threaten other populations around them.[32]

Yes, the Jewish people are behind it all.

Dr. Jones summarized his views on a radio broadcast that goes by the name *Aryan Insights*. (Yes, this is the actual name!) As the webpage linking this broadcast explains:

> Dr. Jones speaks to Sven Longshanks about a wide range of subjects from his books and interviews, centering around the revolutionary activity of the Jew through the centuries. Dr. Jones' understanding of why the Jew behaves as he does, is based upon the Jewish rejection of Logos in the form of Christ.[33]

So according to Jones, every white nation where Jews lived was plagued by the Jews' revolutionary activity, which resulted in "over a hundred separate expulsions of them from Europe." And the Jews always had Christians as their targets, provoking them to attack one another while living among them, but when living among Arab nations, provoking the Arabs to attack Christians nearby. In short, Jones argued, where you see revolution and upheaval, the Jews are behind it, from Poland to England, "where the Jews used Freemasonry to foment the Protestant revolution and overturn our entire scientific tradition."[34]

What's more, according to Jones, the Jewish people were behind the sexual perversions in France, working through the Marquis de Sade, and in America they were behind the civil rights movement. They used folk music to undermine the culture, and "they are now going back to using Negroes again with the Black Lives Matter movement, which is financed by George Soros."[35]

To say it again: the Jewish people are behind it all!

This reminds me of a joke my father told when I was growing up. A prison psychologist sits down with an inmate who has been convicted of sex crimes. The psychologist shows him a picture of a straight line and asks him what he sees. The inmate replies with a filthy, sexual description, to the shock of the psychologist.

The psychologist then shows the inmate a picture of a circle, then a square, then a triangle, and in each case the prisoner responds the same way, telling the psychologist he sees some vulgar, sexual image.

The psychologist then says to him, "Sir, I can see you have a filthy mind!"

The inmate responds, "But you're the one showing me the filthy pictures!"

In the same way, if you want to find a Jewish person behind every nefarious plot in world history, you can do so. But if you read history (or monitor contemporary events) realistically, you'll come to a very different conclusion.

WHAT ARE WE TO MAKE OF THIS?

What, then, are we to make of the Talmudic and kabbalistic texts that speak of a future Jewish rule over the world? First, we can recognize that they have absolutely nothing to do with secular, nonreligious Jews who simply have some degree of power or influence and want to impact the world according to their values, just as a host of powerful atheists, Muslims, Hindus, Christians, and others seek to do. No big deal and nothing conspiratorial.

Second, we must remember an important tradition found in the early rabbinic writings, commonly known as the Three Oaths. The website Torah Jews explains that according to the Talmud, God required three oaths from the world, two from Israel and one from the nations: "To what do these three oaths refer? One, that Israel should not go up as a wall. One, that the Holy One, blessed is He, made Israel swear not to rebel against the nations of the world. One, that the Holy One, blessed is He, made the gentiles swear not to subjugate Israel too much."[36] As explained in the expanded Steinsaltz translation:

> **One,** so **that the Jews should not ascend** to Eretz Yisrael [the land of Israel] **as a wall,** but little by little. **And** another **one, that the Holy One, Blessed be He, adjured the Jews that they should not rebel against** the rule of **the nations of the world. And** the last **one** is **that the Holy One, Blessed be He, adjured the nations** of the world **that they should not subjugate the Jews excessively.**[37]

So based on the homiletical interpretation of certain biblical texts (Song of Sol. 2:7; 3:5; and 8:4; this is the same verse repeated three times), the Talmudic rabbis deduced that God had imposed these three oaths. The first apparently meant that the Jewish people should not return en masse to their ancient homeland (there is debate in terms of what it means to go to the land "as a wall," and that debate carried over to the modern Zionist movement).[38] The second, which is quite straightforward, said that they should not rebel against the nations that ruled over them in exile. And the third was that the nations should not subjugate the Jews who lived there excessively.

This is one reason that for many centuries, traditional Jews have *not* sought to rebel against the nations that had authority over them, especially in light of the terrible suffering that ensued as a result of their two failed revolts against Rome (AD 66–70 and 132–135). This alone refutes E. Michael Jones' whole argument of Jewish subversiveness. And again, it is only when the Jewish people have forsaken their heritage and traditions that they have acted subversively, seeking to overthrow the existing order (as in Jewish involvement in the rise of communism in Russia). But either way, as you read Jewish history in an unbiased way, you see that the normal pattern was that Jewish people simply sought to live their lives and practice their traditions with as little outside interference as possible. They hardly tried to take over the nations in which they lived.

That, however, is not enough for those who truly believe in the danger of a Jewish takeover. In her book *Kabbalah Secrets Christians Need to Know*, Deanne Loper writes:

> One of the most revealing contemporary sources concerning the millennial reign of the *Moshiach* in the world to come [a concept Loper rejects as unbiblical] is Rabbi Michael Higger's controversial book, *The Jewish Utopia*, published in 1932. Higger was a Talmudic scholar and his book is based on rabbinic interpretations of biblical prophecy as set forth in the *Babylonian Talmud*, the *Palestinian Talmud*, the *Midrash* and other apocalyptic writings. Many Christians have been alarmed by Higger's Jewish supremacist vision of a future utopian kingdom in which only the *righteous* will be allowed to exist in the *idea era* on earth; the word *righteous* refers only to those who support a politicized global domination of all other nations by Israel.[39]

To back this up, she cites this passage from Rabbi Higger's book, published in 1932, in caps and bold (her emphasis):

> **ONLY THOSE WHO ARE CONVINCED OF ISRAEL'S DIVINE PURPOSE IN THE WORLD, WILL BE WELCOME TO JOIN ISRAEL IN THE UPBUILDING OF AN IDEALLY SPIRITUAL LIFE ON EARTH. ISRAEL, THE IDEAL, RIGHTEOUS PEOPLE, WILL THUS BECOME SPIRITUALLY THE MASTERS OF THE WORLD.**[40]

Does this sound scary? Does this confirm your worst fears about "the Jews"? The problem is that when you read Higger's book and take time to look up the sources he cites, a totally different picture emerges. According to Higger, who held a PhD from Columbia University and was an ordained rabbi, one people alone is capable of leading the world into a utopia, and that is the Jewish people. That's because they alone were given the Torah and they alone had the witness of the prophets, and therefore they alone had the potential to rise to the loftiest ethical heights and lead the rest of the nations in this pursuit.

The last thing in Higger's mind was that a Jewish cabal—in particular, a Torah-rejecting, God-denying Jewish cabal—would take over the world and suppress the other nations or that the Jews would execute their political enemies. Rather, in keeping with the Messianic vision found elsewhere in the Scriptures, God would judge both wicked Jews and wicked Gentiles before establishing His righteous kingdom on the earth. The picture would reflect what Isaiah prophesies:

> For as the new heavens and the new earth that I make shall remain before me, says the LORD, so shall your offspring and your name remain. From new moon to new moon, and from Sabbath to Sabbath, all flesh shall come to worship before me, declares the LORD. And they shall go out and look on the dead bodies of the men who have rebelled against me. For their worm shall not die, their fire shall not be quenched, and they shall be an abhorrence to all flesh.
>
> —ISAIAH 66:22–24

That's why Higger also writes, "No line will be drawn between bad Jews and non-Jews. There will be no room for the unrighteous, whether Jewish or non-Jewish, in the Kingdom of God. All of them will have disappeared before the advent of the ideal era on this earth."[41] And "in a Jewish Utopia, therefore, there will be no wicked people. Nature itself will be against the wicked. All the goodness will be bestowed only upon the upright and just; and darkness, the opposite of light, will be the fate of the unrighteous."[42] Indeed, he explains, "The ideal society of mankind on earth, based on the principles of genuine justice and righteousness will then become a fact. The Messiah idea will be revealed."[43]

And how, he asks, will all this happen?

> The question arises: How will that ideal civilization take root?...The answer is: One nation would have to establish its life on a Utopian foundation, thereby leading, the way for the rest of the world to follow its example....Israel is the only nation that is suited for that purpose.

The religious experiences of Israel and the ideology of that people as voiced by the prophets, qualify it to lead the world in establishing a universal Utopia.[44]

Yes:

The world will be one open city, free for intercourse of trade, migration, and education. Genuine liberty and freedom will be the watchwords of the new social order in the world. The whole earth will be for the whole human race. The nations will consequently change their attitude toward Israel. Instead of despising Israel, they will pay their due respect to the ideal people.[45]

This hardly sounds oppressive, let alone ominous to me. As Higger writes, "To the delight and astonishment of the Jew and Gentile alike, Israel will now live in peace and safety. Mankind will be united in the opinion that this could be accomplished only by the will and plan of God."[46]

And how will the leaders of Israel govern? Will they be tyrannical? He explains:

Finally, the leaders in Israel will have to change their attitude toward the great masses of the people. They will have to be more sympathetic and less severe in discharging their duties, disregarding personal honor and self-interest. Instead of looking for faults in the people, the scholars guiding the nation will have to stress the good qualities of the members of their communities.[47]

Yes:

Simultaneous with the plan of a free, ideally righteous Israel, leading the world to an ideal life wherein the righteous would prosper and the wicked suffer, [comes] the essential requirement for a spiritual and holy Zion, guiding the other countries of the world in their spiritual development toward the realization of a World Utopia.[48]

At this time, "Man, with his new, holy spirit, will become a new creature."[49] What's more:

God will then be recognized as Protector of the dwelling and home of every individual. The Lord will be universally known as the Good One, who bestows only goodness and real happiness upon the world.... Thus, just as in the past the Divine Presence of God dwelt in Jerusalem, so, in the ideal era to come, the Divine Presence will fill the whole world, from one end to the other.[50]

Now go back and reread Loper's words, along with the Higger quote in bold caps, and ask yourself if she has painted a true or false picture of the expected "Jewish utopia."

I fully understand that Higger's view of a Jewish utopia would be *Jewish*, meaning I understand that he would believe that in the idyllic, Messianic age, the nations of the world would embrace a Jewish rather than Christian view of God. In other words, God would not be worshipped as a Trinity. But what's so scandalous about this? Christians believe that one day every knee will bow and every tongue confess that Jesus is Lord to the glory of the Father (Phil. 2:9–11). And Muslims envision the day when all true believers will be Muslim. Why it is surprising that a Jewish scholar would have a Jewish view of the world to come?

Traditional Jews believe that when the Messiah comes, Christians, Muslims, and idol worshippers will realize their errors and confess these words from Jeremiah 16:19: "O LORD, my strength and my stronghold, my refuge in the day of trouble, to you shall the nations come from the ends of the earth and say: 'Our fathers have inherited nothing but lies, worthless things in which there is no profit.'" In contrast, as a Jewish follower of Jesus, I look forward to the day when my Jewish people will recognize their errors concerning the Messiah and, in the words of Zechariah 12:10, will look to the One they pierced in deep repentance.

Let me present this to you through the eyes of an ultra-Orthodox teacher, Rabbi Yitzchak Ginsburgh, a man often considered to be on the extreme right by other rabbis.[51] In his book *Kabbalah and Meditation for the Nations*, he states that "the belief in a trinity is nothing short of idolatry as defined by the Torah."[52] And he believes that in the Messianic age, belief in the Trinity will be abandoned. But in his view, this does not mean that Jews will violently subjugate the world and force everyone to worship the one true God. Instead, he writes:

> But even when the non Jewish world at large does not yet possess conscious affinity and subordinance to the Jewish people, it is still possible for us to extract the spark of goodness from the shell of evil. For example, the major religion of Western culture believes in an individual Jew and worships him as a god. This is certainly a great transgression of the most fundamental of the *Bnei Noach* commandments, the commandment that forbids idolatry (as noted earlier). But within this evil context we can perceive an element of good. The believers in this religion desire, whether consciously or unconsciously, to cling to a Jew for inspiration and salvation.
>
> The true rectification of the non-Jewish world will come when it recognizes the Divinely ordained purpose of *every* Jew to enlighten

> the world and bring about universal peace and prosperity as has been prophesized. The non-Jew will then be drawn, in love, to the Jew.
>
> With an existential feeling of attachment to the Jewish people—who in their own consciousness represent the epitome of lowliness before God and man—the world will acknowledge the obligations of the Kingdom of heaven as explained in the Torah. The nations of the world will then merit true insight and partake in the ultimate redemption.[53]

What is so dangerous about this vision from a traditional rabbi? What does it have to do with Jewish businessmen like Michael Bloomberg or George Soros having a large influence on society today? What does it have to do with a godless Karl Marx writing the *Communist Manifesto?* Absolutely nothing. Yet this is the vision of traditional Judaism for the Messianic age, the vision articulated by Rabbi Higger as well. And note that according to Rabbi Ginsburgh, rather than the Jewish people thinking of themselves as superior, "in their own consciousness [they] represent the epitome of lowliness before God and man."

Others, however, find Higger's vision threatening. As noted in an online review of Higger's book, "If you believe in the Son of God, and God come in the flesh in the form of Christ's humanity, you won't qualify for the New World Order!"[54]

At this point, though, you should be able to recognize the leap in logic required by this line of thinking. Jewish tradition believes that when the Messiah comes, He will judge the unrepentant wicked and lead Israel and the rest of the world into the full knowledge of the one true God, as revealed in the Torah and the Prophets. Thus, based on this scenario, sincere Christians (and others) would recognize the errors of their beliefs and would turn to Yahweh in repentance. But this is completely and totally unrelated to an alleged Jewish desire to take over the world, as in largely secular Jewish business leaders like Mark Zuckerberg of Facebook or Sergey Brin and Larry Page, cofounders of Google, wanting to have massive influence through the internet. (And correct me if I'm wrong, but massively influential tech leaders such as Bill Gates and Jeff Bezos are *not* Jewish. I guess they are just secretly *controlled* by "the Jews"!)

Do you see the point? Rabbinic texts speaking of a future Messianic age in which the whole world will worship the God of Israel and will respect and honor the Jewish people have *no* connection whatsoever to non-Orthodox Jews like Jerrold Nadler and Adam Schiff trying to remove President Trump from office. As for religious Jews, it is absolutely true that they are seeking to have more and more influence and control in Israel. There's no doubt about that. But are they seeking to take over other countries? Are religious Jews in

America seeking to dominate and control the nation? Not in the least. For the most part, they want to be left alone to practice their faith.

As for religious Jews within Israel, while I differ strongly with some of their policies and do not support their growing dominance, in their view Israel is called to be a holy nation, not a secular nation, and therefore it is right and just that Torah law be enforced throughout the country. And they are also seeking to do what all the other political parties do: gain greater influence and power by getting more votes and carrying more weight in a government coalition.

Either way, to repeat: 1) religious Jews, in Israel or the Diaspora, are not trying to take over the world; 2) religious Jews are praying for the coming of the Messiah, whom they believe will lead Israel and the nations into the true knowledge of God; 3) secular Jews, who have disproportionate influence in some sectors of American (and, at times, European) society, are not working in collusion toward a Jewish-led, one-world government; and 4) where secular Jews and conservative Christians clash is generally over spiritual and moral values, in which case the conservative Christians are much closer to religious Jews! On this last point, it's interesting to note that while secular Jews in America vote overwhelmingly for Democrats, Orthodox Jews now vote overwhelmingly Republican.[55]

The bottom line is simply this: The idea that "the Jews want to take over the world" is an antisemitic myth. Don't give it any credence.

CHAPTER 8

SINCE WHEN IS IT SINFUL TO BE A CHRISTIAN ZIONIST?

WHAT DOES IT mean to be a Zionist? According to the respected Bible teacher David Pawson, "'Zionism' is a comparatively recent word, coined to describe the return of the Jews to the land of their ancestors and the re-establishment of the nation-state of Israel, with Jerusalem (Zion) as their capital. A 'Zionist' is one who takes part in this or supports those who do."[1] Being a Christian Zionist (or Messianic Jewish Zionist) means you believe this is God's will, according to the Bible.

So Zionism has nothing to do with ethnic supremacy or racial superiority, nor does it give Israel the right to mistreat the Palestinians, let alone set up an apartheid (or, worse still, genocidal) state.[2] God forbid. But it does mean that God keeps His promises and that He who scattered the Jewish people from the land will regather them to the land, just as it is written: "He who scattered Israel will gather them and will watch over his flock like a shepherd" (Jer. 31:10, NIV).

And while the term *Zionism* may be recent, the belief is not recent, as we will discover. Also, Zionism is not the product of dispensationalism, which as a system is less than two hundred years old,[3] although the claim is commonly made that Christian belief in a restored Israel is the product of pretribulation dispensational beliefs alone. As a commenter on social media claimed in response to a *Line of Fire* broadcast:

> What a joke,.. absolutely NO ONE with any real Biblical knowledge thinks God put "Jews" back in that land... no one, this is a 150 year old made up doctrine that was completely unknown to any Christian for 1800 years. The Zionist themselves said they were sick of waiting and needed to be their own messiah and get themselves a country so they

> wouldn't keep getting kicked out of countries they ransacked through all their schemes, a point Mr Brown always forgets to mention, they want you to believe all those countries, for no reason at all just segregated Jews and ultimately kicked them out simply because they didn't like Jews.. what a JOKE! No there is no Biblical Israel outside of Jesus the Messiah and his followers of all races and those people are called Christians, just as Isaiah 65 so clearly tells us, His New people would be called by a New Name but would still be Israel, because true Israel always has been and always will be a spiritual nation. Don't let the Zionist fool you.[4]

To the contrary, some of the most prominent church leaders who lived from the second to fifth centuries predicted the national restoration of Israel, as did Puritan leaders in the 1600s, including their top theologian, John Owen, and Anglican, Baptist, and Presbyterian leaders in the 1800s. (None of them were dispensationalists, meaning none of them believed the church age represents a parenthetical age in God's dealing with Israel and that before the full focus turns back to Israel, the church will be removed from the earth, which is known as the pretribulation rapture.)[5]

In the words of Charles Spurgeon from an 1864 sermon:

> I think we do not attach sufficient importance to the restoration of the Jews. We do not think enough about it. But certainly, if there is anything promised in the Bible it is this. I imagine that you cannot read the Bible without seeing clearly that there is to be an actual restoration of the Children of Israel.[6]

And he was speaking of a literal restoration of the Jewish people to the physical land of Israel, along with their turning as a nation to Jesus the Messiah.

Today, however, the term *Christian Zionist* (or just *Zionist*) is used as an insult and means of vilification. I hear it all the time, as if people have found me out, exclaiming, "You are a Zionist!" Oh, the shame!

Allow me to illustrate this again with some representative YouTube comments:

- "You're a filthy liar, corrupt to the core, and no matter how much religion you preach, what good is it when you can't even speak the truth. . . . I have yet to meet an honest Zionist Christian, you're all infected by the Zionists, devilish souls."

- "Crypto jews ashkenazi - Khazars Kabbalah wizards. Christians please wake up. You are being deceived by Zionism."
- "I just started listen to Dr Brown and it is a shame he showed his true colours about defending the world biggest terrorist state."
- "Brown is a Zionist agent that infiltrated the Christians. The goyim KNOWS mikey…repent…only JESUS CHRIST AS OUR SAVIOR God in the flesh can save you for eternity…you're leading saints away…you will be judged in front of the throne of Jesus Christ in heaven."
- "This Brown guy is a liar and his mustache should be stapled to his intestines. Go ask the natives about manifest destiny. Zionists are no different than jingoists."[7]

To be sure, these are not the quotes of Christian leaders, teachers, pastors, or scholars. But they do not occur in a vacuum. Instead, the fact that they are so common points to the widespread dissemination of these concepts among professing Christians today. And that means that there *are* Christian leaders, teachers, pastors, or scholars who are putting forth similar concepts and ideas, as indicated by this comment: "I agree with [Rev. Stephen] Sizer, so called Christians who are Zionists are apostates, the 'Judeans' in Israel, are Pharisees and Talmudists. Jesus called them Children of the Devil. Ergo, Christian Zionists are supporting Satanists."[8]

Who exactly is Stephen Sizer? As noted on the *Jewish News* website on September 19, 2019, Reverend Sizer is a "disgraced" Anglican vicar who in 2015 was banned by the Anglican Church "from 'writing, preaching, teaching, emailing, tweeting, posting on Facebook or commenting in any way in relation to the current situation in the Middle East' after [he] posted a link to an article titled '9-11/Israel Did It.'"[9]

Sizer was once in the Christian Zionist camp, titling his PhD thesis "The Promised Land: A Critical Investigation of Evangelical Christian Zionism in Britain and the United States of America since 1800."[10] He followed up his doctoral dissertation with *Christian Zionism: Road-map to Armageddon?* (2006) and then, for a wider Christian audience, *Zion's Christian Soldiers? The Bible, Israel, and the Church* (2007).[11]

Sizer now seems convinced that 1) God does not bless those who bless Israel; 2) the Jewish people are no longer God's chosen people; 3) the land of Israel was not given exclusively to the Jewish people; 4) Jerusalem is not the exclusive, eternal, undivided capital of Israel; 5) the Jewish temple must be rebuilt before Jesus returns; 6) believers will be raptured before the final Armageddon war; and 7) God does not have a separate plan for Israel and the church.[12]

To be sure, some of these points relate primarily to dispensationalism rather than the broader views of Christian Zionism (in particular, points 5, 6, and, in part, 7).[13] But the most important positions Sizer rejects are, in fact, the foundational positions of Christian Zionism. Is there any truth to Sizer's claims?

Let me first point out that Sizer does not simply reject the claims of Zionism. He is militantly anti-Zionist and arguably antisemitic. In fact, Sizer once stated:

> There are certainly churches in Israel/Palestine that side with the occupation [of the West Bank, Gaza, and the Golan Heights], that side with Zionism. One of my burdens is to challenge them theologically and show that they've repudiated Jesus, they've repudiated the Bible, and they are an abomination.[14]

So according to Dr. Sizer, if you are a follower of Jesus living in Israel today and you side with the nation of Israel, you have "repudiated Jesus," you have "repudiated the Bible," and you "are an abomination." How extraordinary! It looks like the horrific Internet comments cited previously are not so exceptional after all. Instead, they reflect the views of men like Sizer, who in 2014 "attended a gathering of antisemites in Iran for a conference with seminars such as 'Mossad's Role in the 9/11 Coup d'Etat,'" during which the panelists discussed several themes including "Zionist Fingerprints on the 9/11 Cover-up."[15]

To be sure, there are Christian leaders who affirm some of Sizer's positions, including Tony Higton, who retracted some of his earlier criticism of Sizer, stating:

> Sizer is right to criticize the serious failings of some Christian Zionism. I agree with him in rejecting the following errors which are held by many Christian Zionists: Lack of godly compassion for the Palestinians, and of concern for their human rights and about their legitimate aspirations. A negative attitude toward Palestinians, and Arabs in general, to the point of racism. Uncritical support for Israel (a secular, sinful state like any other), justifying all its actions against the Palestinians.[16]

I agree with Higton here, believing that having God's heart for Israel also requires having God's heart for the Palestinians. As my close friend and colleague Scott Volk has written, "If we look at Israel through a political lens, we will end up hating either Arabs or Jews (or both!). If we look at Israel through a biblical lens, we will end up loving both Arabs and Jews."[17]

But there is no question whatsoever that the militant, often indiscriminate comments made by Sizer, grounded in his rejection of God's promises to Israel, have fueled the fires of Christian antisemitism today.[18] As British journalist Melanie Phillips notes in an article dated March 4, 2009:

> Last weekend the Revd Stephen Sizer, vicar of Christ Church, Virginia Water appeared at an anti-Israel meeting with an Islamist called Ismail Patel. Patel has not only accused Israel of "genocide" and "war crimes" but considers Disney to be a Jewish plot and supports Hamas, Iran and Syria.
>
> Sizer is a virulent opponent of Christian Zionism and of Israel, which he has said he hopes will disappear just as did the apartheid regime in South Africa. He has also applauded Iranian President Ahmadinejad for having "looked forward to the day when Zionism ceased to exist."[19]

The fires of militant anti-Zionism (and antisemitism) are also fueled by videos like pastor Steven Anderson's *Marching to Zion*, which has been viewed more than half a million times and is an attack on Judaism as well as on Zionism.[20] As the ADL explains:

> Anderson denigrates Judaism in a number of clips on YouTube publicizing "Marching to Zion." The titles betray their anti-Semitic agenda, including: "The Jews are the Racists," "Taking Part in the Jews' Evil Deeds," "Jews are Antichrists," and "Jewish Synagogue = Synagogue of Satan." He paints Jews as an evil force and claims God has rejected Jews, since Jews do not accept Jesus as the Messiah.[21]

Now, it is true that Anderson pastors a small congregation and is a fringe player among American evangelicals. He is known for his fanatical "King James only" stance and for rejoicing in the murder of homosexuals and calling for their execution by law. As he said after the massacre at the gay Pulse bar in Orlando, "The good news is there are 50 less pedophiles in this world. Because these homosexuals are a bunch of disgusting perverts and pedophiles." He continued, "The bad news is a lot of the homos in the bar are still alive, so they're going to continue to molest children and recruit children into their filthy homosexual lifestyle."[22]

Anderson even preached a sermon in 2009 in which he claimed, based on the translation of certain verses in the King James Version, that it was important for Christian men to urinate standing up rather than sitting down.[23] He was quite passionate in his position! Yet he has gained a significant online following, with many professing Christians echoing his antisemitic and anti-Zionistic comments.

How is it, then, that there can be so much hostility toward the state of Israel in the church today? Part of it comes from biased theology, based on the notion that the church has forever displaced Israel. (See chapter 10 for more on this.) And part of it comes from biased politics, as Israel is falsely branded as a terrorist, genocidal, apartheid state. So from the theological side, we are told that God is finished with the Jewish people as a nation and therefore has nothing to do with bringing them back to the land. Worse still, we are told that the Jewish people are under a curse for rejecting the Messiah, even guilty of deicide, killing God. They are children of their father the devil and are, by nature, evil and untrustworthy.[24]

From the political side, Israel is viewed through the lens of revisionist history and portrayed as the evil oppressor, the giant Goliath terrorizing the little innocent Davids. Every bad report about Israel is believed while the Palestinians are painted in the purest, most pristine, guiltless terms. Evil Israel must go!

STEVEN ANDERSON'S *MARCHING TO ZION*

Since Pastor Anderson's video is often cited by Christian antisemites, I'll take some time to review the contents with you, correcting his most egregious errors. But I warn you in advance: Anderson espouses some very ugly, very false ideas. In sum, Anderson does not see the return of the restoration of modern Israel as a blessing from God. Rather, he asks whether "darker forces were at work," and it is the goal of his one hour and forty-five minute video to argue that point.[25]

To start, based on snippets of video interviews conducted with local rabbis and Jewish leaders, most of whom are quite liberal (including a nonreligious humanist!) and whom Anderson tricked into participating in his film, he makes ridiculous statements such as, "Jews stopped believing in the Torah starting in Genesis, chapter 1."[26] Of course, he could have come to the same bogus conclusions about Christians by interviewing liberal pastors who do not take Genesis 1 literally and thus determine that "Christians stopped believing in the Torah in Genesis 1." But Anderson gives such a misleading picture of Judaism that he shows the aforementioned Jewish humanist saying, "Ouch," about circumcision to "prove" that Jews don't believe in it today.[27] He presents an outlying view as mainstream, yet people take this seriously.

Anderson also claims, based on interviews with nontraditional rabbis, that Jews do not believe in a literal Adam and Eve, Noah's flood, the Tower of Babel, or offering animal sacrifices. And he responds by asking, "What part of the Torah do they believe in?"[28] But once again, had he asked liberal pastors their views on these subjects, he would have received the same answers. And had he talked with more traditional rabbis, he would have found they believe that God dictated the Torah to Moses and that every word of it is true and that they pray daily for the rebuilding of the temple so they can offer animal sacrifices again. (According to the Torah, without the prescribed altar and place of worship, animal sacrifices cannot be offered.) What's more, had Anderson talked with ten-year-old boys from ultra-Orthodox homes, he would have found them to be more familiar with the contents of the Torah than most of the pastors in his own ministry network.

But it would seem Anderson has no desire to be fair, which is why he had to trick the few rabbis he could find into appearing in his video. It appears he wants only to make the world think the Jewish people are evil. So why should he seek truth? The same can be said for some of his pastoral colleagues who state that Jews don't believe in God or the Old Testament, despite the fact that religious Jews pray to God three times daily and study the Torah almost every waking hour—and continue to do so even in times when their faith costs them their lives.

To be sure, as a Jewish believer in Jesus, I have challenged rabbinic authority and pointed out how, in practical application, rabbinic traditions can take precedence over Scripture.[29] At the same time, I recognize how central the Scriptures are to rabbinic Judaism and how many of the promises of the Hebrew Bible are repeated to the Lord in prayer by religious Jews daily. In contrast, Anderson has only one goal in his video: to portray the Talmud as evil and filled with blasphemies against Jesus, thereby discrediting the Jews. (For my response to antisemitic claims about the Talmud, see chapter 6.)

Anderson's film even manages to quote Jewish professor Peter Schäfer verbatim from his book *Jesus in the Talmud*, but the quotes are taken so out of context as to make Schäfer sound like he hates Jesus and is proud of the Jewish role in crucifying Jesus. In actuality, Schäfer is presenting a possible Talmudic perspective on why, in the eyes of these ancient rabbis, Jesus deserved to die. This, then, serves as the platform for Anderson to rail on "the Jews," all of whom were responsible for the death of Jesus. (Regarding this point, see chapter 9, especially the discussion of Matthew 27:25.) He even shows a pastor, Tim Coleman, saying that since the devil hates Christ and the Jews are the children of the devil, they hate Him too.[30]

But this is only the beginning. Matters get progressively worse. According to Anderson, Christians throughout history have not viewed the Jews as God's chosen people. Rather, he says, because the Jews rejected Christ, God forever rejected the Jews, and Christian leaders have recognized this. Apparently Anderson has forgotten Paul's very clear words: "As far as the gospel is concerned, they are enemies for your sake; but as far as election is concerned, they are loved on account of the patriarchs, for God's gifts and his call are irrevocable" (Rom. 11:28–29, NIV).

Anderson has also discarded the words of God Himself, spoken through prophets such as Jeremiah and Isaiah:

> This is what the LORD says, he who appoints the sun to shine by day, who decrees the moon and stars to shine by night, who stirs up the sea so that its waves roar—the Lord Almighty is his name: "Only if these decrees vanish from my sight," declares the Lord, "will Israel ever cease being a nation before me."
>
> This is what the LORD says: "Only if the heavens above can be measured and the foundations of the earth below be searched out will I reject all the descendants of Israel because of all they have done," declares the LORD.
>
> —JEREMIAH 31:35–37, NIV

> "For a brief moment I abandoned you, but with deep compassion I will bring you back. In a surge of anger I hid my face from you for a moment, but with everlasting kindness I will have compassion on you," says the LORD your Redeemer.
>
> "To me this is like the days of Noah, when I swore that the waters of Noah would never again cover the earth. So now I have sworn not to be angry with you, never to rebuke you again. Though the mountains be shaken and the hills be removed, yet my unfailing love for you will not be shaken nor my covenant of peace be removed," says the LORD, who has compassion on you.
>
> —ISAIAH 54:7–10, NIV

The fact that God has been so merciful to Israel, despite her many failings, should encourage Christians as well. He will show mercy to the church too!

But Anderson will not hear this for a second. Instead, to support his position, he quotes some of the vilest words written by a major Christian leader in history, the horrific antisemitic writings of Martin Luther, cited in chapter 1. Rather than refute these words and grieve over them—as generations of Lutheran leaders have done[31]—he cites them to back his claim that the Jews are evil. Yes, you heard that right: to support his view that the Jewish people are evil, pastor Steven Anderson quotes Martin Luther, who counseled German princes to set synagogues on fire, deprive Jews of good jobs, round them up into ghettos, and forbid their rabbis to teach under penalty of death. That would be like me quoting the words of the grand wizard of the Knights of the Ku Klux Klan to argue that African Americans are evil. How utterly sick.

But this explains why other Christians come to such perverse conclusions about the Jewish people: they come under the influence of people like Steven Anderson and Texe Marrs, who is also featured in this video. (For more on Marrs, see chapter 4.) Marrs even laughs at Luther's hate-filled, violence-inciting words, saying that Luther got so angry, he actually said we should go and burn all the copies of their Talmuds.[32] Yes, he laughs at this! Perhaps he would have laughed when the Nazis burned Talmuds too? My friend, this is terribly twisted.

According to Anderson and Marrs, however, there is no reason to think the Lord views the Jewish people as chosen in any way, as they claim the idea that the Jews are still God's chosen people was not taught by the church until the rise of dispensationalism less than two hundred years ago.[33] Apparently Anderson and Marrs forgot the words of Paul in Romans 9, where he said this of his nonbelieving fellow Jews:

> For I could wish that I myself were cursed and cut off from Christ for the sake of my people, those of my own race, the people of Israel. Theirs *is* the adoption to sonship; theirs the divine glory, the covenants, the receiving of the law, the temple worship and the promises. Theirs *are* the patriarchs, and from them is traced the human ancestry of the Messiah, who is God over all, forever praised! Amen.
>
> —Romans 9:3–5, NIV, EMPHASIS ADDED

Yes, the promises still belong to Israel, even in unbelief.

Are Jews lost without Jesus, like everyone else? Absolutely. Is there any salvation for Jewish people outside of Jesus? Absolutely not. But to repeat Paul's words from Romans 11:28–29, even if they are presently enemies because of the gospel, they are still loved for the sake of the fathers. And the promises are still theirs, including the preservation of the Jewish people, no matter what; their regathering to the land, even in unbelief; and their renewal in faith at the end of the age. God said it, and therefore I believe it. We do well to stay with the Word!

In contrast, Anderson claims that every major church father in history believed the Jewish people had forfeited their chosen status and were forever rejected by the Lord.[34] Here too, however, he displays his ignorance of church writings, since many of these same leaders who spoke harshly about the Jewish people also believed they would be restored by God.

In his book *Has the Church Replaced Israel?*, Michael Vlach, a professor at the Master's Seminary in California, provides eight pages of citations from early church leaders who spoke of Israel's future restoration, including:

- Justin Martyr (100–165), who "held that the tribes of Israel would be gathered and restored in accord with what the prophet Zechariah predicted."[35]
- Tertullian (c. 155–c. 220), who writes, "For it will be fitting for the Christian to rejoice, and not to grieve, at the restoration of Israel, if it be true, (as it is), that the whole of our hope is intimately united with the remaining expectation of Israel."[36]
- Origen (c. 184–c. 253), who writes, "Those, however, who, dwelling *beyond the rivers of Ethiopia,* shall even so come to the Lord, bearing sacrifices, can also be taken as denoting those who will come after the fullness of the Gentiles—for which *the rivers of Ethiopia* are a figure—has come in, and all Israel shall be saved."[37]
- Chrysostom (c. 347–407), "who often made harsh statements against the Jews, [but] still believed in a future salvation of the Jews. He linked the coming salvation of the Jews with the coming of Elijah."[38]
- Jerome (c. 347–420), who according to St. Bernard said, "When the Jews receive the faith at the end of the world, they will find themselves in dazzling light, as if Our Lord were returning to them from Egypt."[39]
- Augustine (354–430), who had many things to say about Israel's future salvation (along with some very negative things about the Jewish people), including, "The time will come, the end of the world will come, and all Israel shall believe; not they who now are, but their children who shall then be."[40]

And on and on the citations continue, including Ambrose, Cyril, and other significant leaders in the first five centuries of church history.

Ironically (and quite tellingly), Anderson cites some of these very same leaders, in particular Chrysostom and Augustine, to support his argument that *no* church leaders believed Israel was still chosen by God,[41] without realizing that every one of them (and many more) said the opposite of what he claims. This is the destructive power of selective ignorance, especially when mingled with antisemitic attitudes. The potion is deadly.

But the selective ignorance continues, as Anderson claims that there is no merit for the idea that God will bless those will bless Israel, pointing out that in Genesis 12:3, where the Lord says to Abram, "I will bless them that bless thee, and curse him that curseth thee" (KJV), the Hebrew for *thee* is singular. This promise is only for Abraham, Anderson argues, adding, "Many evangelical Christians today do not get their doctrine on Israel from anything that's written in the New Testament; they're getting it from the notes of the Scofield Reference Bible" (which apply the promise to the people of Israel).[42]

Putting aside the fact that most Christians today have probably never heard of the Scofield Reference Bible (it helped disseminate dispensational teaching one hundred years ago, but as of March 26, 2020, one version of it was #264 among Christian Bibles on Amazon.com[43]), Anderson has failed to read the biblical text carefully. First, in Genesis 12:1–3, God tells Abraham that He will make him into a great nation. Second, the same promise is spoken by Isaac, Abraham's son, over Jacob, his son, in Genesis 27:29. Third, in Numbers 24:9, Balaam spoke these words *over the nation of Israel* while still in the wilderness: "Blessed are those who bless you, and cursed are those who curse you." The promise is certainly national!

That's why the Lord spoke similar words through His prophets, warning the nations about the negative consequences of mistreating His people, even when Israel sinned. We read in Jeremiah:

> "I am with you and will save you," declares the LORD. "Though I completely destroy all the nations among which I scatter you, I will not completely destroy you. I will discipline you but only in due measure; I will not let you go entirely unpunished....
>
> "But all who devour you will be devoured; all your enemies will go into exile. Those who plunder you will be plundered; all who make spoil of you I will despoil."
>
> —JEREMIAH 30:11, 16, NIV

And then Zechariah prophesies:

> Then the angel who was speaking to me said, "Proclaim this word: This is what the LORD Almighty says: 'I am very jealous for Jerusalem and Zion, and I am very angry with the nations that feel secure. I was only a little angry, but they went too far with the punishment.'"..."For whoever touches you touches the apple of [God's] eye."
>
> —ZECHARIAH 1:14–15; 2:8, NIV

As the notes for Zechariah 2:8 in the NET Bible explain, "The pupil is one of the most vulnerable and valuable parts of the body, so for Judah to be considered the 'pupil' of the LORD's eye is to raise her value to an incalculable price (cf. NLT 'my most precious possession')."[44] So much for dismissing the promise as belonging only to Abraham.[45] The Lord continued it through Old Testament history, and there is no reason to argue that He ever revoked the principle, since it was founded on His faithfulness, not the faithfulness of Abraham and his descendants.[46]

This, of course, does not settle the matter for Anderson, who wrongly cites Galatians 3:16 and 3:29 to argue that 1) God made promises to Abraham and to his seed Jesus Christ and *not* to Israel, looking to pastor Roger Jimenez (who was my guest on *Line of Fire* on August 17, 2016, and who, like Anderson, rejoices in the death of homosexuals, believes they should be executed by the government, and claims that they cannot be saved by the blood of Jesus) for support; 2) those in Christ, whether Jewish or Gentile, are Abraham's seed; and 3) Jewish people today who do not believe in Jesus are not Abraham's seed and do not receive the promise of Genesis 12:1–3.[47]

We'll look more carefully at Galatians 3 in the next chapter, but for the moment I would simply point out that 1) already in the Torah, in Numbers, we saw that Genesis 12:1–3 applies to the nation of Israel as a whole;[48] 2) there are many verses in the Old Testament explicitly identifying Abraham's seed as the physical nation of Israel; 3) the fact that Abraham also has a spiritual seed—namely, those who put their faith in Jesus as Messiah and Lord—does not negate the fact that he has a physical seed as well, and over and over again God applied the promise to inherit the land of Israel to that physical seed; and 4) in this very video, Jimenez quotes the words of Jesus in John 8:37, where He says to His Jewish hearers, "I know that ye are Abraham's seed" (KJV).[49]

Of course, Anderson has no problem applying all the divine curses to Israel. Somehow when it comes to bad things, the Jews are still "the Jews." But when it comes to the blessings, to the good things, no, those belong only to Christians. That is Christian Antisemitism 101—and yet again, for Anderson that is the launching point for his tirade against the Jews.

Errors and Outright Lies

Why have Jewish people been persecuted and mistreated over the centuries? Why have they been banished from country after country? According to Anderson, it is "because of their blasphemy toward Christianity and because of their predatory lending practices."[50] It's not that Christians ever sinned against Jews. It's not that Muslims ever sinned against Jews. It's not that the devil wanted to wipe the Jewish people off the map. Not a chance. It is *all* the fault of the Jewish people. They are so evil! And what about all the countries in which Jewish people lived in poverty, the countries in which they were the tail, not the head? They were still guilty of "predatory lending practices," since that's what the Jews always do.

I could point out, of course, that one reason Jewish people became prominent moneylenders in some countries was because they were not allowed to work many other jobs, so banking became a major profession. I could also ask Anderson that if the Jews were so cursed throughout history, how did they end up (allegedly) controlling whole nations with their wealth? (According to the video, by the mid-1800s, the Rothschilds were the richest family in the world.[51]) But to raise these points would be to dignify Anderson's libels, which simply repeat the standard antisemitic canards that have been circulated for centuries.[52]

Outrageously, as the documentary traces the founding of the state of Israel, including the United Nations' Partition Plan, which would have formed two states in what was called Palestine, Texe Marrs claims that Israel became a state first and—get this—"they never allowed Palestine to become a state."[53] How utterly outrageous, and what a blatant, rank lie.

The Arab leadership categorically rejected the two-state solution, with their leaders saying things like this on October 11, 1947: "This war will be a war of extermination and a momentous massacre which will be spoken of like the Mongol massacres and the Crusades."[54] In stark contrast, the Jewish leadership embraced the two-state solution. As stated by Golda Meir on November 29, 1947, "We are happy and ready for what lies ahead. Our hands are extended in peace to our neighbors. Both States can live in peace with one another and cooperate for the welfare of their inhabitants."[55]

David Ben-Gurion even encouraged Arabs living in what would become Israel to remain in their homes and villages: "If the Arab citizen will feel at home in our state…if the state will help him in a truthful and dedicated way to reach the economic, social, and cultural level of the Jewish community, then Arab distrust will accordingly subside and a bridge will be built to a Semitic, Jewish-Arab alliance."[56]

The sentiments of the Arab leadership were diametrically opposed to this, as they had been for decades. As Middle East scholar Daniel Pipes writes, quoting Efraim Karsh, author of *Palestine Betrayed*:

> Far from being the hapless victims of a predatory Zionist assault, it was Palestinian Arab leaders who, from the early 1920s onward, and very much against the wishes of their own constituents, launched a relentless campaign to obliterate the Jewish national revival which culminated in the violent attempt to abort the U.N. partition resolution.[57]

Indeed, "The Jewish-Zionist-Israeli side perpetually sought to find a compromise while the Palestinian-Arab-Muslim side rejected nearly all deals; and…Arab intransigence and violence caused the self-inflicted 'catastrophe.'"[58]

That's why, almost as soon as the state of Israel was announced, surrounding Arab nations launched attacks against the fledgling nation, seeking to wipe Israel off the map. And it was the bad decision making of the Arab leadership that robbed the people of their own state in 1947. It was not the Jews who thwarted them. Talk about turning historical facts upside down. Not only so, but the Arab leadership rejected outright an earlier two-state proposal in 1937, one that was much more to their advantage and very difficult for the Jews. Yet many Jewish leaders welcomed the proposal (while many others rejected it). All the Arab leadership, however, said no. But why let the truth confuse the standard antisemitic line? It seems Marrs was willing to bend the facts until the narrative fit his bias.

How is it, then, that Israel was restored as a nation? Anderson and his pastoral colleagues are emphatic: God scattered the Jewish people because of their unbelief, and they cannot be regathered until they believe in Jesus.[59] That means—and I quote—that it was "the spirit of antichrist that brought them back to the Promised Land; it was the United Nations that brought them back," that reestablished the state of Israel in 1948.[60] Yes, the spirit of antichrist!

Tragically, Anderson forgets that God brought the Jewish people back from Babylonian captivity in unbelief because His name was being blasphemed. And so He is free to do what He wants whenever He wants, expressly because He is God. (See Ezekiel 36:22–32, which is still being fulfilled in our day.) In addition, Anderson digs his own pit, noting that it was God who scattered the Jewish people in judgment.[61] But if that is true—and it is—then *no one* other than God can regather them, not the Jewish people themselves, not the United Nations, and not the Antichrist.

You see, the Word makes clear that when God blesses, no one can curse, and when He curses, no one can bless. (See especially Leviticus 26 and Deuteronomy 28.) In the same way, when He wounds, no one can heal, and when He heals, no one can wound; when He opens a door, no one can shut it, and when He shuts a door, no one can open it. (See Deuteronomy 32:39 and Revelation 3:7.) So if the Jewish people have been scattered by God in judgment, no one (most of all the Jewish people themselves) can regather them. To claim otherwise is to claim that the divine edict is meaningless and can be overthrown by mere mortals.

And since the Bible is explicit that the exile from the land was a divine judgment (among many scriptures, see 2 Chronicles 7:17–22), the only explanation for the regathering to the land is that God Himself did it. As declared through the prophet Jeremiah, "For I am with you to save you, declares the LORD; I will make a full end of all the nations among whom I scattered you, but of you I will not make a full end. I will discipline you in just measure, and I will by no means leave you unpunished" (Jer. 30:11). And, "Hear the word of the LORD, O nations, and declare it in the coastlands far away; say,

'He who scattered Israel will gather him, and will keep him as a shepherd keeps his flock'" (Jer. 31:10).

But what's really scary is this: we are barely forty minutes into this one-hundred-minute video and it already contains some of the most glaring, shocking, unhistorical, blatantly false statements imaginable—and yet tens of thousands of Christians likely believe this video preaches the gospel truth. Do you understand even better now why you are reading this book?[62] That being said, I'll refute briefly the most serious errors that follow in the next hour-plus of video.

CLAIM 1: The Star of David is actually the star of the idol Remphan (also spelled Rephan), mentioned in the Septuagint (the Greek translation of the Hebrew Bible) at Amos 5:26 (and cited in Acts 7:43).

There is literally zero evidence for this claim, and it is difficult even to trace where the myth began. But wherever it started, we actually know nothing whatsoever about this "star of Remphan." In Hebrew it is actually the star of *kiyyun*, which appears to be a derogatory spelling of the ancient Near Eastern god called Kaiwan. As for this deity called Remphan, we're not even sure how to spell the name, let alone identify the deity in question or the star associated with it.

As professor Samuel A. Meier explained in the *Anchor Yale Bible Dictionary*:

> **REPHAN** (DEITY) [Gk *Rhaiphan* (Ῥαιφαν)]. A deity whom Stephen claimed that Israel worshipped in the wilderness (Acts 7:43). Greek texts of the OT preserve a variety of transliterations for the name of a deity which appears in the Hebrew text of Amos 5:26 as *kiyyûn* (consonantal text *kywn*). This Greek tradition is the source for the name Rephan in Acts 7:43 where Amos 5:26 is quoted. A common confusion in the text of the OT between the letters *kap* and *reš* accounts for the confusion in the initial letter, and the Greek letter *phi* points to a pronunciation of the Hebrew *waw* as consonant. Although the final vowel is consistently represented in Greek as *alpha*, there is no agreement as to the first vowel, the following forms being attested in Acts and Amos: *rompha (n), rempha (m/n), raiphan, rephan, raphan*. Since there is no deity known who bears such a name, the Hebrew text should be given priority over the Greek transliterations. The Hebrew consonants in Amos 5:26 correspond to an Akkadian name for the planet Saturn, which was recognized as a deity.[63]

It is true that the six-pointed Star of David is not referenced in the Bible and that it was used in different ancient religions along with occult practices right to this day.[64] But in itself, it is just a symbol and as such can be used for good or evil. The earliest Jewish usage attested so far may be as recent as the fourteenth century, but the symbol did not become widely used in Jewish circles until the last few centuries.[65] Either way, as noted on the My Jewish Learning website:

> After the [antisemitic] Dreyfus Affair in the 19th century [in France], the star was adopted by the Zionist movement at its 1897 Congress, and this gave the symbol more international prominence. In the 20th century, the star became even more evocative of Judaism when it was used by the Nazis to mark Jews for persecution. And after the Holocaust, the same star became part of the flag of the nascent State of Israel.[66]

The bottom line is that there are satanic explanations for the symbolism of the Star of David and holy explanations for the Star of David, but in the end it's just a symbol.[67] It is only those who are already biased against Israel and the Jewish people who will shout, "Look! Here's another proof that the modern state of Israel is of the devil!"

On the documentary, Texe Marrs claims that Remphan is Moloch, the god of child sacrifice, who is actually the devil himself. But to repeat: there is not a stitch of solid evidence to support his claim. Facts, however, don't seem to matter to those who latch on to antisemitism, and so based on these false claims, Marrs then points to the Masonic use of the Star of David and states that Freemasonry is based on Judaism, specifically on the Kabbalah.[68]

So according to this twisted logic, Jews today worship the god of child sacrifice, Moloch, and we know this because they use the Star of David, which we know was the star of Remphan, who is Moloch, and it's confirmed by Freemasonry, which is based on Kabbalah. All of which leads Marrs to say, "If anyone tells me that the Jews were not placed under a great curse by Jesus Himself, it's there."[69]

CLAIM 2: Today's Jews are not really Jews but are the synagogue of Satan.

I address this in depth in the next chapter, looking at the primary verses cited by Anderson. He also makes the absurd statement in this section that "the Jews that think God loves only them."[70] In reality, as noted on the My Jewish Learning website, "A righteous Gentile is a full child of God—to be cherished by all who give God allegiance, regardless of their religious affiliation." And, "God demands goodness of the Jew no less than of the non-Jew, and loves the Gentile no less than the Jew. And so should we."[71]

CLAIM 3: The expected Jewish Messiah describes what the Bible calls the Antichrist.

Anderson claims, "The Jews are ready to accept the Antichrist as their Messiah." And, he avers, when this happens, all the apostate Christians will say, "Look, this is the second coming of Jesus Christ. Look, all the Jews believe on him."[72] And so they too will be led into deception. Put another way, the Jews will lead the whole world into deception. That's what Jews do!

Forget about the fact that the New Testament states plainly that Jesus will come again in the clouds of glory. Forget about the fact that Jesus Himself said that the whole world will see Him when He returns in the sky. And forget about the fact that apostate Christians are already deceived and no longer believe the Bible, in which case they don't need "the Jews" to lead them into error.

No, for Anderson and his ilk, it is the evil Jews who will follow the Antichrist himself, thereby leading the whole world into error. And the modern state of Israel is just the foundation for this great deception. That's why modern Israel is so evil! (Did I already call this logic twisted?)

CLAIM 4: We will have God's wrath upon us if we support Israel.

Anderson is absolutely correct in denouncing statements made by pastor John Hagee claiming that Jews already had a covenant with God and did not need to believe in Jesus.[73] Indeed, there were some serious errors in the first edition of Pastor Hagee's book *In Defense of Israel*.[74] (Thankfully, in the revised and updated edition he corrected those errors and wrote that "redemption for all men comes through Jesus Christ."[75] How this squares with some of his other statements is not for me to explain, but I take his words at face value.) But Hagee is to be applauded for standing with Israel and helping Jews worldwide know that evangelical Christians are their best friends, especially in light of centuries of church-sponsored antisemitism.

In keeping with his misuse of Scripture, however, Anderson cites 2 John 9–11, which speaks of not welcoming or aiding false teachers, and claims that based on this text, it is wrong for Christians to bless Israel, since Israel does not believe in Jesus. What a misapplication of the Word. The video also mocks American politicians who, allegedly out of a desire to please the evangelical voting bloc, go to Jerusalem and "pray to the Jewish God."[76] Actually, that would be the same God the apostles prayed to in New Testament times, also known as the God of the Bible. The fact that Jews who reject Jesus are not rightly connected to their God does not change who He is.

To be totally candid, as I watched this video, I found myself saying over and over, "No, you've got to be kidding!" And it almost feels silly to take the time to rebut these nonsensical statements—except for the fact that it seems many thousands of Christians believe them. The lies *must* be exposed, however ridiculous they may be.

Naturally, Anderson believes all the bad reports about Israel, and so, as pro-Israel quotes from Hagee are being played in the background, the video shows Palestinians carrying babies allegedly killed by the Israelis. There is not the slightest attempt to paint a fair picture of the Middle East conflict or of Israel's constant efforts to spare civilian lives in the midst of constant terrorist attempts to slaughter Israeli civilians. No, Anderson asserts that "the Bible teaches that if we help an ungodly and wicked nation like Israel, we'll have God's wrath upon us."[77]

Another pastor makes the bogus claim that it is illegal in Israel to pass out Christian tracts. (I have many friends who have freely passed out evangelistic tracts in Israel for years.) But as I've asked repeatedly through this book, who cares about facts when demonizing Israel and the Jewish people is the goal?

To be sure, Israel is a Jewish state, not a Christian state. And to the extent that the ultra-Orthodox control the Ministry of the Interior, it is more difficult for Messianic Jews to become Israeli citizens, since they're viewed as Christians and no longer Jews. But Messianic Jews freely evangelize in Israel and share the gospel in many different settings, including on national TV in the equivalent of shows like *American Idol* or *The Voice*.[78] Not only so, but an April 2018 article in the *Jerusalem Post* notes, "Prime Minister Benjamin Netanyahu's new deputy social media adviser Hananya Naftali is a popular Israel advocate online, served in the Armored Corps, fought Hamas in Operation Protective Edge, and calls himself a Jew who loves Jesus."[79]

Still, it is true that there are many things about Israel that are offensive to conservative Christians, and Anderson is right to point out how gay-friendly Israel is, in particular the city of Tel Aviv. (Religious Jews, of course, strongly oppose this gay activism.) But our support for Israel is based on God's promises and God's purposes, not Israel's goodness. It is also based on the fact that the surrounding hostile nations want to wipe Israel off the map. So our support is not an endorsement of everything Israel does or of every Israeli policy. It is a recognition of the hand of God, the promises of God, the plan of God, and the belief that this is the best way to advocate for peace in the Middle East.

CLAIM 5: It is wrong for Christians to speak of God's shekinah glory since that is a Jewish concept.

We are told that the word *shekinah* is not found in the Old Testament but rather is borrowed from Judaism. Therefore, according to Anderson, it is wrong for Christians to refer to the "shekinah glory." Of course, the word *Trinity* does not occur in the New Testament, yet Christians have used it freely for centuries because of what it conveys. In the same way, while the word *shekinah* does not occur in the Bible, the concept of God's manifest presence is certainly there, and of equal importance, the root *sh-k-n*, meaning "to dwell," is found there too. An excellent example is found in Exodus 25:8, where God says to Moses, "And let them make me a sanctuary, that I may dwell in their midst." (The root for "I may dwell" is *sh-k-n*.) That's where we get the concept of the shekinah glory of God—His manifest presence—and it is a beautiful, biblical concept we should embrace.

That doesn't mean that we embrace everything Judaism teaches about the shekinah (in Judaism, normally spelled *Shechinah*), in particular that it speaks of the feminine side of God. In fact, the vast majority of Christians who use the term have no idea what Judaism teaches. But here we have a classic expression of antisemitism, namely that if the Jews embrace something, Christians must reject it. And for Anderson, this concept in particular must be rejected since the God of the Bible is a He, not a She, and there is nothing feminine about Him. (Has He forgotten that when God created us in His image, according to Genesis 1:26–27, He created us male and female?) Rather, Anderson claims this is New Age mysticism, worship of Mother Earth, and the like.[80] There you have it!

CLAIM 6: Today's Jews have no way of proving they are really descendants of Israel.

In another head-shaking, "I don't believe he's saying this" moment in the video, Anderson says the only way a Jew could know he was really Jewish was by use of genealogical records. Yet, Anderson notes, Titus 3:9 tells us to avoid genealogies! I guess the author of Ezra, in the Old Testament, was really off base when he described Ezra as "the son of Seraiah, son of Azariah, son of Hilkiah, son of Shallum, son of Zadok, son of Ahitub, son of Amariah, son of Azariah, son of Meraioth, son of Zerahiah, son of Uzzi, son of Bukki, son of Abishua, son of Phinehas, son of Eleazar, son of Aaron the chief priest" (Ezra 7:1–5). And I guess Paul was equally wrong when he described himself as "of the people of Israel, of the tribe of Benjamin, a Hebrew of Hebrews; as to the law, a Pharisee" (Phil. 3:5).

But hang on. There's more. Not only are we told that Jews can only know that they're really descended from Israel by means of genealogical records but that genealogies should be avoided, we're also told that it doesn't matter, since physical descent no longer counts. Rather, in Jesus, there is no longer Jew or Gentile. So Jews can't prove they're really Jewish, and even if they could, they shouldn't, but even if they were, it doesn't matter.

Even more absurd is Anderson's lengthy argument about family trees, which includes the claim that if you can point to one person in your lineage from two thousand years ago who was from Israel, that makes you a direct descendant of Israel. And while he agrees with the statement that "DNA doesn't lie" (in contrast with all the intermingling and intermarriage and even children born out of wedlock that get jumbled together in genealogies), he completely ignores the DNA evidence for the common origins of a large percentage of today's Jews.[81] Then a colleague of Anderson's mocks the importance of

DNA—which they just brought up—and asks, "What about faith in Christ?" But since when did faith in Christ determine whether you were a physical descendant of Israel?

As for the idea that there is no Jew or Gentile in Jesus, as I explain further in the next chapter, Paul is speaking of spiritual status. He is *not* saying that Jews and Gentiles no longer exist, even within the church, any more than he is saying that males and females no longer exist in the church. After all, when Paul wrote that there was neither Jew nor Gentile, he also wrote that there was no longer male or female (Gal. 3:28). Should we then expect to find unisex bathrooms at Pastor Anderson's church? Or would he let a man marry a man or a woman marry a woman, since there is no longer male or female in Christ?

The bottom line is that, yes, in Jesus, Jew and Gentile become one, equally heirs of Christ and equally loved by God. And yes, faith in Jesus is essential for Jew and Gentile and there is no salvation outside of Him. And yes, *God keeps His promises*, and if He goes back on His promises to the physical descendants of Israel—if He fails to discipline them as He promised; if He fails to preserve them in the nations as He promised; if He fails to bring them back to the land in unbelief, just as He promised; if He fails to make Jerusalem the city of controversy for the whole world, just as He promised; if He fails to turn the hearts of His Jewish people to Yeshua the Messiah, just as He promised—then He cannot be trusted.

Thank God that He Himself is a Zionist.[82] That's why the Jewish people still exist as a people. And that's why the nation of Israel exists as a nation. And that's why all the books by men like Reverend Sizer and videos by men like Pastor Anderson will never stop the plan of God.

I can only pity those who mock that sacred plan. They may intend to do good and may be jealous for the purity of the gospel as they see it. They may be concerned about the mistreatment of the Palestinians and have a heart for justice and equity. But they miss the hand of God at work in the world right before their eyes, and that's why I am a follower of Jesus and a Zionist at the same time. The two go hand in hand.

One day, all believers will enjoy the New Jerusalem forever, when God creates a new heaven and a new earth. Until that time, the earthly Jerusalem matters—to God, to Satan, to the Jewish people, and to the world. It should matter to us as well.

We'll return to this subject in the last chapter of the book.

CHAPTER 9

THE SYNAGOGUE OF SATAN?

HAVE YOU HEARD this argument before? It goes something like this, using what seems to be fair and compelling scriptural logic: The Jewish people rejected Jesus as Messiah and called for His crucifixion, bringing down judgment on their own generation as well as all subsequent generations of Jews (Matt. 27:25). As a result of this, God took the kingdom from them and gave it to the Gentiles who put their trust in the Lord (Matt. 8:10–12; 21:43). As for the Jewish people themselves, Jesus said they are not really Jews at all but rather are the synagogue of Satan (Rev. 2:9; 3:9); they are of their father the devil, which is why they too lie and murder (John 8:44).

Paul, it is said, confirms this, teaching that a Jew is not one outwardly but inwardly, meaning that a Gentile follower of Jesus is more of a Jew than someone born Jewish who rejects Jesus (Rom. 2:28–29). And that's why he explains that "not all who are descended from Israel are Israel" (Rom. 9:6, NIV), that the true seed of Abraham is not Israel but Jesus (Gal. 3:16), and that the church is the Israel of God (Gal. 6:16).

They point out Paul's words in 1 Thessalonians 2:15, where he says the Jews "killed both the Lord Jesus and their own prophets, and have persecuted us; and they do not please God and are contrary to all men" (NKJV). And they say Peter corroborates this, telling his Jewish people:

> The God of Abraham, Isaac and Jacob, the God of our fathers, has glorified his servant Jesus. *You handed him over to be killed,* and *you disowned him before Pilate,* though he had decided to let him go. *You disowned the Holy and Righteous One* and asked that a murderer be released to you. *You killed the author of life,* but God raised him from the dead. We are witnesses of this.
>
> —ACTS 3:13–15, NIV, EMPHASIS ADDED

Need any more be said?

In the words of Christian global analyst Vince Dhimos:

> Christian Zionism is a false Satanic cult that has cost America the lives of its precious sons and trillions in treasure. According to the Bible, a Jew is a person who accepts the Jewish scriptures. Those calling themselves Jews who do not accept the scriptures are described quite plainly in Revelation 3:9, as follows:
>
> *Behold, I will make them of the synagogue of Satan, which say they are Jews, and are not, but do lie; behold, I will make them to come and worship before thy feet, and to know that I have loved thee.*[1]

Is it, then, that the whole problem of antisemitism can be traced back to the New Testament? Perhaps the New Testament itself is antisemitic (as well as anti-Zionistic). In that case, if we believe the New Testament to be God's Word and are rightly interpreting it, then we could say that the Jews are responsible for the death of Jesus, the Jews are children of the devil, the Jews are hostile to all men and displeasing to God, and the Jews are cursed and rejected by God. We could also say that the church is now Israel and that modern Israel has no connection to biblical Israel.

But what if these verses are being grossly misinterpreted, wrenched out of their context and wrongly applied? What if the New Testament actually reaffirms God's promises to Israel and speaks of a bright future for the Jewish people, including a restoration to the physical land of Israel? Let's examine each of these texts in context. What does the Word of God say? In some of my other publications, I have provided in-depth, academic treatments of many of the most controversial verses, but rather than repeat all the details here, I'll present a summary of the key arguments.[2]

Are All Jews in All Generations Responsible for the Death of Jesus?

Matthew records that a Jewish crowd urged Pilate to release Barabbas rather than Jesus at the time of the Passover:

> Pilate said to them, "Then what shall I do with Jesus who is called Christ?" They all said, "Let him be crucified!" And he said, "Why? What evil has he done?" But they shouted all the more, "Let him be crucified!"
>
> So when Pilate saw that he was gaining nothing, but rather that a riot was beginning, he took water and washed his hands before the crowd, saying, "I am innocent of this man's blood; see to it yourselves." And all the people answered, "His blood be on us and on our children!"
>
> —MATTHEW 27:22–25

What do we make of this passage? We know that elsewhere Matthew records that a large percentage of the Jewish population thought Jesus was a prophet. (See Matthew 21:45–46, and for more on this, see the next section.) So this crowd hardly represented the whole nation. More importantly, there is not any hint in the text that this crowd had the authority to speak for all future generations of the Jewish people. Not a chance.

Does Matthew present this account to point to Jewish responsibility in the crucifixion of Jesus? Absolutely. There *was* Jewish responsibility in the Messiah's death, in particular on the part of the Jewish leaders. The New Testament states this consistently, just as the Old Testament prophets often called out the guilt of Israel's leaders. This was a serious, grave sin with lasting effect.

But at worst, the words "His blood be on us and on our children!" simply mean this: "We take full responsibility for this decision. Let the consequences come on us and our children." And at worst, that is exactly what happened, as Jerusalem was leveled forty years later and hundreds of thousands of Jewish lives were lost in the revolt against Rome.

Under no circumstances, however, does Matthew 27:25 teach that all Jewish people worldwide were responsible for the death of Jesus in the first century. More emphatically still, Matthew 27:25 does *not* teach that all Jews through all future generations were responsible for the death of Jesus. Perish the thought.

Did God Take the Kingdom From Israel and Give It to the Gentiles?

Matthew 21 begins with an account of the triumphal entry of Jesus into Jerusalem as the Jewish crowds hailed Him as Messiah. Next, Jesus enters the temple to clear out the corrupt money changers. There He heals the sick and is welcomed by the children—all of them Jewish—while the Jewish leaders reject Him. After this He curses the fig tree, which to the disciples' shock has withered by the next day.

Matthew then records that as Jesus was teaching in the temple courts, the Jewish leaders challenged His authority. After exposing their hypocrisy, He taught two parables. In the first, He stated that the tax collectors and prostitutes—again, all of them Jewish—would enter the kingdom ahead of the religious leaders. In the second parable, Jesus told the story of a landowner who rented out his property but his tenants were ungrateful, beating and killing the owner's servants and ultimately killing his son. Jesus then said to the crowds listening, "Have you never read in the Scriptures: 'The stone that the builders rejected has become the cornerstone; this was the Lord's doing, and it is marvelous in our eyes'?" (Matt. 21:42, quoting Psalm 118:22–23).

And then Yeshua uttered these oft-quoted words: "Therefore I tell you, the kingdom of God will be taken away from you and given to a people producing its fruits" (Matt. 21:43). Does this indicate that the Lord was taking the kingdom of God away from the Jews and giving it to the Gentiles? Not at all. He was speaking of a change in leadership.

How do we know this? We keep reading! Matthew continues, "When *the chief priests and the Pharisees* heard his parables, *they* perceived that he was speaking about *them*. And although *they* were seeking to arrest him, *they* feared the crowds, because they held him to be a prophet" (Matt. 21:45–46, emphasis added). That's it!

The crowds were *Jewish crowds,* and they held Jesus to be a prophet. Indeed, they had just welcomed Him into Jerusalem as the Messiah. In contrast, throughout this entire chapter, Yeshua's conflict was with the *Jewish leaders*. And they clearly understood that He was directing His rebuke to them. The kingdom would soon be taken from them and "given to a people producing its fruits."

And who were those people? In the first place, it was the Jewish followers of Jesus, men like Peter and Jacob (James),[3] John and Paul! As the Lord said to His disciples at the Last Supper, "You are those who have stayed with me in my trials, and *I assign to you, as my Father assigned to me, a kingdom,* that you may eat and drink at my table in my kingdom and sit on thrones *judging the twelve tribes of Israel*" (Luke 22:28–30, emphasis added; see also the discussion of Acts 1:6 in chapter 11).

It is true that over the centuries, the church became largely Gentile as the gospel spread through the nations of the world. But at no point did God displace Israel with the church, and Matthew 21:43 does *not* support such a view.

What about Matthew 8:10–12? After Jesus heard the faith-filled words of a Roman soldier—not a Jewish teacher but a Gentile soldier—the text states that

> he marveled and said to those who followed him, "Truly, I tell you, with no one in Israel have I found such faith. I tell you, many will come from east and west and recline at table with Abraham, Isaac, and Jacob in the kingdom of heaven, while the sons of the kingdom will be thrown into the outer darkness. In that place there will be weeping and gnashing of teeth."

And that is exactly what has happened for much of the last two thousand years, as the Jewish people have rejected Jesus as Messiah, excluding themselves from the kingdom now and in the world to come, while many Gentiles from around the world have been feasting at the table of the Lord's grace. But this text certainly does not state that *all* the sons of the kingdom—meaning the people of Israel—will be cast out. Hardly!

The very man writing these words, Matthew, was a son of the kingdom, as have been several million Jewish believers in Jesus since then. Nor does the text say that there will not be a future turning of the Jewish people. To the contrary, it will be just as Paul explains in Romans 9–11. Jewish branches have been cut off, and Gentile branches have been grafted in. But when the fullness of the Gentiles comes in, there will be a massive regathering of the Jewish people. God will keep His Word! Matthew also speaks of the future time when Israel will be restored. (See Matthew 19:28.)

Did Jesus Teach That the Jews Were Children of the Devil, Calling Them the "Synagogue of Satan"?

In John 8, Jesus was speaking with some Jews who believed in Him on some level, and He was challenging them to continue in His teaching, thereby proving themselves to be real disciples (John 8:31–32). But the more He spoke with them, the clearer it became that they were not real believers at all, as He said to them, "You are looking for a way to kill me, because you have no room for my word" (John 8:37, NIV).

When they claimed that Abraham was their father and, even more, that God was their Father, Jesus replied:

> "If God were your Father, you would love me, for I came from God and I am here. I came not of my own accord, but he sent me. Why do you not understand what I say? It is because you cannot bear to hear my word. *You are of your father the devil,* and your will is to do your father's desires. He was a murderer from the beginning, and does not stand in the truth, because there is no truth in him. When he lies, he speaks out of his own character, for he is a liar and the father of lies. But because I tell the truth, you do not believe me. Which one of you convicts me of sin? If I tell the truth, why do you not believe me? Whoever is of God hears the words of God. The reason why you do not hear them is that you are not of God."
>
> —John 8:42–47, emphasis added

Let's think this through and ask some simple questions. Did Jesus ever say to every Jew on the planet, "You are of your father the devil"? No, He did not. (Once again, if you differ with me, show me why. Give me some scriptural texts to support your views.) Is it right to say, "The Jews are of their father the devil"? No, it is not. Yeshua simply said to Jewish men who wanted to kill Him—despite having some faith in who He was—that they showed themselves to be children of the devil, not children of God.

You might say, "But doesn't this hold true for every Jewish person who rejects Jesus as the Messiah? Wouldn't they all fall under the category of 'children of the devil'?"

Yes, in that sense, they would—*but so would every single Gentile on the planet who rejects Jesus.* Writing to the Gentile believers in Ephesus, Paul says:

> And you were dead in the trespasses and sins in which you once walked, following the course of this world, *following the prince of the power of the air, the spirit that is now at work in the sons of disobedience*—among whom we all once lived in the passions of our flesh, carrying out the desires of the body and the mind, *and were by nature children of wrath,* like the rest of mankind. But God, being rich in mercy, because of the great love with which he loved us even when we were dead in our trespasses, made us alive together with Christ.
>
> —EPHESIANS 2:1–5, EMPHASIS ADDED

Similarly, 1 John 5:19 says this: "We know that we are from God, and *the whole world lies in the power of the evil one*" (emphasis added). Indeed, John explains, "By this it is evident who are the children of God, and *who are the children of the devil*: whoever does not practice righteousness is not of God, nor is the one who does not love his brother" (1 John 3:10, emphasis added). And on one occasion, Jesus addressed His own disciple Peter as Satan, since it was the devil speaking through Peter at that time (Matt. 16:23).

To single out the Jews, then, as children of the devil is to be unscriptural and bigoted. To recognize that all human beings who do not know the Lord and who act accordingly are children of the devil is to be accurate and fair. That's why Jesus died for all of us. All of us were lost, all of us were under Satan's power, and all of us needed redemption and forgiveness.

What about Revelation 2:9 and 3:9, where Jesus brought a word of encouragement to Christians suffering persecution in Smyrna and Philadelphia? He said, "I know your tribulation and your poverty (but you are rich) and the slander of those who say that they are Jews and are not, but are a synagogue of Satan" (Rev. 2:9). And, "Behold, I will make those of the synagogue of Satan who say that they are Jews and are not, but lie—behold, I will make them come and bow down before your feet, and they will learn that I have loved you" (Rev. 3:9).

So Yeshua was speaking of certain people "who say that they are Jews and are not" and was opposing the believers in these two cities, calling them the "synagogue of Satan" and promising they would be judged. That's it.

Did Jesus say that all Jews worldwide were the synagogue of Satan? No, He did not. Did He say that all Jews in all generations were the synagogue of Satan? Absolutely not. Do we even know if these people who opposed the gospel were actually Jews? It's possible they were not even Jews at all but simply claimed to be so, just as there were those in Ephesus who claimed to be apostles and were not (Rev. 2:2).

So either Jesus was speaking to particular groups of ethnic Jews who were acting contrary to their calling as Jews, rebuking them strongly by saying to them prophetically, "You're not real Jews; you're the synagogue of Satan," or He was speaking to Gentiles who were opposing the gospel and claiming to be Jews, saying, "Actually, you're not Jews at all; you're the synagogue of Satan." But again, it is an abusive and dangerous misuse of God's Word—in this case, of the very words of Jesus—to brand all Jews today the "synagogue of Satan."

Tragically, I see this happen online every day, as professing Christians throw that term around with disparagement, using it to refer to all Jews who do not believe in Jesus. Yet, to repeat: We don't even know if the people in question were Jewish at all. They could have been Gentiles in some kind of Jewish-related cult, similar to some cultic groups today who claim to be Jews but in reality are not. But even if Jesus was referring to ethnic Jews, He was rebuking them for acting contrary to their high calling. He was not saying that all Jews who did not follow Jesus were the "synagogue of Satan."

This would be similar to a pastor today calling out his compromised congregation, saying, "You say you are Christians, but you are not! Look at how you are living. You're more like the church of the evil one than the church of the living God!"[4] And this would be similar to how the prophets rebuke God's people in the Old Testament, saying that they are Israel in name only, despite the fact that they are still Israel in the physical, ethnic sense. (See Hosea 1:8–9 in the NIV, where God calls sinful Israel by the name of "Not My People," even though in other passages, such as Isaiah 1:2–3, He makes clear that His sinning people are still His people.)

Did Paul Teach That Jews Weren't Really Jews and Israel Wasn't Really Israel?

In Romans 1–3, Paul is demonstrating how every human being, Jew and Gentile alike, is sinful in God's sight and in need of redemption. In Romans 2, he focuses on his fellow Jews, asking, "Now you, if you call yourself a Jew; if you rely on the law and boast in God...do you dishonor God by breaking the law?" (Romans 2:17, 23, NIV). Then he says this:

> For circumcision indeed is of value if you obey the law, but if you break the law, your circumcision becomes uncircumcision. So, if a man who is uncircumcised keeps the precepts of the law, will not his uncircumcision be regarded as circumcision? Then he who is physically uncircumcised

> but keeps the law will condemn you who have the written code and circumcision but break the law. For no one is a Jew who is merely one outwardly, nor is circumcision outward and physical. But a Jew is one inwardly, and circumcision is a matter of the heart, by the Spirit, not by the letter. His praise is not from man but from God.
>
> ROMANS 2:25–29

This is similar to John the Immerser warning the Pharisees and Sadducees who come to hear him preach, "And do not presume to say to yourselves, 'We have Abraham as our father,' for I tell you, God is able from these stones to raise up children for Abraham" (Matt. 3:9). Both John and Paul are speaking directly to Jewish pride. Being a Jew, they emphasize, does not guarantee you God's favor, nor does it make you righteous. It is your conduct that counts, along with the condition of your heart.

In Romans 2, it is most likely that Paul is contrasting two Jews, both of whom are circumcised in the flesh but only one of whom is circumcised in heart. This would be seen in the translations that add words like *only* and *merely* to verse 28, as does the NIV: "A person is not a Jew who is one only outwardly, nor is circumcision merely outward and physical."

But what if Paul is saying that a Gentile who is circumcised in heart is the real Jew, while the Jew who is not circumcised in heart is not Jewish at all? Wouldn't that change how we interpret the word *Jew* today? And wouldn't that change how we view God's promises in the Bible to the Jewish people? Perhaps they all apply now to Gentile followers of Jesus!

The problem with this line of thinking is that Paul himself rejects it, categorically and clearly. To be sure, Gentile believers in Jesus *do* share in many of God's promises to Israel. As Paul explains to Gentile believers in Rome, you "now share in the nourishing root of the olive tree" (Rom. 11:17). Or, as he writes to the Gentile believers in Ephesus:

> So then you are no longer strangers and aliens, but you are fellow citizens with the saints and members of the household of God, built on the foundation of the apostles and prophets, Christ Jesus himself being the cornerstone, in whom the whole structure, being joined together, grows into a holy temple in the Lord. In him you also are being built together into a dwelling place for God by the Spirit.
>
> —EPHESIANS 2:19–22

In Yeshua, we are all one! We are equals in the Lord—equally loved by God, equally filled by the Spirit, equally called and chosen.

That's what Paul means in Galatians 3:28 when he writes, "There is neither Jew nor Greek, there is neither slave nor free, there is no male and female, for you are all one in Christ Jesus." He means that there is no class system, no caste system, no higher and lower in Jesus. We are spiritual equals, joint heirs of the Messiah, equally loved by God, equally children of God. But men are still men and women are still women, which is why Paul gives distinct teachings to men and women, as well as to husbands and wives, in his letters. The distinctions remain! That's why, to this day, churches have men's meetings and women's meetings (not to mention men's bathrooms and women's bathrooms).

In the same way, there were still slaves and free people among the believers, and Paul gives specific instructions to Christian slaves and (get this) to Christian slave owners. This, of course, was a different type of slavery than the brutal African slave trade. But the point is that there *were* slaves and there *were* free people in the churches, yet in Jesus they were one.

In the same way, there were still Jews and Gentiles in Paul's churches, just as there are Jews and Gentiles in churches today. But in Yeshua, we are equals; we are one. At the same time, our distinctions remain, with each of us uniquely called to specific and sacred missions.

And that's why Paul never calls Gentile believers Jews. Not once.[5] In fact, in the passage where he deals most extensively with God's eternal purposes for Israel (namely, Romans 9–11), he explicitly refers to the Gentile Christians as Gentiles, contrasting them with Israel. (See Romans 11:11–14; this contrast is consistent throughout all of Romans.) Not only so, but throughout all of Paul's writings, whenever he says "Jew," he is speaking of physical, ethnic Jews. In other words, even he if says at one point, "A real Jew is one who is circumcised on the inside," he never stops referring to the Jewish people as a whole as Jews.

It would be like me saying at a men's conference, "You're not a man if you don't care for your wife and your children. You're not a man if you fear people more than you fear God. Men, I'm talking to you!" In the same breath, I addressed all the men there as men—because that's who they were—and then talked about what a real man was.

And that's why they would all understand me when I continued, saying, "Our next men's meeting will be this Friday night. And if you're visiting here, I wanted to let you know that the men's room is downstairs and to your left." I used the word *man* in a special sense while continuing to speak to the men. Simple.

It's exactly the same with Paul, not only in Romans but in all of his letters. If you don't believe me, just keep reading. What's the very next verse after Romans 2:29? It's Romans 3:1. What does Paul write there? "Then what advantage has the Jew? Or what is the value of circumcision?"

So, *in the very next verse*, he refers to ethnic, physical Jews as Jews, since the logical question would be, "Well, if being an ethnic Jew doesn't guarantee your salvation, what's the advantage in being Jewish?" He answers this in verse 2: "Much in every way. To begin with, the Jews were entrusted with the oracles of God" (the Greek for "the Jews" is "they"). Yes, Paul is speaking of physical, ethnic Jews. That is *always* who he refers to when he speaks of Jews. Always.

Let's just survey Paul's use of *Jew* or *Jews* in Romans, outside of 2:28–29. There's no possible debate about the meaning of his words:

- "For I am not ashamed of the gospel, for it is the power of God for salvation to everyone who believes, to the Jew first and also to the Greek" (Rom. 1:16).
- "There will be tribulation and distress for every human being who does evil, the Jew first and also the Greek, but glory and honor and peace for everyone who does good, the Jew first and also the Greek" (Rom. 2:9–10).
- "But if you call yourself a Jew and rely on the law and boast in God" (Rom. 2:17).
- "What then? Are we Jews any better off? No, not at all. For we have already charged that all, both Jews and Greeks, are under sin" (Rom. 3:9).
- "Or is God the God of Jews only? Is he not the God of Gentiles also? Yes, of Gentiles also" (Rom. 3:29).
- "Even us whom he has called, not from the Jews only but also from the Gentiles?" (Rom. 9:24).
- "For there is no distinction between Jew and Greek; for the same Lord is Lord of all, bestowing his riches on all who call on him" (Rom. 10:12).

We could repeat this exercise through every single letter of Paul's, and the results would be the same: When Paul speaks of Jews, he is differentiating them from Gentiles. Always. Every single time. Without exception. (For the question of whether he ever uses the term to speak of the Jewish leaders in particular, or more specifically of Judean Jews, see the next section.) To claim based on Romans 2:28–29 that Jews around the world today are not really Jews in God's sight is, once again, to misuse and abuse God's Word.

What about Romans 9:6, where Paul states that "they are not all Israel, which are of Israel" (KJV; the TLV reads, "Not all those who are descended from Israel are Israel"). Here Paul is addressing the important question "Did God's Word fail?" After all, God made promises to the nation of

Israel, promises of salvation and blessing, yet when the Messiah came, the nation as a whole rejected Him. What, then, happened to those promises? Did they fail?

Paul's answer is decisive: "But it is not as though the word of God has failed. For not all who are descended from Israel belong to Israel" (Rom. 9:6). In other words, there is a remnant within the nation, a remnant of true believers. They constitute the Israel within Israel, and they are the ones who receive the promises.

But Paul is not saying the church was Israel—again, there is not one single example of this anywhere in the Bible—nor is he saying that the nation as a whole is no longer regarded as Israel. To the contrary, throughout the rest of Romans, anytime he speaks of Israel, he speaks of the nation as a whole. But don't trust me on this; take out your Bible and read the verses for yourself. These are the rest of the times that Paul uses the term *Israel* or *Israelites* in Romans: 9:27, 31; 10:1,[6] 19, 21; 11:1–2, 7, 25–26.

There can be no doubt about Paul's language. After speaking of the believing remnant within the nation as Israel, every time he uses the term *Israel* after that (as well as before that, in 9:4), he is referring to the nation as a whole, noting that God reached out to them in their unbelief and disobedience (Rom. 9:27; 10:21), that they did not attain what they sought after (9:31), that they did not understand (10:19), that Elijah appealed to God against them (11:2), that those who didn't believe were hardened (11:2) but that the hardening was only in part (11:25), and that all Israel would be saved (11:26). Israel means Israel!

Did Paul Say the Jews Killed Jesus and the Prophets, Displease God, and Are Hostile to All Mankind?

If there is any single passage in the New Testament that seems to back the claims of the antisemites, it is 1 Thessalonians 2:14–16. There Paul writes:

> For you, brothers, became imitators of the churches of God in Christ Jesus that are in Judea. For you suffered the same things from your own countrymen as they did from the Jews, who killed both the Lord Jesus and the prophets, and drove us out, and displease God and oppose all mankind by hindering us from speaking to the Gentiles that they might be saved—so as always to fill up the measure of their sins. But wrath has come upon them at last!

Some scholars doubt that Paul could have written these words, arguing that it is a later addition and not part of his original letter. But there is no solid evidence to support this, so we must deal with the text as it stands.

However, before we focus on these verses, let's remember that Paul also says this about the Jewish people:

> I am speaking the truth in Christ—I am not lying; my conscience bears me witness in the Holy Spirit—that I have great sorrow and unceasing anguish in my heart. For I could wish that I myself were accursed and cut off from Christ for the sake of my brothers, my kinsmen according to the flesh. They are Israelites, and to them belong the adoption, the glory, the covenants, the giving of the law, the worship, and the promises. To them belong the patriarchs, and from their race, according to the flesh, is the Christ, who is God over all, blessed forever. Amen.
>
> —ROMANS 9:1–5

Notice again those words: "the adoption, the glory, the covenants, the giving of the law, the worship, and the promises" belong to the Israelites (he is speaking in the present tense, not the past tense; this remains Israel's heritage). Paul also writes this: "As regards the gospel, they are enemies for your sake. But as regards election, they are beloved for the sake of their forefathers. For the gifts and the calling of God are irrevocable" (Rom. 11:28–29). So they are hardly cursed and rejected by God forever—quite the contrary!—and they are still chosen and loved by the Lord, even while in a state of unbelief and while acting as enemies of the gospel.

Note also Paul's words in Romans 11:16, where Paul writes (speaking of Israel): "If the dough offered as firstfruits is holy, so is the whole lump, and if the root is holy, so are the branches." As New Testament scholar C. K. Barrett explains, "You cannot divide a living organism, such as a tree; the trunk and branches which grow from holy roots must themselves be holy."[7] God will keep His promises, and Israel will be redeemed.

What, then, is Paul's point in 1 Thessalonians 2? In short, he is encouraging the believers in Thessalonica that just as they have suffered at the hands of their own countrymen, so have Paul and his Jewish colleagues. (See also 1 Thessalonians 1:6–7; 2:1–2; 3:2–4, 7.) Yet that is not the end of the story, and judgment will come on their persecutors (2 Thess. 1:4–8), just as it is coming on the Jews who rejected Jesus and oppose the gospel.

But who, exactly, is Paul speaking of? Is he indicting all Jewish people around the world? Of course not. First, there were thousands of Jews like Paul who believed in Jesus as the Messiah. Second, much of the Jewish population around the world at that time was still quite ignorant about Jesus and did not fit this description. (See Paul's discussion years later with the Jewish leaders in Rome in Acts 28:17–22.) Third, there is a specific connection between "Judea" (Greek *Ioudaia*) in 1 Thessalonians 2:14a and "Jews" (Greek *Ioudaios*) in 2:14b. That's why the NKJV, which is a conservative translation, renders the verse, "For you, brethren, became imitators of the churches of God *which are in Judea* in Christ Jesus. For you also suffered the same things from your own countrymen, just as they did from *the Judeans*" (emphasis added). Or as the Tree of Life Version translates it, "For you, brothers and sisters, became imitators of God's communities in Messiah *Yeshua that are in Judea*—for you suffered the same things at the hands of your own countrymen as they did *from the Judean leaders*" (emphasis added).

Fourth, in these verses Paul can be understood as saying that, in general, "the Jews" killed Jesus and the prophets and now they persecute us, which as we have seen is not accurate. Or he can be understood to be speaking about a certain group of Jews, specifically the Judean Jews (or the Jewish leaders) who rejected Jesus, killed prophetic voices like Stephen, and now oppose Paul and his Jewish coworkers. This would be entirely accurate, also in keeping with Israel's history, where the leaders consistently rejected God's prophetic witness. (See, for example, Zechariah 1:2–4.)

So there is no denying that there has been a consistent pattern of Jewish disobedience and rebellion, rejecting the Lord and His Word and His messengers. Jesus addressed this forcefully as well when rebuking the hypocritical religious leaders. (See Matthew 23:29–36.) I do not minimize this in the least. And there are Jewish leaders who do this until this day, actively opposing the gospel in every way they can. Paul could well include them in his description. But that is a far cry from making the blanket statement (wrenched right out of its larger context) that "*the Jews*...killed both the Lord Jesus and the prophets, and drove us out, and displease God and oppose all mankind."

The correct interpretation, as stated by the New Testament scholar Gordon Fee, is this:

> It is not all Jews who are in view, but those who in particular were responsible for the death of Jesus and the prophets. And if that is so, then one's first interpretive instincts should be to see whether one can make sense of the whole passage with this usage in view. In any case, this is the perspective from which the rest of Paul's long sentence will be interpreted in the comments that follows. Thus, it is not the Jewish community as such, nor as a whole, who are singled out here, but especially a part of the Judean sector of the community, whose leaders violently opposed Christ and his early followers.[8]

DOES THE BOOK OF ACTS SAY THE JEWS KILLED JESUS?

Preaching to a Jewish crowd in Jerusalem—a group that had assembled from around the world less than two months after the crucifixion—Peter spoke these stinging words:

> "Men of Israel, hear these words: Jesus of Nazareth, a man attested to you by God with mighty works and wonders and signs that God did through him in your midst, as you yourselves know—this Jesus, delivered up according to the definite plan and foreknowledge of God, you crucified and killed by the hands of lawless men."
>
> —ACTS 2:22–23

And then this: "Let all the house of Israel therefore know for certain that God has made him both Lord and Christ, this Jesus whom you crucified" (Acts 2:36). That seems pretty clear!

Some time later, speaking to another group of Jews at the temple in Jerusalem, Peter said this:

> "The God of Abraham, the God of Isaac, and the God of Jacob, the God of our fathers, glorified his servant Jesus, whom you delivered over and denied in the presence of Pilate, when he had decided to release him. But you denied the Holy and Righteous One, and asked for a murderer to be granted to you, and you killed the Author of life, whom God raised from the dead. To this we are witnesses."
>
> —ACTS 3:13–15

Then, speaking to the Jewish leadership in Jerusalem, the Sanhedrin, Peter said, "The God of our fathers raised Jesus, whom you killed by hanging him on a tree" (Acts 5:30). Once again, this seems pretty clear. And speaking to this same audience—the Sanhedrin—Stephen said, "Which of the prophets did your fathers not persecute? And they killed those who announced beforehand the coming of the Righteous One, whom you have now betrayed and murdered, you who received the law as delivered by angels and did not keep it" (Acts 7:52–53).

Based on these verses, we could say that the "men of Israel" or "all the house of Israel" committed terrible sins against the Messiah. They "crucified and killed" Him "by the hands of lawless men" (meaning the Romans); they "denied" Him and "delivered Him over" to Pilate; they "betrayed and murdered" Him. Without a doubt, then, we can see that Peter and Stephen, themselves Jews, placed the responsibility for Yeshua's death at the hands of their own people, in particular the leadership. But does this mean that they blamed all Jews worldwide for crucifying the Messiah? Hardly.

First, when preaching to Jews in a synagogue in Pisidian Antioch—outside the land of Israel and probably more than fifteen years later—Paul said this:

> "Fellow children of Abraham and you God-fearing Gentiles, it is to us that this message of salvation has been sent. The people of Jerusalem and their rulers did not recognize Jesus, yet in condemning him they fulfilled the words of the prophets that are read every Sabbath. Though they found no proper ground for a death sentence, they asked Pilate to have him executed. When they had carried out all that was written about him, they took him down from the cross and laid him in a tomb. But God raised him from the dead, and for many days he was seen by those who had traveled with him from Galilee to Jerusalem. They are now his witnesses to our people.
>
> "We tell you the good news: What God promised our ancestors he has fulfilled for us, their children, by raising up Jesus. As it is written in the second Psalm:
>
> You are my son; today I have become your father.
>
> —Acts 13:26–33, niv

Notice that Paul did not blame his Jewish hearers for the death of Jesus. He explained to them what the Jewish leadership in Jerusalem did, holding them responsible. As for the Jews in Pisidian Antioch, they had nothing to do with it, just like a secular Muslim living in Indonesia on September 11, 2001, had nothing to do with bin Laden's terrorist attacks in America on that fateful day. Not only so, but Paul presented this whole story as good news: "What God promised our ancestors he has fulfilled for us, their children, by raising up Jesus." What a contrast from blaming "the Jews" for the death of Jesus and saying that for that sinful act, the Jewish people, as a people, were cursed and rejected by God.

In short, when preaching to a Jewish crowd in Jerusalem with Jewish leaders present or, even more specifically, when preaching to the Jewish leadership council, Peter and Stephen spoke in terms of what "you" did—meaning the Jewish people, because of their leaders. They were speaking to the nation, headquartered in Jerusalem, and indicting the leaders in particular while addressing the people as a whole. But outside of that context, they did not speak in this way, since the men responsible for turning Jesus over to the Romans were not part of their audience.

In keeping with this, when Paul arrived in Thessalonica, Luke tells us that "as usual, Paul went to the synagogue, and on three Sabbath days reasoned with them from the Scriptures, explaining and showing that the Messiah had to suffer and rise from the dead: 'This Jesus I am proclaiming to you is the Messiah'" (Acts 17:2–3, HCSB). The text does not say he blamed the Jews there for the Messiah's death. Rather, Paul reasoned with them from the Scriptures, demonstrating that Yeshua was the prophesied Messiah.

In the same way, quite a few years later, when Paul was a prisoner in Rome, he met with the Jewish leaders there. We read in Acts 28:

> When they had appointed a day for him, they came to him at his lodging in greater numbers. From morning till evening he expounded to them, testifying to the kingdom of God and trying to convince them about Jesus both from the Law of Moses and from the Prophets. And some were convinced by what he said, but others disbelieved.
>
> —ACTS 28:23–24

Here too his message to them was not, "You crucified the Messiah!" To the contrary, they lived in Rome and had no direct connection to Yeshua's death. Rather, he preached Jesus to them from the Scriptures. His issue with them, as was Peter's ultimate issue, was that they rejected his message in the here and now. They rejected the resurrected Messiah.

It's the same thing when sharing the gospel with Jewish people today. The message to them is not, "You killed the Messiah!" Rather, our message is, "Yeshua is our prophesied Messiah, as written in the Scriptures! Our forefathers rejected Him, but you can receive Him today." The issue, again, is how they respond today, not what their ancestors in Jerusalem did two thousand years ago.

Second, Peter made a startling statement in Acts 3, right after delivering the strong message we just quoted, namely, "You killed the Author of life, whom God raised from the dead." He continued:

> "And now, brothers, I know that you acted in ignorance, as did also your rulers. But what God foretold by the mouth of all the prophets, that his Christ would suffer, he thus fulfilled. Repent therefore, and turn back, that your sins may be blotted out, that times of refreshing may come from the presence of the Lord, and that he may send the Christ appointed for you, Jesus, whom heaven must receive until the time for restoring all the things about which God spoke by the mouth of his holy prophets long ago."
>
> —ACTS 3:17–21

I know you acted in ignorance, Peter proclaimed. What a word! So repent, that God can bring upon you the promised blessing (not cursing). And he offered this word of assurance:

> "You are the sons of the prophets and of the covenant that God made with your fathers, saying to Abraham, 'And in your offspring shall all the families of the earth be blessed.' God, having raised up his servant, sent him to you first, to bless you by turning every one of you from your wickedness."
>
> —Acts 3:25–26

He did not say, "You are forever cursed for your rejection of the Messiah." To the contrary, he said, "I know you acted in ignorance, but you are still God's children, His chosen ones." That's why, after the Messiah's resurrection, God "sent him to you first, to bless you by turning every one of you from your wickedness." And that's why, about twenty-five years later, Paul could still write that the gospel was to the Jew first and also to the Gentile (Rom. 1:16).

Third, we must never forget the larger New Testament perspective that emphasizes:1) God sent His Son Jesus to die for our sins as an act of His infinite love (John 3:16); 2) Jesus said no one took His life from Him but that He laid it down freely (John 10:17–18); 3) this was the Father's preordained plan (1 Pet. 1:19–20; Acts 4:27–28); and 4) it was our sins that nailed Him to the cross (Isa. 53:6; 1 Pet. 2:24). So rather than blaming or cursing the Jews for the death of Jesus, a true Christian thanks God for sending His Son and praises the Son for dying for us.

It is clear, then, that the preaching of Peter and Stephen, beginning less than two months after Yeshua's crucifixion and based in Jerusalem, addressed their people's guilt in a corporate way because of the sins of the leaders. But make no mistake about it: they were addressing people who were directly related to the murder of the Messiah, in particular the Jerusalem-based leadership. This would be in keeping with these words of lament spoken by Jesus at the end of His rebuke of the hypocritical leaders: "O Jerusalem, Jerusalem who kills the prophets and stones those sent to her! How often I longed to gather your children together, as a hen gathers her chicks under her wings, but you were not willing!" (Matt. 23:37, TLV). The Lord holds Jerusalem responsible for these deaths since the city represents the national leadership.

This, then, is quite distinct from indicting the entire nation, let alone indicting all Jewish people throughout the ages. But it does give us insight into the mindset of Peter and Stephen when they were preaching in Jerusalem shortly after the crucifixion and addressing some of these very same leaders face-to-face. What a far cry this is from a telling a Jewish person today, "You killed Jesus!"

Did Paul Claim That Only Christ, Not Israel, Was Abraham's Seed in Galatians 3:16?

I recently wrote a lengthy academic article on Galatians 3:16, demonstrating how it was impossible to argue that Paul was denying the plurality of Abraham's seed.[9] This can be seen when we read the verse in a translation, such as the English Standard Version: "Now the promises were made to Abraham and to his offspring. It does not say, 'And to offsprings,' referring to many, but referring to one, 'And to your offspring,' who is Christ." There you see the problem in a nutshell. We all know that the word *offspring* is a collective noun. It can potentially speak of one individual child, as in, "Sam was the only offspring of Jeff and Judy." But in common English usage we do not say "offsprings," which is why we can say, "Although Sam was an only child, he was the father of many offspring, including eight children, seventeen grandchildren, and forty-one great-grandchildren."

It's the same with the Hebrew word *zera*, meaning "seed" or "offspring," and the Greek word *sperma*, with the same meanings. The only time the plural would be used would be in the case of agricultural seeds. But when it comes to children, to descendants, *seed* (or *offspring*) is collective. Paul knew this, just as the Galatians knew this and just as we know it with the word *offspring*.

After all, in this very same chapter, in verse 29, he writes, "And if you are Christ's, then you are Abraham's *offspring*, heirs according to promise" (Gal. 3:29, emphasis added). He understands the word is used in the plural! Not only so, but also in Romans 4:16: "That is why it depends on faith, in order that the promise may rest on grace and be guaranteed to *all his offspring*—not only to the adherent of the law but also to the one who shares the faith of Abraham, who is the father of us all" (emphasis added).

Notice also that Jesus, when rebuking His double-minded Jewish audience, said, "I know that you are offspring of Abraham; yet you seek to kill me because my word finds no place in you" (John 8:37). He told these men—plural—that they were Abraham's offspring. But of course! Who would deny this for a split second? There are scores and scores of verses in the Old Testament that speak of Abraham's seed/offspring in the plural, speaking of the people of Israel. (For one example among many, read Genesis 12:7; 13:15; 15:5, 13, 18, and remember that God promised Abraham that his offspring would be uncountable, like the sand of the seashore or the stars in the sky.) Not only so, but this is the common language of the New Testament. See Acts 3:25; 7:5–6; and 13:23; each example refers to Abraham's offspring or seed in a plural way.

What, then, is Paul's point in Galatians 3:16? He is using a hyperliteral reading of the text, which was common among the ancient rabbis, to make a homiletical point, as if I said, "Now look, brothers. The text says 'brethren.' It doesn't say 'brethrens.' God is talking to you!" In normal speech we do not say *brethrens,* just as we do not say *offsprings,* and everyone would know this. But in the case of *offspring,* it can, in fact, refer to one individual as well.

That is Paul's point. When God promised to bless the world through Abraham's offspring, He had in mind one particular offspring among that offspring, namely the Messiah. And through Him, blessing would come to the whole world. That was super important for these Gentile believers to grab hold of, since some misguided Jewish believers were pressuring them to become circumcised and obey the Law of Moses to be saved (similar to what Paul warns about in Philippians 3:1–3; see note 6).

Not so, Paul boldly proclaims. The key is to be in the Messiah, the particular offspring through whom the promises were fulfilled. And if you are in Him, then you become part of Abraham's larger offspring. It is absurd and almost blasphemous to suggest that Paul is voiding out hundreds of verses in the Old Testament—promises written by God Himself to the people of Israel, Abraham's offspring—with a single stroke of his pen.

Perish the thought. For Paul, the foundation of everything God was doing was revealed in the Hebrew Scriptures. And those very Scriptures assure us that the God who cannot lie—our heavenly Father!—will fulfill His word to Israel, meaning the day will come when Israel will be saved. Hasten it, Lord!

CHAPTER 10

ANTISEMITISM, REPLACEMENT THEOLOGY, AND THE ROOT OF INSECURITY

In 2003, William I. Brustein, then a professor of sociology, political science, and history at the University of Pittsburgh, published a book with Cambridge University Press titled *Roots of Hate: Anti-Semitism in Europe Before the Holocaust*.[1] In the book, Professor Brustein identifies four major roots of antisemitism in Europe before the Holocaust: the religious root, the racial root, the economic root, and the political root. But he starts his discussion by focusing on the religious root, writing, "Of the four roots of anti-Semitism, religious anti-Semitism has the longest history in Western Christian societies."[2] How can this be?

He explains, "Religious anti-Semitism encompasses hostility that stems from the Jewish people's refusal to abandon their religious beliefs and practices and, specifically within Christian societies, from the accusation of Jewish collective responsibility for the death of Jesus Christ." And he makes this startling claim: "Official Christian antipathy toward Judaism began to gather steam within one hundred years of the death of Christ."[3]

I ask again: How can this be? How can it be that Christians, who were called to follow the example of Jesus and show love to all, including their spiritual opponents, so quickly turned against the Messiah's own people? How can it be that Christians, now majority Gentile, sharing in the spiritual heritage of Israel, could demonize the people of Israel?

Remarkably, the apostle Paul warns against this very thing in his letter to the Romans, where he teaches that Gentile ignorance could lead to arrogance against the Jewish people. And it is this arrogance, based on ignorance, that paved the way for the rise of Christian antisemitism. Allow me to explain.

Exhorting the Gentile Christians in Rome, Paul writes, "Do not be arrogant, but tremble." Yes, he continues, "I do not want you to be ignorant of this mystery, brothers and sisters, so that you may not be conceited" (Rom. 11:20, 25, NIV). What exactly is Paul warning about? Why is he so concerned that these Gentile believers might become arrogant? And what is the nature of the "mystery" that was so crucial to understand, to the point that ignorance of this truth would lead to the very arrogance of which Paul warns?

When we understand the answers to these questions, we understand the root of Christian antisemitism. And when we understand this, we understand one of the main reasons the church has left such a tragic and bloody trail of hatred toward the Jewish people. But to understand this warning, we need to understand the background to Paul's letter to the believers in Rome.

On the one hand, in this extraordinary epistle, Paul is addressing weighty theological issues, wanting to be sure the church in Rome understands the foundations of the gospel. And so he begins by focusing on God's judgment on a sinning world. (See Romans 1:18–3:26, where Paul explains that both Jew and Gentile stand guilty before a holy God.) Then he moves to justification by faith in Jesus the Messiah for Jew and Gentile alike (Rom. 3:27–5:21), then our victory over sin and life in the Spirit (Romans 6:1–8:39), and finally God's plan for Israel, including Israel's current rejection and future restoration (Rom. 9:1–11:36). After this, Paul offers practical application of his teaching (Rom. 12:1–16:27) but with frequent reference to the special relationship between Jew and Gentile in the Messiah.

So one of the foundational topics Paul addresses is the subject of Israel. This is a big issue for the apostle, and he wants it to be a big issue for the Roman believers too. Did God's Word fail? Did the promises to Israel not come to pass? Or did they only come to pass for a remnant within Israel? In that case, what about the rest of the nation? Was there any future hope for them? And what were the implications for Gentile believers? Where did they fit?

But Paul is not only focused on theological issues regarding Jews and Gentiles. Instead, he is concerned with practical issues, including, "If Jewish and Gentile believers follow different customs and traditions, how can they live together in one spiritual community? How can the family of God find unity in diversity?"

These, of course, were questions that many different congregations faced. But when it came to Rome, the situation was unique. It started out just like many other local assemblies, in that the first believers were all Jewish. After all, this was a message about the Messiah of Israel, based on promises given to Israel in the Hebrew Scriptures, and that message was being declared by Jewish followers of Yeshua. Of course it started with Israel. That's why Paul writes in Romans 1:16, "For I am not ashamed of the gospel, because it is the power of God that brings salvation to everyone who believes: first to the Jew, then to the Gentile" (NIV). And so in Rome, as in many other major cities in the ancient world, the good news about the Jewish Messiah was first received and believed by Jews and then by Gentiles, and the first leaders in the early church were themselves Jewish.

But then something happened. Sometime in the AD 40s, all Jews were expelled from Rome by the emperor Claudius (see Acts 18:2), which meant the Jewish believers in Jesus were also expelled.[4] Roughly ten years later, the Jews were allowed to return, only this time the situation in the Roman church was reversed. In the beginning there was a congregation of Jewish believers in Jesus to which Gentile believers were joined. Now there was a congregation of Gentile believers to which Jewish believers were rejoined. How would they be received by the Gentile majority?

It is this context that explains some of Paul's teaching in Romans 14 about differences in dietary customs and recognizing certain days as more sacred than others. And it is in this context, looking to the present as well as to the future, that Paul writes:

> Accept one another, then, just as Christ accepted you, in order to bring praise to God. For I tell you that Christ has become a servant of the Jews on behalf of God's truth, so that the promises made to the patriarchs might be confirmed and, moreover, that the Gentiles might glorify God for his mercy. As it is written: "Therefore I will praise you among the Gentiles; I will sing the praises of your name."
>
> —Romans 15:7–9, niv

With this in mind, let's look carefully at Paul's warning to the Gentile Christians in Rome in chapter 11 of his letter. Are you ready to dig in to the Word?

Is God Finished With the Jewish People?

In Romans 11:11–16, after speaking of the divine hardening that came upon unbelieving Israel, Paul asks if God is finished with the Jewish people (he had previously said no to this same question in Romans 11:1):

> So I ask, did they stumble in order that they might fall? By no means! Rather, through their trespass salvation has come to the Gentiles, so as to make Israel jealous. Now if their trespass means riches for the world, and if their failure means riches for the Gentiles, how much more will their full inclusion mean!
>
> Now I am speaking to you Gentiles. Inasmuch then as I am an apostle to the Gentiles, I magnify my ministry in order somehow to make my fellow Jews jealous, and thus save some of them. For if their rejection means the reconciliation of the world, what will their acceptance mean

> but life from the dead? If the dough offered as firstfruits is holy, so is the whole lump, and if the root is holy, so are the branches.

In the NIV, Romans 11:11a reads: "Again I ask: Did they stumble so as to fall beyond recovery? Not at all!" And it says in the NET Bible, "I ask then, they did not stumble into an irrevocable fall, did they? Absolutely not!" To quote New Testament scholar C. K. Barrett again, with the words of Paul in bold:

> **I must repeat my question then: Did they stumble so as to fall altogether?** There is no doubt that the Jews, or the majority of them, have stumbled (cf. ix. 32 f.) and lost their place; the Gentiles are overhauling them. But does this mean that they are now out of the race? that they are for ever outside the sphere of salvation? It is probable that some Christians gave a positive answer to this question; there are passages in the gospels which suggest this (e.g. Matt. xxi. 43; xxvii. 25). But this was not Paul's solution of the problem. He answers his own question: **Certainly not**. What then of the facts? The defection of the Jews is temporary, and while it lasts serves a definite and important purpose.[5]

Paul then emphasizes how glorious the salvation of the Jewish people will be—speaking of Israel's end-time turning to the Messiah, stating it will mean "life from the dead," something even greater than "the reconciliation of the world." This is absolutely massive and underscores why Israel's salvation is so important. And to emphasize the certainty of all this, Paul writes in Romans 11:16, "If the dough offered as firstfruits is holy, so is the whole lump, and if the root is holy, so are the branches."

Commenting on this verse, the nineteenth-century theologian Charles Hodge writes:

> The restoration of the Jews, which will be attended with such beneficial results for the whole world, is to be expected, because of their peculiar relation to God as his chosen people. God, in selecting the Hebrew patriarchs, and setting them apart for his service, had reference to their descendants, as well as to themselves; and designed that the Jews, as a people, should, to the latest generations, be specially devoted to himself. They stand now, therefore, and ever have stood, in a relation to God which no other nation ever has sustained; and, in consequence of this relation, their restoration to the divine favour is an event in itself probable, and one, which Paul afterwards teaches (ver. 25), God has determined to accomplish.[6]

What a glorious future there is for the people of Israel. They *will* be grafted back in to their own olive tree, as Paul writes, using a common metaphor for Israel in the Bible. But where will this leave the Gentile Christians? Will they become second-class citizens? Will they be relegated to a lower position in the body of Christ? Will they end up serving the Jews, who in turn serve God?[7]

We could liken the situation to an apartment building with one hundred units, all of which were once rented by Jews but from which most of the Jewish renters were forced to leave. Now most of the apartments are rented by Gentiles. What if the original renters come back? What will happen to the new renters? Or maybe the old renters won't be coming back at all. Perhaps the old (Jewish) renters were bad, which is why they were kicked out. Perhaps the new (Gentile) renters are good, which is why they now live in these apartments.

Here's how Paul puts it in Romans 11, continuing with the image of the root and the branches:

> But if some of the branches were broken off, and you, although a wild olive shoot, were grafted in among the others and now share in the nourishing root of the olive tree, do not be arrogant toward the branches. If you are, remember it is not you who support the root, but the root that supports you. Then you will say, "Branches were broken off so that I might be grafted in." That is true. They were broken off because of their unbelief, but you stand fast through faith. So do not become proud, but fear. For if God did not spare the natural branches, neither will he spare you. Note then the kindness and the severity of God: severity toward those who have fallen, but God's kindness to you, provided you continue in his kindness. Otherwise you too will be cut off. And even they, if they do not continue in their unbelief, will be grafted in, for God has the power to graft them in again. For if you were cut from what is by nature a wild olive tree, and grafted, contrary to nature, into a cultivated olive tree, how much more will these, the natural branches, be grafted back into their own olive tree.
>
> —Romans 11:17–24

Paul issues a clear warning against pride, writing, "Do not be arrogant toward the branches." Don't think you're better than those Jewish branches, Paul exhorts, since you can be cut off just as they were. Not only so, but this is their own tree, and it is more natural for them to be grafted back in to their own cultivated olive tree than it was for you Gentiles who were grafted in from a wild olive tree.

And then Paul gives one more warning, followed by a glorious promise:

> Lest you be wise in your own sight, I do not want you to be unaware of this mystery, brothers: a partial hardening has come upon Israel, until

> the fullness of the Gentiles has come in. And in this way all Israel will be saved, as it is written, "The Deliverer will come from Zion, he will banish ungodliness from Jacob"; "and this will be my covenant with them when I take away their sins." As regards the gospel, they are enemies for your sake. But as regards election, they are beloved for the sake of their forefathers. For the gifts and the calling of God are irrevocable.
>
> —ROMANS 11:25–29

What is Paul's point? First, let's focus on his warning against pride, which is the second time this has come up in just a few verses. As rendered in some other translations, the beginning of Romans 11:25 reads, "I do not want you to be ignorant of this mystery, brothers and sisters, so that you may not be conceited" (NIV); "So that you may not claim to be wiser than you are, brothers and sisters, I want you to understand this mystery" (NRSV); "I want you to understand this mystery, dear brothers and sisters, so that you will not feel proud about yourselves" (NLT).

Do you understand the force of Paul's words? He is saying, in essence, "My Gentile brothers and sisters, it's essential that you grasp what I'm saying. Otherwise, you will become proud. You see, Israel is not hardened for all time, nor is the hardening on every individual Israelite. Even now, there is a remnant that believes, and at the end of the age, when the fullness of the Gentiles comes in, the hardening will lift and all Israel will be saved."

Being ignorant of this, the Gentile Christians might think, "God is finished with Israel! We are the new Israel! God has forever cut off the Jewish branches. This is now a Gentile tree!"

Paul's warnings are strong and clear: Do not be arrogant toward the Jewish branches. And understand this mystery of Israel's partial hardening, lest you become wise in your own eyes. Be on guard against pride! Put another way, *both insecurity and ignorance lead to arrogance.*

FAULTY FOUNDATIONS

These, then, are the roots of replacement theology, namely insecurity and ignorance. And it is replacement theology—the idea that the church (which today has perhaps less than ten thousand Gentiles for every Jew) has replaced Israel in God's plan of salvation—that has opened the door to antisemitism throughout church history, right until today.

In terms of the concept of replacement theology, Professor Michael Vlach writes:

> At the heart of the controversy is the question, Does the church replace, supersede, or fulfill the nation Israel in God's plan, or will Israel be saved and restored with a unique identity and role? The position that

> the church is the "new" or "true" Israel that replaces or fulfills national Israel's place in the plan of God has often been called "replacement theology" or "supersessionism."[8]

He adds:

> Several theologians have offered definitions of *supersessionism* or *replacement theology*. According to Walter C. Kaiser Jr., "Replacement theology...declared that the Church, Abraham's spiritual seed, had replaced national Israel in that it had transcended and fulfilled the terms of the covenant given to Israel, which covenant Israel had lost because of disobedience." [Ronald] Diprose defines *replacement theology* as the view that "the Church completely and permanently replaced ethnic Israel in the working out of God's plan and as recipient of OT promises to Israel."[9]

To be sure, the term *replacement theology* is very unpopular today, and *supersessionism*, which expresses the idea that the church has superseded Israel in God's plan, is not well-known to the general public. Contemporary theologians often prefer the term *fulfillment theology*, meaning that Jesus fulfills the promises to Israel and so Jews and Gentiles *in Him* are the new people of God, giving full expression to Israel's destiny and calling. Others speak of *expansion theology*, meaning that God has expanded the borders of the people of God, both ethnically and geographically. Ethnically, God's congregation—His *ekklesia*, or church—has expanded from being almost entirely Jewish to now include people from all over the world. Geographically, rather than the people of Israel being promised their own distinct homeland, the church now inherits the whole earth. Some even teach that Jesus is the promised land, so the geographical emphasis virtually disappears.[10]

Jesus is the promised land? Really? On a practical level, I have asked elsewhere:

> What might this mean to one of the 800,000 Jews who, in 1948, were forcibly expelled from their homes throughout the Middle East? As most of them sought refuge in the land of their forefathers, the land promised to the descendants of the patriarchs, should they have been told, "But Jesus is now your promised land!"? One might as well as tell a starving person that "Jesus is the bread of life!"
>
> Did these Jewish refugees not need a place to live? Should they have been encouraged to live in the "land of Jesus" rather than seek a homeland? And how is it that Israel's scattering was physical and literal but its regathering is spiritual and ethereal?[11]

Yet I have had biblical scholars and theologians tell me these very things in public debate and dialogue: "It's true that the Lord *literally* scattered the Jewish people from their homeland twenty-five hundred years ago. But when He promised to *regather* them to their homeland, He meant that spiritually." Seriously.

Others read the Old Testament as if it means this: When God said (in one and the same verse, such as Jeremiah 31:10), "I will scatter you in judgment," He was referring to the Jewish people. When He said, "I will regather you in mercy," He was referring to the church. In other words, the bad stuff is for the Jews. The good stuff is for the church.

Do you see how this contributes to negative attitudes toward the Jewish people? And do you see how replacement theology opened the door wide to antisemitism?

Another variation of replacement theology being taught today can be found in *preterism,* which interprets passages like Matthew 24 with reference only to the destruction of the second temple in AD 70, with no reference to the second coming and which sees no national future for Israel. Some emphasize strongly that Israel's rejection of Jesus was the third strike, meaning that as a people, they were forever cut off and judged, with the destruction of the second temple sealing their doom. Individual Jews can be saved, but there remain no national promises for Israel, and under no circumstances is Israel's return to the land a fulfillment of prophecy.

As expressed by Kenneth Gentry, ThD (who is not a full preterist, which is a truly heretical position), "Matthew 24:1–34 (and parallels) in the Olivet Discourse was fulfilled in the events surrounding the fall of Jerusalem in A.D. 70. In Revelation, most of the prophecies before Revelation 20 find fulfillment in the fall of Jerusalem."[12]

In the words of preterist scholar David Chilton:

> The Book of Revelation is not about the second coming of Christ. It is about the destruction of Israel and Christ's victory over His enemies in the establishment of the New Covenant temple....Revelation prophesies the judgment of God on apostate Israel; and while it does briefly point to events beyond its immediate concerns, that is done merely as a "wrap-up," to show that the ungodly will never prevail against Christ's Kingdom.[13]

Yes, he says, God is finished with Israel! To quote Chilton again, "Ethnic Israel was excommunicated for its apostasy and will never again be God's Kingdom."[14] Ethnic Israel is forever cursed! Notions like this, indeed, open the door very wide to antisemitism, for very obvious reasons. And they fly in the face of Paul's warnings in Romans 11, not to mention his words of assurance. To quote him once more, this time from the NLT, which is a close paraphrase:

> And so all Israel will be saved. As the Scriptures say, "The one who rescues will come from Jerusalem, and he will turn Israel away from ungodliness. And this is my covenant with them, that I will take away their sins." Many of the people of Israel are now enemies of the Good News, and this benefits you Gentiles. Yet they are still the people he loves because he chose their ancestors Abraham, Isaac, and Jacob. For God's gifts and his call can never be withdrawn.
>
> —Romans 11:26–29

Thank God that Paul is right and that David Chilton is wrong. And thank God that Israel has been preserved because of the Lord's goodness, not because of its own goodness. This gives hope to each of us! After all, if God can't be trusted to keep His promises to Israel, *based on His covenant faithfulness*, why should He be trusted to keep His promises to the church?

But it is not my purpose here to refute replacement theology in all of its manifestations, both past and present. To do so would take a full-length book, and there are a number of important studies refuting these errors. I would especially recommend:

- Michael Vlach, *Has the Church Replaced Israel?*[15]
- Ronald Diprose, *Israel and the Church: The Origins and Effects of Replacement Theology*[16]
- Andrew D. Robinson and Paul R. Wilkinson, *Israel Betrayed* (two volumes)[17]
- Gerald McDermott, ed., *The New Christian Zionism: Fresh Perspectives on Israel and the Land*[18]
- Barry Horner, *Future Israel* and *Eternal Israel*[19]

I would also encourage you to work through chapters 12–14 in the new edition of my book *Our Hands Are Stained With Blood*, since it expands on some of the material discussed here.

My main goal in this chapter is simply to identify the root of Christian antisemitism, namely replacement theology, which in turn has at its root insecurity and ignorance. May those faulty foundations be uprooted and replaced by God's eternal truth!

To be perfectly clear, and to repeat what I have stated many times before, there are fine Christians today who hold to a form of replacement theology and are *not* antisemitic. Some of them are my colleagues in the Lord, excellent teachers in other respects and certainly devoted to Jesus. At the same time, there can be no doubt that, historically speaking, replacement theology opened the door for Christian antisemitism. And there can be no doubt that this theology influences one's attitude toward Israel today.

In short, I do not know a single Bible teacher who believes that Israel today is the fulfillment of biblical prophecy and also holds to replacement theology. How could they? If they believed that God was finished with ethnic Israel, why would He preserve them as a nation and then bring them back to the land *in fulfillment of biblical prophecy?* That would be a total contradiction. In the same way, I do not know of a single Bible teacher who holds to replacement theology and also believes the modern state of Israel is a fulfillment of biblical prophecy. More importantly, I do not know a single Christian leader who is hypercritical of Israel—who demonizes the modern state of Israel and believes all kinds of false charges against the Jewish state—who does not also hold to some form of replacement theology.

To illustrate this last point, let me give you a down-to-earth, everyday example straight from the keyboard of a professing Christian. In fact, I found these comments posted by Barbara on my YouTube channel as I was writing these very sentences and stopped for a moment to check our YouTube feed. Barbara was responding to one of my videos exposing the antisemitic rhetoric of Rick Wiles. (See chapters 4 and 7.) In her first of two comments, she espouses classic replacement theology, including her misuse of the words of Jesus:

> Nowhere in the New Testament does it say Jews are the chosen people. In fact if you want to know what he called those who tried to kill him read REVELATION 2:9 and 3:9. I can't quote Jesus because you and your followers will call me an anti-Semite!!! Apparently quoting Jesus gets you persecuted by the authorities.

Then in that same spirit, and doubtless influenced by that false theology, she unloads on Israel in her second comment, quoting Jesus again for support:

> Jews and Arabs got along pretty well until 1948? Can you GUESS WHY? Why has 7 decades of GENOCIDE, land theft and the ethic [*sic*] cleansing. You support that too, Dr. Brown? Have you never read that:
>
> "Behold, your house is left unto you desolate. For I say unto you, Ye shall not see me henceforth, till ye shall say, Blessed is he that cometh in the name of the Lord."
>
> Matthew 23:5-6, 14, 23-25, 27-28, 33-34, 38-39 KJV
>
> Has this happened yet? Has Jesus come back and has the physical state of Israel come in the name of the Lord? Not to my knowledge it hasn't.[20]

So her wrong theology blends with her wrong history, resulting in these standard (and quite dangerous) misconceptions: today's Jews are not really Jews, and modern Israel is not really Israel. Not only so, but the Jews are committing genocide against the Palestinians and engaging in ethnic cleansing, and that is something she claims I support. And if I rightly call her out for her antisemitism, then I'm threatening her free speech.

Of course, it's clear that Barbara is not a professional theologian (or historian!). But her erroneous ideas are a direct result of the theological (and historical) errors of others. And so while these theological errors could be likened to a concentrated amount of poison, when that poison is loosed into a large city's water system, it could prove deadly to millions of people.

With regard to Barbara's theological errors, we have addressed them elsewhere in the book,[21] as well as in this chapter. (She would do well to reread Romans 11!) But she also fails to realize that implicit in the Lord's words in Matthew 23:37–39 (a passage she cites) is the idea that *a repentant, Jewish Jerusalem must welcome Him back*. That is confirmed by the picture painted in Zechariah 12, in which it is a Jewish Jerusalem that will look to the One they pierced and deeply repent. That means, then, that the Jewish people will come back to the land *in unbelief* before turning to the Lord in repentance and faith. (On this, see also Isaiah 4:2–4; Jeremiah 33:6–9; Ezekiel 36:24–26; 37:1–14; Joel 2:18–29; and Zechariah 13:8–9.)[22]

With regard to Barbara's historical errors, it was radical Muslims who began attacking the local Jewish population of Palestine in the late 1920s, and it was the Arab leadership that refused a two-state solution in 1937 and again in 1947, instead declaring war on Israel in 1947–48 (and this was despite the fact that the many Jewish leaders wanted to adopt the first proposal and did accept the second proposal).[23] As for the claim that Israel has been guilty of genocide and ethnic cleansing, the one hundred fifty-six thousand Arabs who remained in Israel and became part of the new state have grown more than ten times, to almost two million, enjoying more freedoms than any other Arabs in the region. As for the population that identifies as Palestinian and lives in Gaza and the West Bank (biblically, Judea and Samaria), they now number around five million.[24] So much for ethnic cleansing and genocide.

But once again, wrong theology—replacement theology—goes hand in hand with demonizing the Jewish people. This will repeat itself again and again, which is why we must pull this wrong theology up from the roots.

Consider this beautiful prophecy spoken to Jerusalem and the Jewish people in the midst of exile and judgment. Please read it slowly and reverently:

> "Sing, O barren one, who did not bear; break forth into singing and cry aloud, you who have not been in labor! For the children of the desolate one will be more than the children of her who is married," says the LORD. "Enlarge the place of your tent, and let the curtains of your habitations be stretched out; do not hold back; lengthen your cords and strengthen your stakes. For you will spread abroad to the right and to the left, and your offspring will possess the nations and will people the desolate cities.
>
> "Fear not, for you will not be ashamed; be not confounded, for you will not be disgraced; for you will forget the shame of your youth, and the reproach of your widowhood you will remember no more. For your Maker is your husband, the LORD of hosts is his name; and the Holy One of Israel is your Redeemer, the God of the whole earth he is called. For the LORD has called you like a wife deserted and grieved in spirit, like a wife of youth when she is cast off, says your God. For a brief moment I deserted you, but with great compassion I will gather you. In overflowing anger for a moment I hid my face from you, but with everlasting love I will have compassion on you," says the LORD, your Redeemer.
>
> "This is like the days of Noah to me: as I swore that the waters of Noah should no more go over the earth, so I have sworn that I will not be angry with you, and will not rebuke you. For the mountains may depart and the hills be removed, but my steadfast love shall not depart from you, and my covenant of peace shall not be removed," says the LORD, who has compassion on you.
>
> —ISAIAH 54:1–10

This should bring great encouragement to a Jewish person reading these words today, especially during times of exile and pain: "God will not forsake us forever! He will not always be angry! His mercy will triumph in the end, and we will be restored!"

But that is not the case if you hold to replacement theology. These promises are now applied exclusively to the church! That's why one of the chapters in *Our Hands Are Stained With Blood* is called "Thou Shalt Not Steal." The church can make spiritual application of all the divine promises. But the church cannot steal them from Israel.

It's the same with another beautiful passage from Isaiah, this time from chapter 62:

> For Zion's sake I will not keep silent, and for Jerusalem's sake I will not be quiet, until her righteousness goes forth as brightness, and her salvation as a burning torch. The nations shall see your righteousness, and all the kings your glory, and you shall be called by a new name that the mouth of the LORD will give. You shall be a crown of beauty in the hand of the LORD, and a royal diadem in the hand of your God. You shall no more be termed Forsaken, and your land shall no more

> be termed Desolate, but you shall be called My Delight Is in Her, and your land Married; for the LORD delights in you, and your land shall be married. For as a young man marries a young woman, so shall your sons marry you, and as the bridegroom rejoices over the bride, so shall your God rejoice over you.
>
> On your walls, O Jerusalem, I have set watchmen; all the day and all the night they shall never be silent. You who put the LORD in remembrance, take no rest, and give him no rest until he establishes Jerusalem and makes it a praise in the earth. The LORD has sworn by his right hand and by his mighty arm: "I will not again give your grain to be food for your enemies, and foreigners shall not drink your wine for which you have labored; but those who garner it shall eat it and praise the LORD, and those who gather it shall drink it in the courts of my sanctuary."
>
> —ISAIAH 62:1–9

Again, what beautiful words of comfort and what great promises concerning Jerusalem.[25] But not for those who hold to replacement theology. Instead, Jerusalem and Zion now represent the church and not a single word of this can be applied to the physical people of Israel, the physical land of Israel, or the physical city of Jerusalem.

This, then, is an easy way to see if you hold to a form of replacement theology. When you read these verses, how do you interpret them? Do you understand them the way Isaiah would have understood them? The way the original hearers would have understood them? The way generations of readers have understood them? Or do you now apply them exclusively to the church? There's your answer.

You might say, "But I'm only doing what the New Testament does, since it reinterprets the promises in this same way."

Actually, if that was the case, and if the New Testament radically rewrote the Old Testament, we would know that it was not God's Word. A God like that could hardly be trusted. Perhaps there will be a Third Testament that will radically rewrite the New Testament! Perish the thought.

Jesus also emphasized that He did not come to abolish the Torah or the Prophets (meaning the Old Testament as a whole) but rather to fulfill them (Matt. 5:17–20). And He reaffirmed to His disciples that the kingdom would be restored to Israel one day. (See Luke 22:28-30, which helps to explain Acts 1:6–8.)[26] Further, we saw what Paul wrote about Israel's national future in Romans 11. Their restoration will mean life from the dead. They will turn as a people and be saved. And even now, as enemies of the gospel, they are still loved by God because of the patriarchs: "For God's gifts and his call can never be withdrawn" (Rom. 11:29, NLT).

If God can withdraw His promises to Israel, some of which are unconditional (especially the land promises),[27] He can withdraw His promises to the church. Perish that thought as well.

I encourage you again to work through the contents of some of the books I cited above, looking up every relevant verse and seeing how the New Testament authors treat the Old Testament text. If you do, you will see that the New Testament authors did not rewrite the Hebrew Bible or negate its promises. They simply saw the realizing of many of the relevant promises to the Gentiles, promises that applied to the Messianic era, and they understood that those promises were now being fulfilled as well. The Messianic era had begun! And they made beautiful, spiritual application of many Old Testament verses without robbing those verses of their original intent.

May I also encourage you to ask yourself how you would feel about the modern state of Israel if you believed that God Himself brought His ancient people back to their homeland in explicit fulfillment of His loving promises? It doesn't mean you would have to sanction everything Israel did. And it certainly wouldn't mean that you would be hostile to the Palestinians. But is it possible your attitude toward Israel and the Jewish people might be different? And what if you were convinced that the Jewish people, as a people, still played an important role in God's future plans?

What if you were convinced that, just as the gospel must go into all the nations before Yeshua returns (Matt. 24:14; 28:19; Acts 1:8), a Jewish Jerusalem must one day welcome Him back? Would that influence how you pray? How you read Romans 1:16, that the gospel is for the Jew first and also for the Greek? How you read Psalm 122, calling for prayer for Jerusalem, or a passage like Isaiah 62, quoted previously, calling for unceasing prayer for Jerusalem until God establishes it as the praise of all the earth? I can assure you that if you joined me one day for a tour of Israel (or joined any solid, believing tour of the land) and you realized that history would one day culminate there, your spiritual perspective would be rocked. But it is all true!

And that's why finding your security in Jesus as a Gentile believer—equal in standing with your Jewish brothers and sisters, equally loved by God, equally chosen, equally a member of the body of Christ, a branch of the Vine, and a stone in His spiritual temple—is so important. There is plenty of room for billions of Gentile believers and millions of Jews! The one does not displace the other, and the Father can keep His promises to one and to all. And just as the church does not displace Israel, Israel does not displace the church. There's room at the table for both.

THE TRUTH ABOUT ISRAEL'S HARDENING

It is true that Paul's teaching in Romans 11, namely that God hardened the hearts of the people of Israel because of their rejection of the Messiah, has contributed to the negative attitudes many Christians have toward the Jewish people and reemphasizes the common Old Testament description of Israel being stiff-necked. (See Exodus 32:9; 33:3, 5; 34:9; Deuteronomy 9:6, 13; 10:16; 31:27; 2 Kings 17:14; 2 Chronicles 30:8; 36:13; Nehemiah 9:16-17, 29; and Jeremiah 7:26; 17:23; 19:15.) This notion of divine hardening made it easier for church leaders to demonize the Jews, as if they of all people were under God's judgment, to the point that they were eternally blinded to His truth. But that is to grossly misread Paul's intent.

Notice first that Israel's hardening comes as the direct result of Israel's sin, just as Pharaoh hardened his own heart before God began to strengthen his sinful resolve and then gave him over fully to his stubbornness and pride.[28] In other words, the hardening is not arbitrary or unfair. Neither is it illogical or something a Jewish person should protest.

What I mean is this. Judaism as a religion has rejected Jesus as Messiah and exists apart from Him and without Him. If Jewish leaders believe they did the right thing in rejecting Him—and in continuing to reject Him—then they should be pleased that they have taught their children for generations not to believe in Jesus, either by speaking against Him, by ignoring Him, or by simply putting their entire focus elsewhere. If Jewish leaders were wrong in rejecting Jesus as Messiah, then they have been perpetuating their error in each generation. In that way, they have been hardened as a direct result of their decision to reject Yeshua twenty centuries ago.

Second, according to Paul, no Jewish person need remain in a hardened state. As he writes to the Corinthians:

> We are not like Moses, who used to put a veil over his face in order for *Bnei-Yisrael* [the children of Israel] not to look intently upon the end of what was passing away. But their minds were hardened. For up to this very day the same veil remains unlifted at the reading of the ancient covenant, since in Messiah it is passing away. But to this day, whenever Moses is read, a veil lies over their heart. But whenever someone turns to the Lord, the veil is taken away.
>
> —2 Corinthians 3:13–16, tlv

If a Jewish person will truly turn to the Lord, the veil will be removed, and that's why in every generation there has been a remnant that has believed. But this is not only true of the Jewish people. Paul writes just a few verses later that "even if our gospel is veiled, it is veiled to those who are perishing. In their case the god of this world has blinded the minds of the unbelievers, to keep them from seeing the light of the gospel of the glory of Christ, who is the image of God" (2 Cor. 4:3–4). So Paul sees *all nonbelievers*, including the entire Gentile world, as being blinded by Satan. (Elsewhere, he describes them as being dead in sin and subservient to the flesh and the devil, deserving of God's wrath; see Ephesians 2:1–3.)

Third, the whole reason Paul needs to explain Israel's hardening is because of Israel's calling. They of all people should have recognized the Messiah! But that is also why Paul explains that they of all people will most readily receive Him as King. They are being grafted back in to their very own tree. They are coming back home. This is not something foreign or alien. It is their very heritage.

Fourth, nowhere does Paul speak of his people the way the Lord described them in passages like Ezekiel 2:3–10 and 3:4–9. Not even close! In fact, if you take a minute to read these verses, you might be shocked by how negatively God describes His own children. Oh my! He calls them a nation of rebels who always transgress. He labels them impudent and stubborn, a rebellious house (a charge repeated over and over), having hard foreheads and stubborn hearts—and to be contrasted with the Gentiles. "If I sent you to them," God says, "they would listen!" (See Ezekiel 3:6.)

Or what about words like these, spoken by the Lord about His people Israel: "And now, go, write it before them on a tablet and inscribe it in a book, that it may be for the time to come as a witness forever. For they are a rebellious people, lying children, children unwilling to hear the instruction of the LORD" (Isa. 30:8–9).

Can you imagine if these words had been written in the New Testament? Yet they are God's very words, spoken about His own beloved people, right in the pages of the Hebrew Scriptures. We can say, then, Paul's words are mild in comparison, not making a statement about the intrinsic nature of the people of Israel but rather explaining how they have been judicially hardened. There is no fuel for the antisemites here.

AN HONEST QUESTION ABOUT PERSONAL SECURITY

Is it possible, though, that there is something else going on at the root of this wrong theology, something much less theological and much more personal? Is it possible that some Gentile believers have been personally jealous of their Jewish friends, classmates, or colleagues?

John Zmirak is a conservative Catholic intellectual who writes regularly for Stream.org, as I do, offering insights on the culture, the world, and the Catholic Church. As I was addressing Christian antisemitism back in April 2019, he sent me this note:

> As a Gentile, allow me to let you in on a secret: MUCH of anti-Semitism is just Envy. Not financial envy. IQ envy, talent envy, influence envy. People see the special gifts God gave His people, and bristle at it.
>
> I'll never forget the fervent secular Zionist who first pointed that

> out to me. He said, "You gentiles hate us because we're smarter than you!" I smiled and said, "Well I don't, and in my case, you aren't." That REALLY ticked him off, and he named two Jewish professors who were DEFINITELY smarter than me. Since they taught at the University of Chicago, I allowed that he was probably right.[29]

Do you think there could be some truth to this? An article on the Canadian Jewish News website notes, "The voluminous Wikipedia entry, List of Jewish Nobel laureates, states that 'as of 2017, Nobel Prizes have been awarded to 902 individuals, of whom 203 or 22.5% were Jews, although the total Jewish population comprises less than 0.2% of the world's population. This means the percentage of Jewish Nobel laureates is at least 112.5 times or 11,250% above average.'"[30]

The article, written Mark Mietkiewicz on December 10, 2018, discusses the various theories as to why this is the case, seeking to evaluate the data fairly. Since Judaism puts a strong emphasis on study, some believe it is here specifically where Jews have benefited. They have sharper minds, either by gifting or by hard work. As claimed by Israeli scientist Aaron Ciechanover, the 2004 Nobel Prize co-winner for chemistry, "The human brain is the only natural resource that Israel possesses."[31]

That can be debated, and it is debated by Jews as well.[32] But the high Jewish success rate, at least in terms of twentieth-century intellectual achievements and Nobel Prize awards, cannot be debated. Nor can the fact that on average, American Jews earn more than non-Jews, as demonstrated in a Pew Research survey in 2016. According to Pew's data, only 16 percent of American Jews had a household income of less than $30,000. In contrast, Hindus were at 17 percent, Episcopalians at 19 percent, members of the Presbyterian Church (U.S.A.) were at 24 percent, Mormons at 27 percent, Southern Baptists at 32 percent, Muslims at 34 percent, Catholics at 36 percent, members of the Assemblies of God at 43 percent, and Jehovah's Witnesses at 48 percent.[33] (This is a sampling of the data, as other groups were listed as well, with Jewish Americans leading the way.)

When it came to household incomes over $100,000, the disparity was even greater, with Jewish households at 44 percent, fully 8 percent higher than the next group (Hindus at 36 percent). Skipping down the list, Muslims and Mormons were at 20 percent, Catholics at 19 percent, Southern Baptists at 16 percent, Assemblies of God at 10 percent, and Jehovah's Witnesses at just 4 percent.[34]

Is it a stretch to believe that with human nature being as corrupt as it is, antisemitism can also be rooted in envy and resentment, even among Christians? Perhaps the theological insecurity Paul warns about in Romans 11 has a parallel in social and economic insecurity.

In late 1982, the Holy Spirit was poured out mightily in a church where I served as an elder, leading to a deep spirit of repentance in our midst. To my shock (and my wife Nancy's as well), longtime friends of ours confessed that they had been jealous of us, since we had a nicer house than they did. (Trust me, the house was nothing to boast about; it was all relative.) Some also confessed to us that they had always been jealous of other Jewish people, since the Jewish kids in their schools (and beyond) did better than they did. It really caught us off guard, especially since they were our friends and fellow congregants.

Is it possible some of this is lurking in the hearts of Christians today, not just the overt antisemites but also those with more minor anti-Jewish attitudes? Be assured that this is not a judgment I make, nor is it a thought that I think. That's why I cite the words of my colleague John Zmirak. And that's why he, not I, was the one to bring the issue of envy into the equation. But it's only appropriate to encourage you to search your own heart to see if there might be some bad roots contributing to a wrong theological attitude.

Whatever the case may be, the bottom line is that all of us have sinned and need God's mercy, that Jesus died for Jew and Gentile alike, that we are equally loved by the Father, and that in the Lord we are absolutely one. There's no room for insecurity at our Father's throne or in our Father's house!

Not only so, but we desperately need one another, since it is only together that we will see God's purposes accomplished. And so, as a Jewish believer in Jesus indebted to the Gentile church for showing me the way of salvation, I appeal to my Gentile brothers and sisters in the Lord: Step into your high calling, and make my people envious by your walk with the Lord, by your love for one another, and by your conduct before the watching world. My people need what you have. And that means we need you to be who you are in Jesus, a holy, royal priesthood, sons and daughters of the Most High God, ambassadors for the Messiah. Let your light shine!

CHAPTER 11

O JERUSALEM, JERUSALEM!

JESUS IS COMING *back to Jerusalem.* As the angels said to the disciples as they watched the Lord ascend to heaven from the Mount of Olives, "Men of Galilee, why do you stand looking into heaven? This Jesus, who was taken up from you into heaven, will come *in the same way as you saw him go into heaven*" (Acts 1:11, emphasis added). Yes, in the same way He left visibly and bodily *from* the Mount of Olives in Jerusalem, He will return visibly and bodily *to* the Mount of Olives in Jerusalem.

As Bible teacher David Pawson notes:

> Once you accept that his return will be physical as well as personal, tangible as well as visible, in a word "bodily," then another adjective has to be added: it will be "local." Once that has been said, the location needs to be identified. I have never heard anyone claim it will be Rome or Geneva, Canterbury or Moscow. Every opinion that I have come across plumps for Jerusalem.[1]

But this is not merely a matter of opinion. Zechariah 14 confirms this explicitly, stating, "On that day, He will set His feet on the Mount of Olives, near Jerusalem on the east" (Zech 14:4, JPS TANAKH). It is also confirmed by other passages, which we will examine shortly, affirming the central importance of Jerusalem during the Lord's millennial reign.

Pawson continues:

> But that raises real problems for the anti-Zionist. It is one of their basic axioms that the land of Israel and its capital city have long since ceased to have any significance for the Lord, even if he still has plans for the Jewish people. The question: "Why on earth would Jesus return to Jerusalem of all places?" becomes a real embarrassment. The only

> possible answer is that the place as well as the people is still integral to his purposes.[2]

Exactly! Why would Jesus return to Jerusalem if the city no longer has significance? Or to turn this question around, to what other location would the Lion of the tribe of Judah and the King of the Jews return? One of the most famous prophecies in the Bible is found on the lips of the prophet Isaiah, presenting a glorious picture of the Messianic reign:

> The word that Isaiah the son of Amoz saw concerning Judah and Jerusalem. It shall come to pass in the latter days that the mountain of the house of the Lord shall be established as the highest of the mountains, and shall be lifted up above the hills; and all the nations shall flow to it, and many peoples shall come, and say: "Come, let us go up to the mountain of the Lord, to the house of the God of Jacob, that he may teach us his ways and that we may walk in his paths." For out of Zion shall go forth the law, and the word of the Lord from Jerusalem. He shall judge between the nations, and shall decide disputes for many peoples; and they shall beat their swords into plowshares, and their spears into pruning hooks; nation shall not lift up sword against nation, neither shall they learn war anymore.
>
> —ISAIAH 2:1–4

How beautiful this day will be, and how this hope has inspired millions throughout the centuries. No more war. No more strife. The nations of the world worshipping the God of Israel. The Messiah ruling and reigning with justice and with truth. And all of this will flow out of Jerusalem!

Christians who demonize the Jews, however, have a very different take. In the words of Rick Wiles:

> For the record, I totally reject Evangelical Zionism. John Nelson Darby was an occultist. Cyrus Scofield was a lying, deceiving swindler and conman. I am not a religious Zionist, nor a secular Zionist. I am a New Zionist! Old Jerusalem is not my eternal capital. Old Jerusalem is the harlot, the great city, Sodom and Egypt, the city that killed our Lord. It will be completely destroyed by fire when Jesus Christ returns to establish His everlasting kingdom on the new earth. Unlike today's Evangelical Zionists, I do not idolize the State of Israel. I desire a better country, that is, an heavenly: wherefore God is not ashamed to be called my God: for he hath prepared for me a city.[3]

Other Christians who are fearful of a "Jewish utopia" have raised similar concerns. Some point to DeAnne Loper, who writes in *Kabbalah Secrets Christians Need to Know*:

> Nearly ten years ago when the Holy Spirit began to reveal to me out of the Scriptures the mysteries of *the great city* Jerusalem, I made efforts to share this information with pastors. In every instance I received the same answer: they could not or would not acknowledge the biblical evidence pointing to Jerusalem as *Mystery Babylon*, the mother of harlots. This overwhelming response is based in tightly held traditions of men and is often rooted in fear.[4]

That is quite a contrast: Jerusalem the praise of all the earth (Isa. 62:7) or Jerusalem the mother of harlots. Which is it? And why does it matter?

If replacement theologians are correct, then there are no future promises for Israel as a nation or for the earthly city of Jerusalem. Jewish individuals can be saved like anyone else, but the only Jerusalem that matters is the Jerusalem from above, the New Jerusalem, our eternal home. As for the earthly city mentioned so often in the Bible, it is of no significance anymore—other than to be judged at the end of this age.

The problem is that for this view to be true, scores of verses from the Hebrew Scriptures would have to be voided out entirely—or at the least reinterpreted so radically as to be completely unrecognizable. Just look at these promises about the future of Jerusalem, all taken from the Book of Isaiah:

> Then the moon will be confounded and the sun ashamed, for the LORD of hosts reigns on Mount Zion and in Jerusalem, and his glory will be before his elders.
>
> —ISAIAH 24:23

> And in that day a great trumpet will be blown, and those who were lost in the land of Assyria and those who were driven out to the land of Egypt will come and worship the LORD on the holy mountain at Jerusalem.
>
> —ISAIAH 27:13

> Behold Zion, the city of our appointed feasts! Your eyes will see Jerusalem, an untroubled habitation, an immovable tent, whose stakes will never be plucked up, nor will any of its cords be broken....
>
> And no inhabitant will say, "I am sick"; the people who dwell there will be forgiven their iniquity.
>
> —ISAIAH 33:20, 24

> On your walls, O Jerusalem, I have set watchmen; all the day and all the night they shall never be silent. You who put the LORD in remembrance, take no rest, and give him no rest until he establishes Jerusalem and makes it a praise in the earth.
>
> —ISAIAH 62:6–7

> But be glad and rejoice forever in that which I create; for behold, I create Jerusalem to be a joy, and her people to be a gladness. I will rejoice in Jerusalem and be glad in my people; no more shall be heard in it the sound of weeping and the cry of distress.
>
> —ISAIAH 65:18–19

> "Rejoice with Jerusalem, and be glad for her, all you who love her; rejoice with her in joy, all you who mourn over her; that you may nurse and be satisfied from her consoling breast; that you may drink deeply with delight from her glorious abundance."
>
> For thus says the LORD: "Behold, I will extend peace to her like a river, and the glory of the nations like an overflowing stream; and you shall nurse, you shall be carried upon her hip, and bounced upon her knees. As one whom his mother comforts, so I will comfort you; you shall be comforted in Jerusalem."
>
> —ISAIAH 66:10–13

> And they shall bring all your brothers from all the nations as an offering to the Lord, on horses and in chariots and in litters and on mules and on dromedaries, to my holy mountain Jerusalem, says the Lord, just as the Israelites bring their grain offering in a clean vessel to the house of the Lord.
>
> —ISAIAH 66:20

None of these prophecies has yet been fulfilled, but all of them will be fulfilled—and not just the prophecies from Isaiah but from all the other prophets that prophesied about Jerusalem's glorious future as well. Yeshua *will* return to Jerusalem, and from there He will rule and reign, sitting on David's throne, as the prophets foretold and as the New Testament reaffirms. In the words of the angel Gabriel to Miriam (Mary), the mother of Jesus, "He will be great and will be called the Son of the Most High. And the Lord God will give to him the throne of his father David" (Luke 1:32)—and that throne is on earth, not in heaven. That is when God will fulfill His many promises to Israel. Those promises remain true as surely as God is true!

The big question is: What right does anyone have—any author or theologian or preacher or scholar or leader or believer—to change the meaning of scores of clear and plain verses in the Bible? What right does anyone have to claim that a later meaning voids out or makes null what God has previously stated? What right does anyone have to so radically reinterpret the plain sense of Scripture verses so as to make them completely unrecognizable?

According to Christopher H. Wright, a top Old Testament scholar, it is the Bible itself that points us to a spiritualizing interpretation of Jerusalem and the promises to Israel. He writes:

> In all of this, then, it is not a case of abolishing and "replacing" the realities of Israel in the Old Testament, but of taking them up into a greater reality in the Messiah. Christ does not deprive the believing Jew of anything that belonged to Israel as God's people; nor does he give to the believing Gentile anything less than the full covenantal blessing and promise that was Israel's. On the contrary, we share together in all of it and more—in him, and for ever.[5]

As nice as this sounds, and with all respect to Dr. Wright's scholarship, something *has* been replaced, based on his interpretation. Israel today is *not* the promised homeland of the Jewish people. The Jews have *no* biblical claim to Jerusalem, nor are there earthbound prophecies concerning Jerusalem still to be fulfilled. In fact, the unbelieving Jew has no promises (contrast Paul's words in Romans 9:1–5), while the believing Gentile gets all the promises that were given to Israel, except in expanded form (meaning, rather than inheriting the land of Canaan, they get the whole world). This is the essence of replacement theology, yet those who hold to it, as sincere as they might be and as many insights they might have into God's Word, miss the forest for the trees.

For good reason, pastor and Bible teacher Peter Wyns writes:

> The late Derek Prince, my grandfather, used to say that Israel was extremely important to God. It is like the first button while buttoning up your shirt. If you get the first button in the wrong hole, then all of the other buttons will end up in the wrong holes. If you don't love Jerusalem, the rest of your theology will be out of whack because Jesus ruling from Jerusalem is central to God's master plan.[6]

At the risk, then, of being redundant, I'm going to cite here the entire text of Zechariah 14, highlighting every time the word *Jerusalem* or *city* (referring to Jerusalem) occurs:

> Behold, a day is coming for the Lord, when the spoil taken from you will be divided in your midst. For I will gather all the nations against *Jerusalem* to battle, and the *city* shall be taken and the houses plundered and the women raped. Half of the *city* shall go out into exile, but

the rest of the people shall not be cut off from the *city*. Then the LORD will go out and fight against those nations as when he fights on a day of battle. On that day his feet shall stand on the Mount of Olives that lies before *Jerusalem* on the east, and the Mount of Olives shall be split in two from east to west by a very wide valley, so that one half of the Mount shall move northward, and the other half southward. And you shall flee to the valley of my mountains, for the valley of the mountains shall reach to Azal. And you shall flee as you fled from the earthquake in the days of Uzziah king of Judah. Then the LORD my God will come, and all the holy ones with him.

On that day there shall be no light, cold, or frost. And there shall be a unique day, which is known to the LORD, neither day nor night, but at evening time there shall be light.

On that day living waters shall flow out from *Jerusalem*, half of them to the eastern sea and half of them to the western sea. It shall continue in summer as in winter.

And the LORD will be king over all the earth. On that day the LORD will be one and his name one.

The whole land shall be turned into a plain from Geba to Rimmon south of *Jerusalem*. But *Jerusalem* shall remain aloft on its site from the Gate of Benjamin to the place of the former gate, to the Corner Gate, and from the Tower of Hananel to the king's winepresses. And it shall be inhabited, for there shall never again be a decree of utter destruction. *Jerusalem* shall dwell in security.

And this shall be the plague with which the LORD will strike all the peoples that wage war against *Jerusalem*: their flesh will rot while they are still standing on their feet, their eyes will rot in their sockets, and their tongues will rot in their mouths.

And on that day a great panic from the LORD shall fall on them, so that each will seize the hand of another, and the hand of the one will be raised against the hand of the other. Even Judah will fight at *Jerusalem*. And the wealth of all the surrounding nations shall be collected, gold, silver, and garments in great abundance. And a plague like this plague shall fall on the horses, the mules, the camels, the donkeys, and whatever beasts may be in those camps.

Then everyone who survives of all the nations that have come against *Jerusalem* shall go up year after year to worship the King, the LORD of hosts, and to keep the Feast of Booths. And if any of the families of the earth do not go up to *Jerusalem* to worship the King, the LORD of hosts, there will be no rain on them. And if the family of Egypt does not go up and present themselves, then on them there shall be no rain; there shall be the plague with which the LORD afflicts the nations that do not go up to keep the Feast of Booths. This shall be the punishment to

> Egypt and the punishment to all the nations that do not go up to keep the Feast of Booths.
>
> And on that day there shall be inscribed on the bells of the horses, "Holy to the LORD." And the pots in the house of the LORD shall be as the bowls before the altar. And every pot in *Jerusalem* and Judah shall be holy to the LORD of hosts, so that all who sacrifice may come and take of them and boil the meat of the sacrifice in them. And there shall no longer be a trader in the house of the LORD of hosts on that day.

Has the Lord spoken clearly or not? Jerusalem occurs *ten times* in just one chapter, all with reference to the return of the Lord.[7] How dare we spiritualize this away! And what are we to make of all the specific geographical descriptions? How did these suddenly become meaningless spiritual metaphors? Why communicate with such detailed, clear language if none of it has a literal application? (I should point out here that all attempts to interpret Zechariah 14 with reference to past events, such as the destruction of Jerusalem in AD 70, fail miserably.)[8]

The Old Testament prophets certainly knew how to use spiritual language, such as Joel prophesying that the Holy Spirit would be poured out on all flesh, as quoted in Acts 2 (Joel 2:28–32 and Acts 2:14–21) or Isaiah prophesying about the vicarious sufferings of Jesus in Isaiah 53. In the same way, if Zechariah 14 was simply pointing to God destroying the wicked and blessing Israel (or, more broadly, blessing the church), why didn't God say that? Why instead did He speak about Jerusalem ten times, first as surrounded by armies, then delivered by the Lord, then the seat of His kingdom on the earth? Could it be that the Lord means what He says?

The answer is absolutely yes, in which case we can say for sure that *there is a glorious future ahead for Israel, right here on this earth, centered in Jerusalem.* The replacement theologians are wrong. And the Christian antisemites are very wrong.

A Promise of Hope or Destruction?

Where, then, did they get such wrong views? Did they manufacture them out of thin air?

Certainly not. Instead, these wrong views are directly related to their larger wrong views about Israel and the Jewish people that we addressed in previous chapters. If replacement theologians get Israel wrong, they certainly get Jerusalem wrong. And they find further support for their views by some negative references to Jerusalem in the New Testament, including the words of Jesus in Matthew 23, where He said:

> "O Jerusalem, Jerusalem, the city that kills the prophets and stones those who are sent to it! How often would I have gathered your children together as a hen gathers her brood under her wings, and you were not willing! See, your house is left to you desolate. For I tell you, you will not see me again, until you say, 'Blessed is he who comes in the name of the Lord.'"
>
> —MATTHEW 23:37–39

But this is *not* a promise of the lasting destruction of Jerusalem and, with it, the cutting off of the Jewish people. To the contrary, it is a warning with a promise: Jerusalem will be destroyed and will not see the Messiah *until* it welcomes Him back as the Messianic King. So terrible judgment *would* come upon the city and the people, especially because of the sins of the leaders. But a Jewish Jerusalem will one day welcome Yeshua back!

Others point to the Lord's prophecy in Luke 21, where He said of His own people, "They will fall by the edge of the sword and be led captive among all nations, and Jerusalem will be trampled underfoot by the Gentiles, until the times of the Gentiles are fulfilled" (Luke 21:24). But once again there is an *until*. The Jewish people *will* be scattered from Jerusalem "until the times of the Gentiles are fulfilled." Then they will be regathered.

Some point to the Lord's words to the Samaritan woman in John 4, where He said:

> "Woman, believe me, the hour is coming when neither on this mountain [meaning Mount Gerizim] nor in Jerusalem will you worship the Father. You worship what you do not know; we worship what we know, for salvation is from the Jews. But the hour is coming, and is now here, when the true worshipers will worship the Father in spirit and truth, for the Father is seeking such people to worship him."
>
> —JOHN 4:21–23

Based on this text, these Christians believe that Jerusalem can never again be central for God's people, since the Lord is seeking only spiritual worship. But that is not the point Jesus was making, since it is not a matter of either-or—unless you literally think Jesus was saying that *no one will worship the Lord in Jerusalem*. Obviously not! Rather, while Jerusalem will always be important (the name of our eternal home is the New Jerusalem), true disciples can worship God from anywhere in the world at any time, as we do today. And during the millennial kingdom, while the nations will stream to Jerusalem to learn from the Messiah (Isa. 2:1–4), the whole earth will also be filled with the knowledge of the glory of God (Isa. 11:9). It will be both-and!

What about Paul's teaching in Galatians, namely that, allegorically speaking, "Hagar is Mount Sinai in Arabia; she corresponds to the present Jerusalem, for she is in slavery with her children. But the Jerusalem above is free, and she is our mother" (Gal. 4:25–26)? This parallels the words of Hebrews 12: "But you have come to Mount Zion and to the city of the living God, the heavenly Jerusalem, and to innumerable angels in festal gathering, and to the assembly of the firstborn who are enrolled in heaven, and to God, the judge of all, and to the spirits of the righteous made perfect" (Heb. 12:22–23).

Who would argue with this? Yes, for sure, Jerusalem at present is not free and has not been free for two thousand years. And yes, for sure, our citizenship is in heaven and we are seated in heavenly places (Phil. 3:20; Col. 3:1). The Old Testament prophets frequently spoke against Jerusalem during seasons of oppression, bondage, and sin. Consider the words of the Lord in Isaiah 1, where Israel's leaders are likened to the leaders of Sodom and Gomorrah and where Jerusalem is described in vivid terms: "How the faithful city has become a harlot; [the city] once filled with justice, righteousness used to lodge in it—but now murderers!" (Isa. 1:21, my translation). But that is why we are called to pray incessantly for Jerusalem, not resting and not giving God any rest until He establishes Jerusalem as the praise of the *whole earth*. (See again Isaiah 62:1–7.)

Obviously, we don't need to pray for the heavenly Jerusalem; we need to pray for the earthly Jerusalem. And when Jesus returns *to earth* from heaven, He will come back to a specific location: the city of Jerusalem. You can count on it! And at that time, *the earth* will be filled with the knowledge of the glory of the Lord. This is something to look forward to! This is something the Lord will do right here on our planet, as Zechariah lays out in such detail in chapter 14. To cite Isaiah 62:7 again: "And give him no rest until he establishes Jerusalem and makes it a praise *in the earth*" (emphasis added).

Still, there are some who point to Revelation 11:8, a verse that they claim describes Jerusalem as "the great city that symbolically is called Sodom and Egypt, where their Lord was crucified." Others even claim that the great harlot of Revelation (chapters 17 and 18) is the city of Jerusalem.[9] But even if that's exactly what these verses are saying (and there is *massive* debate about the identity of the great harlot), my question would be: So what? Again, the Old Testament prophets indicted Jerusalem and its leaders in the strongest of terms. Stop for a moment and read Ezekiel 16. The language is so strong, you might even find it offensive. Yet these same prophets, including Ezekiel, saw a bright future for Jerusalem right here on earth. The judgments are very real, but so are the promises!

As Peter reminds us, Jesus must remain in heaven "until the time for restoring all the things about which God spoke by the mouth of his holy prophets long ago" (Acts 3:21). To ask the question again: What did the prophets speak about? What did they predict? What did they say would happen in the future concerning the city of Jerusalem and the people of Israel? You can be sure all of the prophets' words concerning Israel will come to pass, and much of what they prophesied must take place on this earth, flowing out of Jerusalem. It will happen! Peter also tells us it is the repentance of the Jewish people that will bring the Jewish Messiah (Acts 3:19–20), which agrees with the Lord's words in Matthew 23:37–39, discussed previously. Father, we ask You to hasten that day!

Many have pointed to Yeshua's response to His disciples' question in Acts 1:6, where they asked Him immediately before His ascension, "Lord, will you at this time restore the kingdom to Israel?" (Acts 1:6). He answered, "It is not for you to know times or seasons that the Father has fixed by his own authority. But you will receive power when the Holy Spirit has come upon you, and you will be my witnesses in Jerusalem and in all Judea and Samaria, and to the end of the earth" (Acts 1:7–8).

But this is not a rebuke. Obviously not! Contrast this with the Lord's words to the two disciples He met after His resurrection (but before they realized who He was): "O foolish ones, and slow of heart to believe all that the prophets have spoken!" (Luke 24:25). Or consider His rebuke to Peter when he tried to stand in the way of Him going to the cross: "Get behind me, Satan! You are a hindrance to me. For you are not setting your mind on the things of God, but on the things of man" (Matt. 16:23).

Surely, if the disciples were so wrong, so carnal, so earthly minded after spending *weeks* with Jesus after His resurrection, He would have rebuked them sharply. Surely, if their views were as wrong as the replacement theologians and the Christian antisemites claim, He would have set them straight in the strongest of terms. Imagine if they had said, "Lord, will You at this time send us out to behead all those who reject You?" His reply certainly would not have been, "It's not for you to know the right time for that. You should concentrate on preaching the gospel." Obviously not!

Instead, in Acts 1:7–8, Jesus affirmed the rightness of their question, since God *will* one day restore the kingdom to Israel here on the earth before we enter eternity. He just said that it wasn't for them to know the times and seasons when this will happen. They needed to concentrate on preaching the gospel in the power of the Spirit.

But remember. Less than two months earlier, Jesus sat with these very same men and said to them, "You are those who have stayed with me in my trials, and I assign to you, as my Father assigned to me, a kingdom, that you may eat and drink at my table in my kingdom and sit on thrones judging the twelve tribes of Israel" (Luke 22:28–30). Perhaps that's why they were asking Him about that very same kingdom before He left.

Matthew records a similar comment in a different context in his Gospel, indicating this was something the Lord spoke to His disciples about more than once: "Jesus said to them, 'Truly, I say to you, in the new world [or, in the regeneration], when the Son of Man will sit on his glorious throne, you who have followed me will also sit on twelve thrones, judging the twelve tribes of Israel'" (Matt. 19:28).

This is not a picture of what will happen in eternity in the new heaven and new earth based in the New Jerusalem. No. This is a picture of something that will happen before then, when Yeshua returns and sits on David's throne, ruling and reigning over Israel and the nations as we rule by His side. The promises of the second coming will certainly come to pass, just as certainly as the prophecies of the first coming came to pass. Our God does not lie or misspeak.

At this point, though, one thing should be evident: The clear testimony of the Word will not change the views of many a Christian antisemite. The facts of history will not do it, nor will logic or formal debate. This is a spiritual deception, and these professing Christians need a real change of heart. It is for that change of heart that we must pray, while also presenting the truth with wisdom, long-suffering, and love.

And this brings me to a final observation, one from Israeli rabbi Pesach Wolicki, who works in the field of Jewish-Christian relations. He makes a fascinating point in his November 28, 2019, article in the *Jerusalem Post*, titled "A New Christian Antisemitism." He notes:

> Luther, and Augustine before him, looked at the state of the Jewish people—scattered, powerless, and in a seemingly eternal exile—and drew their theological conclusions based on what they saw and understood from the Bible. They, and many other Christian theologians before and after them taught that the church had replaced Israel as the future recipient of the covenantal promises of the Bible.[10]

In other words, as the Jewish people wandered around the earth, living as outcasts and suffering death and dishonor, this was a sure proof to the church, which by then was building cathedrals and prospering, that the Jews were cursed and that Christians were blessed. The church had become the new Israel. Now, however, with more than six million Jews living in the land and with the nation thriving in so many ways, what do antisemitic Christian leaders say?

In short, their answer today is, "Well, Israel today is unrelated to the Israel of the Bible. Today's Jews are not really Jews."

Rabbi Wolicki notes that, from a historical perspective, such a claim is absurd, writing, "The history of Jewish continuity is a matter of record. Despite...a few relatively short gaps in the written record, there are continuous records of communal life from every century and almost every generation of Jews going back at least 1,500 years."[11]

The earlier history can be traced as well, plus there is DNA testing that can be done and linguistic studies that help place a specific people group in a particular place and time. Without a doubt, despite much intermarriage and dispersion, a straight line can be traced back from Jewish history today to Jewish history in biblical times. The resistance, then, to the notion that Israel today is not really Israel must be theological more than historical.

Wolicki writes:

> According to Dr. Tricia Miller, a Christian academic who monitors Christian attitudes about Israel, this new claim that today's Jews are not really Jews has been circulating for only the past twenty years or so in mainline Protestant circles. It is not difficult to identify the obviously political motives for this new idea.[12]

Of course, the idea that Jews who did not believe in Jesus were not true Jews has been taught by the church for centuries, and we examined the key verses cited in support of this view. (See chapter 9.) But that is different from what Dr. Miller is saying. Rather, throughout church history, no one doubted that "the Jews" were actually Jewish, meaning that they were descendants of Abraham, Isaac, and Jacob who sought to live in obedience to the Torah. To the contrary, it was their Jewishness that singled them out for scorn, mockery, and contempt. They were seen as evil by nature!

Today, however, the notion of "fake Jews" has taken on a more sinister meaning: they are not Jewish in any sense of the word—not spiritually, not ethnically, not physically.

Historically, then, as the Jewish people suffered around the world, "The replacement theology of the past was supported by the reality of the Jewish predicament in a seemingly endless exile. However anti-Jewish, it was a justifiable interpretation of the realities of history as they seemed at the time."[13]

Things did look bad for Israel, and so the idea that it was replaced by the church seemed to have some grounds for support. However, Rabbi Woliki writes:

> With this theology now rendered untenable by current events, the antisemitic theologians of the PCUSA and their ilk have taken a new approach. Rather than adjust their theology based on the new realities that God has brought into the world in our time, they choose the

> reverse. They choose to reinterpret reality to suit their anti-Jewish theological stance. Rather than argue that the church has replaced Israel, they argue that there is no Israel at all.[14]

Exactly! And that is the very argument you have now read for yourself from the pens and lips of contemporary Christians who espouse antisemitism. This lie must be confronted, exposed, and repudiated. As Wolicki ends his article, "It's time to call this new approach by mainline Israel haters what it is: the denial of Jewish identity and Jewish history is the new theological antisemitism."[15]

We have really heard it all, and one way or another the Jewish people get blamed. When we point out how Jews who refused to convert were expelled from countries like Spain, we are told, "You see! The Jews have been kicked out of country after country. They must be doing something wrong!" This would be like blaming a black student who was kicked out of twenty white supremacist schools: "It's obviously his fault! Why else do you think he got expelled so many times?"

When the Jewish people are dispersed from the land and subject to much pain and suffering, that is proof that they are under an eternal curse. But when they are back in the land and prospering, there's an answer for that too: "They're not really Jews!" So their suffering is proof that the Jewish people are cursed, and their prosperity is proof that they're not really Jewish! The antisemites want it both ways. Consequently, during World War II, the Nazis were killing Jewish people precisely because *they were Jewish*. Today, those who hate Jewish people are killing them because *they are fake Jews*. We must realize, then, that at the root of antisemitism is the father of lies himself, and it is Satan we must oppose in Spirit and in truth.

May this be the generation of Christians that says, "Enough is enough." May this be the generation of Christians that stands with the Jewish people rather than with their enemies. May this be the generation that provokes the people of Israel to jealousy by the beauty and reality and passion of their Christian faith. May this be the generation that makes Jesus-Yeshua known to His lost sheep. It's time!

NOTES

Chapter 1

1. See John Chrysostom, "Homilies Against the Jews," HolyWar.org, accessed June 27, 2020, https://web.archive.org/web/20120113053046/http://www.holywar.org/txt/homily1.html. Speaking of the synagogue, he said, "Here the slayers of Christ gather together."
2. There is debate among scholars as to the exact background of the sermons. Was Chrysostom concerned about Christians in his congregation becoming interested in Judaism? Was he concerned about Jewish Christians influencing his people with what he thought were wrong ideas? Or was he merely threatened by the existence of Judaism? For further discussion, see Robert L. Wilken, *John Chrysostom and the Jews: Rhetoric and Reality in the Late Fourth Century* (Berkeley, CA: University of California Press, 1983).
3. Chrysostom, "Homilies Against the Jews."
4. Chrysostom, "Homilies Against the Jews."
5. Chrysostom, "Homilies Against the Jews."
6. See Walter Laqueur, *The Changing Face of Anti-Semitism: From Ancient Times to the Present Day* (Oxford: Oxford University Press, 2006), 47–48.
7. Susan Jacoby, "The First Victims of the First Crusade," *New York Times*, February 13, 2015, https://www.nytimes.com/2015/02/15/opinion/sunday/the-first-victims-of-the-first-crusade.html.
8. Jacoby, "The First Victims of the First Crusade."
9. Martin Luther, "That Jesus Christ Was Born a Jew, 1523," accessed June 27, 2020, https://www.uni-due.de/collcart/es/sem/s6/txt09_1.htm.
10. Martin Luther, "On the Jews and Their Lies, 1543," accessed June 27, 2020, https://web.archive.org/web/20110219063044/http://www.humanitas-international.org/showcase/chronography/documents/luther-jews.htm. There are numerous editions of this book in English, with many variations, none of which affect the overall counsel given by Luther. The German original was entitled *Von den Jüden und Ihren Lügen*. In the pre-internet days, the only place I could find Luther's volume in English was in a neo-Nazi catalog.
11. Daniel Jonah Goldhagen, *Hitler's Willing Executioners: Ordinary Germans and the Holocaust* (New York: Random House, 1996), 111.
12. *Nuremberg Trial Proceedings*, vol. 12, April 29, 1946, as quoted by the Avalon Project at Yale Law School, accessed June 27, 2020, https://avalon.law.yale.edu/imt/04-29-46.asp. See further Michael L. Brown, *The Real Kosher Jesus: Revealing the Mysteries of the Hidden Messiah* (Lake Mary, FL: Frontline, 2012), 1–5.

13. Martin Luther, *On the Jews and Their Lies*, foreword by Texe Marrs (Austin, TX: RiverCrest Publishing, 2014). For a 2019 Marrs radio show featuring the book, see "Martin Luther on the Jews and Their Lies—By Texe Marrs," BitChute video, 59:30, posted by "Rick Heskey," August 18, 2019, https://www.bitchute.com/video/Qsj5OK0yM1Rw/. See further "Anti-Semitic Pastor Promoting New Film on Jews," Anti-Defamation League, November 19, 2014, https://www.adl.org/blog/anti-semitic-pastor-promoting-new-film-on-jews.
14. Martin Luther, *On the Jews and Their Lies*, trans. Martin Bertram (n.p.: CreateSpace Independent Publishing Platform, 2017). At the time of this writing, this book was no longer available on Amazon.
15. Randall McGoy, review of Luther, *On the Jews and Their Lies* (Bertram), September 23, 2018.
16. Review of Luther, *On the Jews and Their Lies* (Bertram), June 22, 2018. At the time of this writing, this book and this review were no longer available on Amazon.
17. United States of America v. John Timothy Earnest, US District Court, Southern District of California, May 9, 2019, https://www.justice.gov/opa/press-release/file/1161421/download.
18. I wrote about this further in Michael Brown, "To the American Jewish Community: The Synagogue Shooter Was Not a Christian," The Stream, April 28, 2019, https://stream.org/to-the-american-jewish-community-the-synagogue-shooter-was-not-a-christian/.
19. John Earnest, "An Open Letter," Free PDF, April 28, 2019, http://www.freepdf.info/index.php?post/Earnest-John-An-open-letter. See also Michael Davis, "The Anti-Jewish Manifesto of John T. Earnest, the San Diego Synagogue Shooter," Middle East Media Research Institute, May 15, 2019, https://www.memri.org/reports/anti-jewish-manifesto-john-t-earnest-san-diego-synagogue-shooter.
20. Earnest, "An Open Letter."
21. Earnest, "An Open Letter." For discussion of all these texts, see chapter 9.
22. Earnest, "An Open Letter."
23. We took a screenshot of Robert's comment before removing it; I then tweeted it. See Dr. Michael L. Brown (@DrMichaelLBrown), "The antisemites are sick! Just saw this posted on my YT channel, speaking of the synagogue shooting in Poway…," Twitter, September 29, 2019, 12:39 p.m., https://twitter.com/DrMichaelLBrown/status/1178348499970269184.
24. "Saint John Chrysostomos: Homilies Against the Jews (*Adversus Judaeos Orationes*)," YouTube video, 6:15:24, posted by "Sperling," January 6, 2017, https://www.youtube.com/watch?v=IenDVBABess&feature=youtu.be.

Chapter 2

1. Malcolm Hay, *Europe and the Jews: The Pressure of Christendom on the People of Israel for 1900 Years* (Boston: Beacon, 1961). It was republished under different names over the years.
2. You can find my "ASKDrBrown" channel on YouTube at https://www.youtube.com/channel/UCbINn3x-intLp88Zrf8acpg.
3. See "What Are the Noahide Laws?," YouTube video, 3:00, posted by "ASKDrBrown," September 19, 2019, https://www.youtube.com/watch?v=ulSoYZkfGHw; "The Truth About the Noahide Laws," YouTube video, 57:32, posted by "ASKDrBrown," April 15, 2019, https://www.youtube.com/watch?v=k3b2X9l0wSk; and "Debunking Noahide Laws Hysteria," YouTube video, 57:49, posted by "ASKDrBrown," September 26, 2019, https://www.youtube.com/watch?v=OxX42zF4zbw.
4. "Owen Benjamin's Anti-Semitic Meltdown," YouTube video, 11:08, posted by "ASKDrBrown," April 1, 2019, https://www.youtube.com/watch?v=gxFHMUUoD-I.
5. For audio, see "Dr. Brown Discusses Antisemitism With Dr. E. Michael Jones," *The Line of Fire* (podcast), April 18, 2019, http://thelineoffire.org/2019/04/18/dr-brown-discusses-antisemitism-with-dr-e-michael-jones/; for video, see "Dr. Brown Discusses Antisemitism With Dr. E. Michael Jones," YouTube video, 49:56, posted by "ASKDrBrown," April 18, 2019, https://www.youtube.com/watch?v=X1nThdq_cBY.
6. "Are Dr. E. Michael Jones and Owen Benjamin Telling the Truth?," YouTube video, 25:59, posted by "ASKDrBrown," May 11, 2019, https://www.youtube.com/watch?v=76Zafbcl6zs.
7. "Rick Wiles Slanders Israel, Jews," YouTube video, 8:33, posted by "ASKDrBrown," March 1, 2019, https://www.youtube.com/watch?v=SGJnWJR-X44; "Global Zionism Exposed: Fourth Beast Rising," TruNews, February 20, 2019, https://www.trunews.com/stream/global-zionism-exposed-fourth-beast-rising.
8. "TRUNEWS and Rick Wiles EXPOSED!!," YouTube video, 10:34, posted by "ASKDrBrown," July 12, 2019, https://www.youtube.com/watch?v=sHEAV3weHSk; "One Nation Under Zion: Did Israel Annex USA?," TruNews, June 18, 2019, https://www.trunews.com/stream/one-nation-under-zion-did-israel-annex-usa.
9. "One Nation Under Zion: Did Israel Annex USA?"
10. BDS stands for Boycott, Divestment, and Sanctions and is one of the most concerted and targeted efforts to hurt and destabilize the nation of Israel. See Jonathan Bernis, "What You Need to Know About the BDS Movement," Jewish Voice, accessed June 29, 2020, https://www.jewishvoice.org/read/article/what-you-need-know-about-bds-movement.
11. *Chabad* and *Lubavitch* refer to the same group of ultra-Orthodox Jews who help spread the message of their late Rebbe (Grand Rabbi), Menachem Mendel Schneerson, who died in 1994. See https://www.chabad.org/.

CHAPTER 3

1. Jaffrey Salkin, "Deborah Lipstadt Teaches Us How to Spell Antisemitism," Religion News Service, January 22, 2019, https://religionnews.com/2019/01/22/antisemitism-deborah-lipstadt/.
2. Michael Berenbaum, "Anti-Semitism," *Encylopaedia Britannica,* last updated April 21, 2020, https://www.britannica.com/topic/anti-Semitism.
3. According to the International Holocaust Remembrance Alliance, "The philological term 'Semitic' referred to a family of languages originating in the Middle East whose descendant languages today are spoken by millions of people mostly across Western Asia and North Africa. Following this semantic logic, the conjunction of the prefix 'anti' with 'Semitism' indicates antisemitism as referring to all people who speak Semitic languages or to all those classified as 'Semites.' The term has, however, since its inception referred to prejudice against Jews alone"; IHRA Committee on Antisemitism and Holocaust Denial, "Memo on Spelling of Antisemitism," International Holocaust Remembrance Alliance, April 2015, https://www.holocaustremembrance.com/sites/default/files/memo-on-spelling-of-antisemitism_final-1.pdf.
4. Fred Maroun, "The 'Arabs Are Semites Too' Fallacy," *Times of Israel* (blog), January 2, 2015, https://blogs.timesofisrael.com/the-arabs-are-semites-too-fallacy/.
5. *Merriam-Webster,* s.v. "Semitism," accessed June 29, 2020, https://www.merriam-webster.com/dictionary/Semitism. A creative use of the term is found in Jonathan Weisman, *(((Semitism))): Being Jewish in America in the Age of Trump* (New York: St. Martin's Press, 2018).
6. E. Michael Jones, "The Conversion of the Revolutionary Jew," *Culture Wars,* October 2006, available at https://web.archive.org/web/20070210155533/http://www.culturewars.com/2006/Conversion.htm; see further E. Michael Jones, "Jewish Privilege—Excerpt," Culture Wars, July 19, 2019, https://culturewars.com/news/jewish-privilege-excerpt.
7. Simon Plosker, "A UK Paper and 'The Trouble With Jews Today,'" *The Algemeiner,* December 9, 2019, https://www.algemeiner.com/2019/12/09/a-uk-paper-and-the-trouble-with-jews-today/.
8. Jones, "The Conversion of the Revolutionary Jew." In chapter 4, we will return to his shocking position that "every Christian, insofar as he is a Christian, must be anti-Jewish."
9. "Dr. Brown Discusses Antisemitism With Dr. E. Michael Jones."
10. "Dr. Brown Discusses Antisemitism With Dr. E. Michael Jones."
11. "Dr. Brown Discusses Antisemitism With Dr. E. Michael Jones."
12. Lexico, s.v. "anti-Semitism," accessed June 29, 2020, https://www.lexico.com/en/definition/anti-semitism.
13. "Working Definition of Antisemitism," International Holocaust Remembrance Alliance, accessed June 29, 2020, https://www.holocaustremembrance.com/working-definition-antisemitism. The

definition adds, "Rhetorical and physical manifestations of antisemitism are directed toward Jewish or non-Jewish individuals and/or their property, toward Jewish community institutions and religious facilities."

14. Office of International Religious Freedom, "Defining Anti-Semitism," US Department of State, May 26, 2016, https://www.state.gov/defining-anti-semitism/.
15. *Merriam-Webster*, s.v. "anti-Semitism," accessed June 29, 2020, https://www.merriam-webster.com/dictionary/anti-Semitism; see also Geoffrey Nunberg, "Lexical Lessons; What the Good Book Says: Anti-Semitism, Loosely Defined," *New York Times*, April 11, 2004, https://www.nytimes.com/2004/04/11/weekinreview/lexical-lessons-what-the-good-book-says-anti-semitism-loosely-defined.html.
16. Dictionary.com, s.v. "anti-Semitism," accessed June 29, 2020, https://www.dictionary.com/browse/anti-semitism.
17. Wikipedia, s.v. "Antisemitism," last modified June 29, 2020, https://en.wikipedia.org/wiki/Antisemitism.
18. Macmillan Dictionary, s.v. "anti-Semitic," accessed June 30 2020, https://www.macmillandictionary.com/us/dictionary/american/anti-semitic.
19. Kenneth L. Marcus, *The Definition of Anti-Semitism* (Oxford: Oxford University Press, 2015), 192.
20. Marcus, *The Definition of Anti-Semitism*, 192.
21. See, conveniently, Madeline Roache, "Surge in Anti-Semitic Attacks Has Caused a 'Sense of Emergency' Among Jews Worldwide, New Report Says," *Time*, May 2, 2019, https://time.com/5580312/kantor-center-anti-semitism-report/.
22. "Deborah E. Lipstadt," Emory College of Arts and Sciences, accessed June 30, 2020, http://religion.emory.edu/home/people/faculty/lipstadt-deborah.html.
23. *Denial*, directed by Mick Jackson, was released in 2016. For more information, see https://bleeckerstreetmedia.com/denial.
24. Deborah E. Lipstadt, *Antisemitism: Here and Now* (New York: Schocken Books, 2019), ix.
25. Lipstadt, *Antisemitism*, x.
26. Lipstadt, *Antisemitism*, xi.
27. Julia Neuberger, *Antisemitism: What It is. What It Isn't. Why It Matters.* (London: Weidenfeld & Nicolson, 2019), introduction.
28. Neuberger, *Antisemitism*, introduction.
29. Neuberger, *Antisemitism*, introduction.
30. For the "fake Jew" slur, see below, chapter 11. For more on the Black Hebrew Israelites, see Jacob S. Dorman, *Chosen People: The Rise of American Black Israelite Religions* (Oxford: Oxford University Press, 2013); for rebuttals to their theology, from academic to popular, see Vocab Malone, *Barack Obama vs. The Black Hebrew Israelites: Introduction to the History and Beliefs of 1West Hebrew Israelism* (Phoenix: Thureos Publishing, 2017); Robert L. Anderson and Andrew E. Hooper, *The So-Called "Hebrew Israelites" Formerly Known As the*

Black Hebrew Israelites (BHI) (Detroit: Truth Seekers Read Publications, 2019); C. L. Willis, *Black Hebrew Israelites: Debunked, Deflated, and Exposed* (n.p.: Amazon.com Services, 2019).

31. Neuberger, *Antisemitism*, chapter 1.
32. Simon Schama, Simon Sebag Montefiore, and Howard Jacobson, "The Labour Party and Its Approach to Zionism," *The Times*, November 6, 2017, https://www.thetimes.co.uk/article/the-labour-party-and-its-approach-to-zionism-cpx2xnkdm.

CHAPTER 4

1. Wikipedia, s.v. "Israel-Related Animal Conspiracy Theories," last modified June 28, 2020, https://en.wikipedia.org/wiki/Israel-related_animal_conspiracy_theories.
2. Wikipedia, "Israel-Related Animal Conspiracy Theories."
3. See also Gil Yaron, "Secret Agent Plot? Saudi Arabia Claims Bird Working as Israel Spy," *The Star*, January 5, 2011, https://www.thestar.com/news/world/2011/01/05/secret_agent_plot_saudi_arabia_claims_bird_working_as_israel_spy.html.
4. Haim Hillel Ben-Sasson, *Trial and Achievement: Currents in Jewish History* (Jeruslalem: Keter, 1974), 254–255, as quoted in Dennis Prager and Joseph Telushkin, *Why the Jews? The Reason for Antisemitism, The Most Accurate Predictor of Human Evil* (repr., New York: Simon & Schuster, 2003), 102.
5. Michael L. Brown, *Our Hands Are Stained With Blood: The Tragic Story of the Church and the Jewish People*, rev. ed. (Shippensburg, PA: Destiny Image, 2019), 94. For more on the Jews and the Black Death, see Edward H. Flannery, *The Anguish of the Jews: Twenty-Three Centuries of Antisemitism*, rev. ed. (New York: Paulist Press, 1985), 109–111.
6. Mona Eltahawy, "Egyptian Boogie Nights," *U.S. News and World Report*, December 19, 1999, https://web.archive.org/web/20131104064522/http://www.usnews.com/usnews/news/articles/991227/archive_004531.htm.
7. Texe Marrs, *Conspiracy of the Six-Pointed Star: Eye-Opening Revelations and Forbidden Knowledge About Israel, the Jews, Zionism, and the Rothschilds* (Austin, TX: RiverCrest Publishing, 2011).
8. Texe Marrs, *DNA Science and the Jewish Bloodline* (Austin, TX: RiverCrest Publishing, 2013).
9. Texe Marrs, *Holy Serpent of the Jews: The Rabbis' Secret Plan for Satan to Crush Their Enemies and Vault the Jews to Global Dominion* (Austin, TX: RiverCrest Publishing, 2016).
10. Texe Marrs, Blood Covenant With Destiny: The Babylonian Talmud, the Jewish Kabbalah, and the Power of Prophecy (Austin, TX: RiverCrest Publishing, 2018).
11. Texe Marrs, *Protocols of the Learned Elders of Zion* (Austin, TX: RiverCrest Publishing, 2011).
12. Luther, *On the Jews and Their Lies* (Marrs).

13. See Power of Prophecy, accessed June 30, 2020, http://www.texemarrs.com/e_book_cart.html.
14. Marrs, Holy Serpent of the Jews.
15. Texe Marrs, "All Hail the Jewish Master Race!," Power of Prophecy, accessed June 30, 2020, https://www.texemarrs.com/112003/jewish_master_race.htm. For a good response, see "Challenging the Anti-Semitism of Texe Marrs," The Refiner's Fire, accessed June 30, 2020, https://www.therefinersfire.org/texe_marrs.htm.
16. Marrs, Blood Covenant With Destiny.
17. Marrs, Blood Covenant With Destiny.
18. Marrs, Blood Covenant With Destiny.
19. Marrs, Blood Covenant With Destiny.
20. Texe Marrs, *Feast of the Beast* (Austin, TX: RiverCrest Publishing, 2017); product description available at http://www.texemarrs.com/e_book_cart.html.
21. "Texe Marrs Has Gone Home to Be With the Lord," Power of Prophecy, November 25, 2019, https://web.archive.org/web/20191126053037/http://texemarrs.com/.
22. Richard D. Wiles, *Judgment Day 2000: How the Coming Worldwide Computer Crash Will Radically Change Your Life* (Shippensburg, PA: Treasure House, 1998).
23. Dexter Van Zile, "Rick Wiles Promotes Notion of 'Fake Jews' in Recent TruNews Segment," CAMERA, December 11, 2019, https://www.camera.org/article/rick-wiles-promotes-notion-of-fake-jews-in-recent-trunews-segment/; see also "Did President Trump Secretly Convert to Judaism In 2017?," TruNews, May 22, 2019, https://www.trunews.com/stream/did-president-trump-secretly-convert-to-judaism-in-2017, beginning at 1:07:40; and "TruNews Tuesday, May 15, 2018," TruNews, May 15, 2018, https://www.trunews.com/stream/trunews-tuesday-may-15-2018, beginning at 1:48:45.
24. When I cited the Anti-Defamation League's damning exposé against Wiles, he tweeted, "Whenever you see or hear the @ADL bashing Christian leaders, always remember that its Jewish Freemasonry doing the trash talking. I'm proud to be at the top of the ADL's hitlist of enemies. Why does @DrMichaelLBrown side with the Freemason ADL against me?"; TruNews (@TruNews), Twitter, December 11, 2019, 1:19 p.m., https://twitter.com/TruNews/status/1204828103576563718. I responded, "Rick -- forget the ADL. I've been documenting your antisemitic rants this whole year. Please, my brother. Humble yourself. Get right with God. Repent of your lies about Israel and the Jews. If you won't repent, then debate me. Why are you running?"; Dr. Michael L. Brown (@DrMichaelLBrown), Twitter, December 17, 2019, 7:48 p.m., https://twitter.com/DrMichaelLBrown/status/1207100201909006336.
25. For my message there, see "A Loving Challenge to My Palestinian Christian Friends," YouTube video, 29:12, posted by "ASKDrBrown," June 12, 2018, https://youtu.be/HMY1SVEpkY4; for my reflections

after the event, see Michael Brown, "What I Learned at Christ at the Checkpoint," The Stream, May 31, 2018, https://stream.org/learned-christ-checkpoint/.

26. "Rick Wiles Slanders Israel, Jews." See also "Has John Hagee Converted to Judaism?," Facebook video post, 25.:11, posted by "TruNews," May 16, 2018, https://www.facebook.com/watch/?v=2003389349695163.

27. "Ilhan Omar Controversy: Is Valid Criticism of Israel Policies Racist Hate Speech?," TruNews, March 8, 2019, https://www.trunews.com/stream/ilhan-omar-controversy-is-valid-criticism-of-israel-policies-racist-hate-speech.

28. "TruNews Wednesday, May 16, 2018," TruNews, May 16, 2018, https://www.trunews.com/stream/trunews-wednesday-may-16-2018.

29. "Jewish Racial Supremacy: Israeli Rabbi Says Jews Born to Rule Over Goy," TruNews, May 1, 2019, https://www.trunews.com/stream/jewish-racial-supremacy-israeli-rabbi-says-jews-born-to-rule-over-goy; certain brief comments were excluded. In this video, the host, Rick Wiles, plays clips with disturbing quotes from extremist rabbis and others. I do not deny the veracity of these quotes; I simply emphasize they are the opposite of the norm in terms of Israel's national ethics and morality.

30. "Jew Coup: Seditious Jews Orchestrating Trump Impeachment Lynching," TruNews, November 22, 2019, https://www.trunews.com/stream/jew-coup-seditious-jews-orchestrating-trump-impeachment-lynching. For my video response, see "Rick Wiles Meltdown," Facebook video post, 7:20, posted by "AskDrBrown," November 27, 2019, https://www.facebook.com/watch/?v=2448546375419150.

31. "Watch This Shocking Hate: Christian TV Host Rick Wiles Calls Impeachment A 'Jew-Coup,'" Yeshiva World, November 26, 2019, https://www.theyeshivaworld.com/news/featured/1804921/watch-this-shocking-hate-christian-tv-host-rick-wiles-calls-impeachment-a-jew-coup.html.

32. "Jew Coup."

33. "Have Friends of Zionism Become Foreign Agents for Israel?," TruNews, May 17, 2019, https://www.trunews.com/stream/have-friends-of-zionism-become-foreign-agents-for-israel.

34. Ray Sutton, "Does Israel Have a Future?," Covenant Renewal 2, no. 12 (December 1988): 3, as quoted in Theodore Winston Pike, Israel: Our Duty…Our Dilemma (Oregon City, OR: Big Sky Press, 1984), 280, as quoted in Brown, Our Hands Are Stained With Blood, 57.

35. Pike, Israel: Our Duty…Our Dilemma, 280, as quoted in Brown, Our Hands Are Stained With Blood, 57.

36. "Dr. Brown Agrees With Rev. Ted Pike on Homosexual Activism; Disagrees on Antisemitism," YouTube video, 57:21, posted by "ASKDrBrown," May 13, 2019, https://www.youtube.com/watch?v=Dhbwl_Fe2GM.

37. Anti-Defamation League, "E. Michael Jones," 2012, https://www.adl.org/sites/default/files/documents/assets/pdf/combating-hate/E-Michael-Jones.pdf.
38. Anti-Defamation League, "E. Michael Jones."
39. "E. Michael Jones Full Interview With Alex Jones," BitChute video, 45:59, posted by "E Michael Jones," November 30, 2019, https://www.bitchute.com/video/NCFIIdlHYQLY/.
40. E. Michael Jones, "Pornography and Political Control," The Unz Review, December 15, 2019, https://www.unz.com/ejones/pornography-and-political-control-the-hexenhammer-debate/.
41. Anti-Defamation League, "E. Michael Jones."
42. E. Michael Jones, "John and the Logos," Culture Wars, December 1, 2018, https://culturewars.com/news/john-and-the-logos.
43. Lasha Darkmoon, "On the Moral Code: An Exchange Among Lasha Darkmoon, E. Michael Jones, and Kevin MacDonald," Occidental Observer, September 7, 2012, https://www.theoccidentalobserver.net/2012/09/07/on-the-moral-code-an-exchange-among-lasha-darkmoon-e-michael-jones-and-kevin-macdonald/.
44. E. Michael Jones, Ethnos Needs Logos: Why I Spent Three Days in Guadalajara Trying to Persuade David Duke to Become a Catholic (South Bend, IN: Fidelity Press, 2015).
45. Dexter Van Zile, "E. Michael Jones's War on the Jews," *Times of Israel*, July 30, 2019, https://blogs.timesofisrael.com/e-michael-joness-war-on-the-jews/.
46. Van Zile, "E. Michael Jones's War on the Jews." See also "Israel: The Real Cause of the Synagogue Shootings," BitChute video, 58:30, posted by "yagma," December 17, 2018, https://www.bitchute.com/video/BGfLvzKPmD2V/.
47. Van Zile, "E. Michael Jones's War on the Jews."
48. Van Zile, "E. Michael Jones's War on the Jews."
49. E. Michael Jones (@EMichaelJones1), "Black people are attacking Jews in record numbers…," Twitter, December 31, 2019, 8:44 p.m., https://twitter.com/EMichaelJones1/status/1212187882942689281.
50. E. Michael Jones (@EMichaelJones1), "The Christian Science Monitor doesn't really tell us why…," Twitter, January 5, 2020, 2:31 p.m., https://twitter.com/EMichaelJones1/status/1213905856049356800. See also Harry Bruinius and Patrik Jonsson, "Why Anti-Semitism Is Surging Across the Political Spectrum," *Christian Science Monitor*, December 31, 2019, https://www.csmonitor.com/USA/Society/2019/1231/Why-anti-Semitism-is-surging-across-the-political-spectrum.
51. "The Moment Iran Attacked Ain Al-Assad Airbase—E. Michael Jones Reaction," YouTube video, 8:28, posted by "E. Michael Jones," January 8, 2020, https://www.youtube.com/watch?time_continue=389&v=JJsrfdX7O4M&feature=emb_logo.
52. Van Zile, "E. Michael Jones's War on the Jews." Jones lives in South Bend, Indiana.

53. E. Michael Jones, "Sicut Judaeis Non," Culture Wars, July 23, 2019, https://culturewars.com/videos/sicut-judaeis-non.
54. Van Zile, "E. Michael Jones's War on the Jews."

CHAPTER 5

1. "The Noahide Laws and Planned Guillotine Genocide of All Christians and Non Jews Worldwide," *TruthTalk13News* (blog), June 4, 2014, https://truthtalk13.wordpress.com/2014/06/04/the-noahide-laws-and-planned-guillotine-genocide-of-all-christians-and-non-jews-worldwide/.
2. "The Noahide Laws That Should Terrify You!," Patreon post, posted by "Project Weeping Angel," March 7, 2019, https://www.patreon.com/posts/noahide-laws-you-25196813.
3. rshalomw, "The Noahide Laws: Your Life Is in Danger!," *Aheyeh Is the Way the Truth the Life* (blog), July 1, 2013, https://rshalomw.wordpress.com/2013/07/01/the-noahide-laws-your-life-is-in-danger/.
4. Stephen Pidgeon, "The Tyranny of the Noahide (Noachide) Laws (With Video)," Cepher Publishing Group, February 22, 2019, https://www.cepher.net/blog.aspx?post=5294.
5. For example, see Beware of the Noahide Laws!, accessed June 30, 2020, http://www.bewareofthenoahidelaws.followersofyah.com/; and Vincent Bruno, *Stop Noahide Law* (blog), accessed June 30, 2020, http://stopnoahidelaw.blogspot.com/.
6. Robert Pickle, "The Goyim Evangelicals Seek to Be Raped on Yom Kippur and Palestinian Noahide Enforcement," Noahide News, September 29, 2017, https://noahidenews.com/2017/09/29/the-goyim-evangelicals-to-be-raped-on-yom-kippur-and-palestinian-noahide-enforcement/.
7. Some have pointed to Jewish discussions of when it is permitted to lie to back the claim that Jewish leaders will push Christians to accept the Noahide Laws without revealing the real intent of the laws. But this is a complete misunderstanding of the Jewish legal concept of acceptable lying under certain circumstances. See Aryeh Citron, "Telling the Truth…and When It Is Permissible to Be Less Than Honest," Chabad.org, accessed June 30, 2020, https://www.chabad.org/library/article_cdo/aid/1049008/jewish/Telling-the-Truth-and-When-It-Is-Permissible-to-Be-Less-Than-Honest.htm; and Jonathan Sacks, "When Is It Permitted to Tell a Lie?," Chabad.org, accessed June 30, 2020, https://www.chabad.org/parshah/article_cdo/aid/2759422/jewish/When-Is-It-Permitted-to-Tell-a-Lie.htm.
8. An alternative spelling is *Noachide*, reflecting the Hebrew pronunciation, with guttural *ch*.
9. Jeffrey Spitzer, "The Noahide Laws," My Jewish Learning, accessed June 30, 2020, https://www.myjewishlearning.com/article/the-noahide-laws/; "Jewish Concepts: The Seven Noachide Laws," Jewish Virtual Library, accessed June 30, 2020, https://www.jewishvirtuallibrary.org/the-seven-noachide-laws.

10. Wikipedia, s.v. "Seven Laws of Noah," last modified May 11, 2020, https://en.wikipedia.org/wiki/Seven_Laws_of_Noah.
11. "Have the Noahide Laws Been Recognized by Any Governments?," AskNoah.org, accessed June 30, 2020, https://asknoah.org/faq/have-the-noahide-laws-been-recognized-by-any-governments. See also "Proclamation 4921—April 3, 1982," https://www.govinfo.gov/content/pkg/STATUTE-96/pdf/STATUTE-96-Pg2721.pdf; and "Proclamation 5956—Education Day, USA, 1989 and 1990," The American Presidency Project, April 14, 1989, https://www.presidency.ucsb.edu/documents/proclamation-5956-education-day-usa-1989-and-1990.
12. Have the Noahide Laws Been Recognized by Any Governments?" See also "H.J.Res.104—To Designate March 26, 1991, as 'Education Day, USA,'" 102nd Congress, March 20, 1991, https://www.congress.gov/bill/102nd-congress/house-joint-resolution/104/text/enr.
13. Vincent Bruno, "President Trump Silently Affirms the Jewish Noahide Laws," *Stop Noahide Law* (blog), April 4, 2019, https://stopnoahidelaw.blogspot.com/2019/04/president-trump-silently-affirms-jewish.html.
14. Bruno, "President Trump Silently Affirms the Jewish Noahide Laws," with slight alteration to punctuation for clarity.
15. Vincent Bruno, "Vatican States Jewish Noahide Law Is Biblical, but Is It?," *Stop Noahide Law* (blog), March 22, 2019, http://stopnoahidelaw.blogspot.com/2019/03/vatican-states-jewish-noahide-law-is.html. To quote the Vatican, "Jewish tradition emphasizes the Noachide Covenant (cf. Gn 9:9–12) as containing the universal moral code which is incumbent on all humanity. This idea is reflected in Christian Scripture in the Book of Acts 15:28–29"; Commission for Religious Relations With the Jews, "The Delegation of the Holy See's Commission for Religious Relations With the Jews and the Chief Rabbinate of Israel's Delegation for Relations With the Catholic Church: Bilateral Commission Meeting," March 11–13, 2007, http://www.vatican.va/roman_curia/pontifical_councils/chrstuni/relations-jews-docs/rc_pc_chrstuni_doc_20070313_commissione-bilaterale_en.html.
16. "Common Questions and Answers," The Seven Laws of Noah, accessed June 30, 2020, https://www.thesevenlawsofnoah.com/common-questions-answers.
17. Spitzer, "The Noahide Laws."
18. Louis Jacobs, "Historic Jewish Views on Christianity," My Jewish Learning, accessed June 30, 2020, https://www.myjewishlearning.com/article/jewish-views-on-christianity/. For a much more detailed, academic treatment, see Louis Jacobs, "Attitudes Towards Christianity in the Halakhah," Books of Louis Jacobs, accessed June 30, 2020, https://louisjacobs.org/articles/attitudes-towards-christianity-in-the-halakhah/.
19. "Jewish Institute for Global Awareness (JIFGA)," City of Jersey City, accessed June 30, 2020, https://volunteer.jerseycitynj.gov/organizations/index.php?org_id=2769; see further Rodney Pelletier, "New Organization Seeks to Promote Moral Law," Church Militant, June 7,

2016, https://www.churchmilitant.com/news/article/new-organization-seeks-to-promote-moral-law.

20. David Novak, *The Image of the Non-Jew in Judaism: The Idea of Noahide Law*, 2nd ed. (Oxford, UK: The Littman Library of Jewish Civilization, 2011).
21. Wikinoah, s.v. "Christianity and Noahide Law," last modified June 26, 2011, http://www.wikinoah.org/en/index.php/Christianity_and_Noahide_Law.
22. Wikinoah, s.v. "Christianity and Noahide Law."
23. Wikinoah, s.v. "Christianity and Noahide Law."
24. Menachem Mendel Schneerson, "A Moral Code for All Mankind," AskNoah,org, 1990, https://asknoah.org/a-moral-code-to-unite-all-mankind.
25. See Michael L. Brown, *Resurrection: Investigating a Rabbi From Brooklyn, a Preacher From Galilee, and the Event That Changed the World* (Lake Mary, FL: Charisma House, 2020), 45–60.
26. Although the tweet and account are no longer available, The Seven Laws of Noah (@7LawsofNoah) wrote in September 2019, "I never implied that Jews were planning to behead Christians. You are a dumb, brainwashed idol worshipper who can't understand simple language. I was merely pointing out that you were lying when you claimed that most 'major proponents' don't believe that Christians are idolaters," Twitter, September 30, 2019, 11:26 p.m., https://twitter.com/7LawsofNoah/status/1178873793994993664.
27. Fibonacci φ (@Fibonacci222), "Dr Brown is a Zionist Jew and Sophist calling people who seek the truth about the #NoahideLaws 'Conspiracy Theorists,'" Twitter, September 30, 2019, 12:16 a.m., https://twitter.com/Fibonacci222/status/1178523950957174785.
28. "Jewish Sophist Dr. Michael L. Brown Exposed!," BitChute video, 16:26, posted by "cjbbooks," September 30, 2019, https://www.bitchute.com/video/xIZq7ccs0TJk/.
29. Steven Leonard Jacobs, "Jacobs: The Outrageous Claim of Christopher Jon Bjerkness: The Jewish Genocide of Armenian Christians," *Armenian Weekly*, January 12, 2010, https://armenianweekly.com/2010/01/12/jacobs-the-outrageous-claim-of-christopher-jon-bjerkness-the-jewish-genocide-of-armenian-christians/.
30. "The 7 Noahide Laws: Universal Morality," The Seven Laws of Noah, accessed June 30, 2020, https://www.thesevenlawsofnoah.com/.
31. Moshe Weiner, *The Divine Code: The Guide to Observing the Noahide Code, Revealed From Mount Sinai in the Torah of Moses*, 3rd ed. (n.p.: Ask Noah International, 2018), Kindle location 5174–75.
32. Jacobs, "Attitudes Towards Christianity in the Halakhah."
33. Weiner, *The Divine Code*, Kindle location 5767–69.
34. "The Noahide Laws—Introduction With Dr. Stephen Pidgeon," YouTube video, 6:00, posted by "Cepher Publishing Group," June 17, 2019, https://www.youtube.com/watch?v=orw6RkCrOwA&t=60s.

35. Private communication on Facebook Messenger with Rabbi Eli Cohen, May 19, 2019. Used with permission.
36. See Michael L. Brown and Craig S. Keener, *Not Afraid of the Antichrist: Why We Don't Believe in the Pre-Trib Rapture* (Grand Rapids, MI: Chosen Books, 2019).
37. See Tzippe Barrow, "Man Convicted of Bombing Israeli Messianic Pastor's Home Demands Release From Prison," CBN News, April 24, 2018, https://www1.cbn.com/cbnnews/israel/2018/april/man-convicted-of-bombing-israeli-messianic-pastors-home-demands-release-from-prison.
38. Adam Eliyahu Berkowitz, "Sanhedrin Calls on President Trump to Uphold Seven Noahide Laws," Breaking Israel News, January 26, 2017, https://www.breakingisraelnews.com/82693/sanhedrin-blesses-trump-calls-president-uphold-seven-noahide-laws/.
39. Berkowitz, "Sanhedrin Calls on President Trump to Uphold Seven Noahide Laws."
40. Arthur Goldberg, "Jewish, Christian, and Muslim Theologians Find Common Moral Ground," Jewish Link, October 11, 2018, https://www.jewishlinknj.com/features/27199-jewish-christian-and-muslim-theologians-find-common-moral-ground. See further Shimon Dovid Cowen, *The Theory and Practice of Universal Ethics: The Noahide Laws* (East St. Kilda, Australia: Institute for Judaism and Civilization, 2014).
41. See Brown, *Resurrection*.
42. Philip Wexler, with Eli Rubin and Michael Wexler, *Social Vision: The Lubavitcher Rebbe's Transformative Paradigm for the World* (New York: Crossroad Publishing Company, 2019), 153–54.
43. Chaim Miller, *Turning Judaism Outwards: A Biography of the Rebbe Menachem Mendel Schneerson* (Brooklyn, NY: Kol Menachem, 2014), 335, with reference to Likutei Sichot, 25:192, n. 56, providing halakhic sources that Christianity is not idolatry.
44. "The Noahide Dinim Sub-Laws," Noahide.org, accessed March 20, 2020, http://noahide.org/the-noahide-dinim-sub-laws/.
45. See especially Michael L. Brown, *Answering Jewish Objections to Jesus, Volume 2: Theological Objections* (Grand Rapids, MI: Baker Books, 2000), 1–51. Of course, I do not believe that we should bow down to statues.
46. As quoted on the AskNoah.org home page, accessed June 30, 2020, https://asknoah.org/.
47. For the record, according to the conspiracy theorists, I'm not the only one who is working for Chabad. According to a comment made by "7Grainsofsalt" on our YouTube channel, "Trump is not an innocent man. lol. He is a puppet of the chabad. This is the 'Order out of chaos'. Wake up to the times we are living in. NWO [New world order] & the new world religion is almost upon us." This comment was made on the video "My Response to the Potential Trump Impeachment," YouTube video, 57:00, posted by "ASKDrBrown," September 30, 2019, https://www.youtube.com/watch?v=FjBQy405je8&lc=z22duzmb5v20vde3zacdp432rx1kwfbuduxn2k51ahpw03c010c

48. Again, see Brown, *Resurrection.*
49. "Noahide Laws Debate | Dr. Michael Brown vs. Adam Green," YouTube video, 1:45:03, posted by "Know More News," October 23, 2019, https://www.youtube.com/watch?v=bHSy1-oaOoE.
50. Comments by Sooth ing and Chris Farley on "Noahide Laws Debate."

CHAPTER 6

1. Michael L. Brown, Answering Jewish Objections to Jesus, Volume 5: Traditional Jewish Objections (San Francisco: Purple Pomegranate Press, 2010).
2. These comments have been removed, but for the original videos, see "The Truth About the Talmud," YouTube video, 22:31, posted by "ASKDrBrown," April 26, 2019, https://www.youtube.com/watch?v=gZ454HzqTlM; "Is the Talmud Anti-Christian?," YouTube video, 2:57, posted by "ASKDrBrown," February 12, 2018, https://www.youtube.com/watch?v=gtzyw4FnzZE; and "Jesus in the Talmud," YouTube video, 3:10, posted by "ASKDrBrown," July 7, 2019, https://www.youtube.com/watch?v=M2jEtSWfekw.
3. A translation of *Toledot Yeshu* can be found at Jewish and Christian Literature, accessed June 30, 2020, http://jewishchristianlit.com//Topics/JewishJesus/toledoth.html; a similar, later work, *Maaseh Yeshu,* can be found at Wikisource, s.v. "Translation: Story of Jesus," last modified March 31, 2018, https://en.wikisource.org/wiki/Translation:Story_of_Jesus.
4. Once again, I refer to you my book *Our Hands Are Stained With Blood,* in the updated, expanded 2019 edition.
5. For a detailed study on the names Yeshu and Yeshua, see Kai KjaerHansen, "An Introduction to the Names Yehoshua/Joshua, Yeshua, Jesus, and Yeshu," Jews for Jesus, March 23, 1992, https://jewsforjesus.org/answers/an-introduction-to-the-names-yehoshua-joshua-yeshua-jesus-and-yeshu/.
6. Gil Student, "The Jesus Narrative in the Talmud," The Real Truth About the Talmud, accessed June 30, 2020, http://talmud.faithweb.com/articles/jesusnarr.html.
7. Gil Student, "Jesus in the Talmud," The Real Truth About the Talmud, accessed June 30, 2020, http://talmud.faithweb.com/articles/jesus.html.
8. Louis Ginzberg, "Some Observations on the Attitude of the Synagogue Towards the Apocalyptic-Eschatological Writings," *Journal of Biblical Literature* 41 (1922), 122.
9. John P. Meier, *A Marginal Jew: Rethinking the Historical Jesus, Volume 1: The Roots of the Problem and the Person* (New York: Doubleday, 1991), 95.
10. Student, "The Jesus Narrative in the Talmud." For additional references, see below.
11. See "686—Debunking the Missionaries #26: The Historical Jesus Part #3 Jesus in the Talmud," YouTube video, 1:05:35, posted by "Tenak Talk," December 1, 2019, https://www.youtube.com/watch?v=E4CgP4Km-Xw.

Rabbi Shulman and I are theological opponents (I would be considered a missionary and he a counter-missionary), yet we are in regular, private contact and I believe it has been helpful in our understanding of each other's positions.

12. When I polled Christians on Twitter about Muhammed, the overwhelming majority said that he was a false prophet who was now in hell. See Michael L. Brown (@DrMichaelLBrown), "As a Christian, if you believe Muhammad is a false prophet, does that mean he is in hell?," Twitter, April 25, 2019, https://twitter.com/DrMichaelLBrown/status/1121489807354531840.
13. Jacob Neusner, *The Mishnah: A New Translation* (New Haven, CT: Yale University Press, 1988), 179.
14. Shabbat 2a–2b, Sefaria, accessed June 30, 2020, https://www.sefaria.org/Shabbat.2a.7?lang=bi&with=Commentary&lang2=en.
15. Islamic websites like Radio Islam have specialized in posting material like this. See the search results on Google for "Talmud site:islam-radio.net," accessed June 30, 2020, https://www.google.com/search?q=talmud&domains=islam-radio.net&sitesearch=islam-radio.net.
16. Jim Townsend, "What Is Judeo-Christianity? Do Christians Really Believe Christ Is in Hell Covered in [Expletive] as the Talmud Claims?," Gentile Defense League, March 3, 2011, https://web.archive.org/web/20110316215129/gentiledefenseleague.org/2011/03/03/what-is-judeochristianity-do-christians-really-believe-christ-is-in-hell-covered-in-shit-as-the-talmud-claims.aspx; Brother Nathanael Kapner, "Satanic Verses of the Jewish Talmud," Real Jew News, accessed June 30, 2020, http://www.realzionistnews.com/?p=156. The 1892 volume compiled by I. B. Pranaitis, *The Talmud Unmasked: The Secret Rabbinical Teachings Concerning Christians* is often cited in support of these views. Spellings have been edited to conform to
17. Freidy Brackman, "Exemptions of Women in Jewish Law," Chabad.org, accessed June 30, 2020, https://www.chabad.org/multimedia/video_cdo/aid/1416866/jewish/Exemptions-of-Women-in-Jewish-Law.htm.
18. Gil Student, "The Talmud Does Not Permit Sex With a Three Year Old," The Real Truth About the Talmud, accessed June 30, 2020, http://www.angelfire.com/mt/talmud/three.html.
19. An expanded translation of the Talmudic text reads, "A girl who is **three years and one day old** whose father arranged her betrothal **is betrothed with intercourse,** as the legal status of intercourse with her is that of full-fledged intercourse." See Sanhedrin 55b, Sefaria, accessed June 30, 2020, https://www.sefaria.org/Sanhedrin.55b.4?lang=bi&with=all&lang2=en.
20. Kiddushin 41a, Sefaria, accessed June 30, 2020, https://www.sefaria.org/Kiddushin.41a.8?lang=bi&with=all&lang2=en.
21. For further discussion, see the videos cited in note 27.
22. Gil Student, "Killing Gentiles Is Forbidden," The Real Truth About the Talmud, accessed June 30, 2020, http://www.angelfire.com/mt/talmud/

kill.html. See also Gil Student, "Theft From Gentiles," The Real Truth About the Talmud, accessed June 30, 2020, http://www.angelfire.com/mt/talmud/theft.html.

23. Student, "Killing Gentiles Is Forbidden."
24. Maurice M. Mizrahi, "Response to Antisemitic Distortions of the Talmud," June 15, 2016, https://s3.amazonaws.com/images.shulcloud.com/618/uploads/PDFs/Divrei_Torah/160615-Response%20to%20anti-semitic%20distortions%20of%20the%20Talmud.pdf.
25. Mizrahi, "Response to Antisemitic Distortions of the Talmud."
26. Gil Student, "Talmud: Statement of Purpose," The Real Truth About the Talmud, accessed June 30, 2020, http://talmud.faithweb.com/.
27. For their discussion of Talmudic and Jewish texts, see "UnSpun 147—Lloyd De Jongh: 'Judaism Pt. 1: The Laws of Noah,'" YouTube video, 1:37:49, posted by "LogosMedia," March 26, 2019, https://www.youtube.com/watch?v=vjZjdmZyzDM&list=PLa3bLMRvk6HobnJlDDzOLozFDkPZaJb1G; for their discussion of Islamic texts, see "UnSpun 137—Lloyd De Jongh: 'Introduction to Islam: Quran, Sunnah, and Sharia, Part 1,'" YouTube video, 1:32:58, posted by "LogosMedia," January 15, 2019, https://www.youtube.com/watch?v=Fmfvu3iJNHU&list=PLa3bLMRvk6Hrmis8oBAletXFeLB8TlNei.
28. See Brown, *Our Hands Are Stained With Blood*, 45–53.
29. "Kiryas Tosh, Canada—'The Rebbe of All Rebbes' VIN News Interview: Insights From the Secretary of the Tosher Rebbe Zt'l," Vos Iz Neias?, August 17, 2015, https://vosizneias.com/2015/08/17/kiryas-tosh-canada-the-rebbe-of-all-rebbes-insights-from-the-secretary-of-the-tosher-rebbe-ztl/.
30. Try reading a classic Jewish work from the twentieth century, like Abraham Joshua Heschel's *The Sabbath* (New York: Farrar Straus Giroux, 2005), and then see if there might be some dimensions to Judaism you're missing. For Jewish perspectives on the Talmud, see Abraham Cohen, *Everyman's Talmud: The Major Teachings of the Rabbinic Sages* (New York: Random House, 1995); Rabbi Adin Steinsaltz, *The Essential Talmud: An Introduction* (Jerusalem: Koren Publishers, 2010); and Rabbi Dov Peretz Elkins, *The Wisdom of Judaism: An Introduction to the Values of the Talmud* (Woodstock, VT: Jewish Lights Publishing, 2007). For further background, see *Introduction to the Talmud* (New York: Artscroll Mesorah Publications, 1995); and Rabbi Adin Steinsaltz, *Reference Guide to the Talmud* (Jerusalem: Koren Publishers, 2014).
31. "Text of the Mourner's Kaddish," My Jewish Learning, accessed June 30, 2020, https://www.myjewishlearning.com/article/text-of-the-mourners-kaddish/.

CHAPTER 7

1. See Brown, Our Hands Are Stained With Blood, 207–17.

2. "The Myth of a Jewish Conspiracy: Holocaust and Human Behavior," Facing History and Ourselves, accessed June 30, 2020, https://www.facinghistory.org/holocaust-and-human-behavior/chapter-4/myth-jewish-conspiracy, quoting Erich Ludendorff, *Kreigsführung und Politik* (Berlin: Berlag von G. C. Mittler & Cohn, 1922), 51, https://archive.org/details/kreigsfhrungun00lude/page/n5/mode/2up.
3. "The Myth of a Jewish Conspiracy."
4. Michael Fox, "'The Elders of Zion': 113 Years of a Lie That Refuses to Die," Haaretz, September 8, 2016, originally published in 2008, https://www.haaretz.com/jewish/.premium-the-elders-of-zion-113-years-of-a-lie-that-refuses-to-die-1.5439695. Used with permission.
5. Fox, "'The Elders of Zion.'"
6. See Esther Webman, ed., *The Global Impact of the Protocols of the Elders of Zion: A Century-Old Myth* (New York: Routledge, 2011).
7. Fox, "'The Elders of Zion.'"
8. For the text of Churchill's article, see Wikisource, s.v., "Zionism versus Bolshevism," last modified April 10, 2017, https://en.wikisource.org/wiki/Zionism_versus_Bolshevism.
9. Fox, "'The Elders of Zion.'"
10. "Will Eisner's *The Plot*," Anti-Defamation League, accessed June 30, 2020, https://www.adl.org/sites/default/files/documents/assets/pdf/education-outreach/Plot-Exhibit-Booklet-Entire-Single-The.pdf. See further "Henry Ford and Anti-Semitism: A Complex Story," The Henry Ford, accessed June 30, 2020, https://www.thehenryford.org/collections-and-research/digital-resources/popular-topics/henry-ford-and-anti-semitism-a-complex-story.
11. "Will Eisner's *The Plot*."
12. "The Myth of a Jewish Conspiracy."
13. "Will Eisner's *The Plot*."
14. *United States of America v. John Timothy Earnest.*
15. I am using this quote with the rabbi's full permission for this book but without identifying him, as per our agreement.
16. For a fair discussion by an Orthodox rabbi, see Moshe Shulman, "The Soul: Is There a Difference Between a Gentile and a Jewish Soul?," Judaism's Answer, 2012, https://judaismsanswer.com/The%20Soul.htm. For an antisemitic perspective, here from the Nation of Islam, see "Racist Rabbis: A Long Legacy of Jewish Race-Haters," Nation of Islam Research Group, May 23, 2018, https://noirg.org/articles/rabbis-who-supported-black-slavery/.
17. David Duke, *Jewish Supremacism: My Awakening on the Jewish Question* (Mandeville, LA: Free Speech Press, 2007). The used copy of this book that I ordered was, ironically enough, signed by Duke himself.
18. See Yitzchak Shpira and Yosef Elitzur, trans., *Torat HaMelech*, November 28, 2010, http://torathamelech.blogspot.com/.
19. "Torat Hamelech," ReformJudaism.org, May 14, 2012, https://reformjudaism.org/blog/2012/05/14/torat-hamelech.

20. "Torat Hamelech."
21. Elad Benari, "Rabbi Opposes Torat Hamelech," Arutz Sheva, June 30, 2011, http://www.israelnationalnews.com/News/News.aspx/145306.
22. Benari, "Rabbi Opposes Torat Hamelech."
23. Yonah Jeremy Bob, "High Court: No Basis to Indict Torat Hamelech Authors for Incitement," *Jerusalem Post*, December 9, 2015, https://www.jpost.com/Israel-News/High-Court-No-basis-to-indict-Torat-Hamelech-authors-for-incitement-436795.
24. JTA, "'Torat Hamelech' Author Indicted for Incitement," Arutz Sheva, June 13, 2017, http://www.israelnationalnews.com/News/News.aspx/230975. See also Raanan Ben-Zur, "Extremist Rabbi Charged With Incitement to Violence," Ynet News, June 13, 2017, https://www.ynetnews.com/articles/0,7340,L-4975221,00.html.
25. "TruNews' Rick Wiles: A Christian Response to Michael Brown's Neo-Nazi Accusations," TruNews, December 11, 2019, https://www.trunews.com/stream/trunews-rick-wiles-a-christian-response-to-michael-browns-neo-nazi-accusations.
26. In my *Line of Fire* interview with Dr. Jones, he agreed that religious Jews who followed the Torah had not rejected biblical morality in the way that secular Jews had, which, as I pointed out, undercut his argument about "the Jews" rejecting Logos, given that Orthodox Jews make up a maximum of 20 percent of world Jewry.
27. Kevin Toolis, "The Most Dangerous Man in the World," *The Guardian*, November 5, 1999, https://www.theguardian.com/lifeandstyle/1999/nov/06/weekend.kevintoolis.
28. Jennie Cohen, "Study Suggests Adolf Hitler Had Jewish and African Ancestors," History.com, last updated August 29, 2018, https://www.history.com/news/study-suggests-adolf-hitler-had-jewish-and-african-ancestors.
29. Jean-Louis Panné, Andrzej Paczkowski, Karel Bartosek et al., *The Black Book of Communism* (Cambridge, MA: Harvard University Press, 1999).
30. Daniel Greenfield, "George Soros Isn't Jewish," Frontpage Mag. December 24, 2019, https://www.frontpagemag.com/point/2019/12/george-soros-isnt-jewish-daniel-greenfield/; see also Daniel Greenfield, "Soros' War Against the Jews," Frontpage Mag, December 31, 2019, https://www.frontpagemag.com/fpm/2019/12/soros-war-against-jews-daniel-greenfield/.
31. Anne B. Gardiner, "The Jewish Origins of Islam," Culture Wars, February 1, 2018, https://culturewars.com/news/jewish-origins-of-islam. The author of the article writes, "In his groundbreaking book, *Le messie et son prophète: Aux origines de l'Islam*, Edouard-Marie Gallez lifts the veil and lets us see the historical roots of Islam. He shows it originating in a vast movement of messianic Jews called 'Ebionites' or 'Nazareens.' These non-rabbinical Jews accepted Jesus as the messiah, but not as the divine Logos." Somehow this "fact" evaded all scholars of Islam until now. Blame those Jews again!

32. Anti-Defamation League, "E. Michael Jones."
33. "Aryan Insights: E Michael Jones—Jewish Agents of Chaos," *Aryan Insights* (podcast), July 18, 2016, https://www.radioalbion.com/2016/07/aryan-insights-e-michael-jones-jewish.html.
34. "Aryan Insights: E Michael Jones—Jewish Agents of Chaos."
35. "Aryan Insights: E Michael Jones—Jewish Agents of Chaos."
36. "The Three Oaths: Claims and Facts," Torah Jews, accessed June 30, 2020, https://www.truetorahjews.org/3oathsclaimsandfacts.
37. Ketubot 111a, Sefaria, accessed June 30, 2020, https://www.sefaria.org/Ketubot.111a.4?lang=bi&with=all&lang2=en.
38. The Daf Shevui commentary notes, "While the meaning of this term is not entirely clear, it is usually understood to mean that Jews should not move to Israel en masse. This midrash was often the source of modern religious anti-Zionist rhetoric. The Zionist movement broke with tradition by moving up to Israel 'as a wall.' . . . The Zionist counterclaim was that in the Holocaust the non-Jews broke their oath, and therefore the Jews were released from their oaths. This was offered as the religious justification of their participation in the Zionist movement, i.e. the breaking of one of the oaths"; Daf Shevui to Ketubot 11a:2, Sefaria, accessed June 30, 2020, https://www.sefaria.org/Ketubot.111a.4?lang=bi&with=Daf%20Shevui&lang2=bi.
39. Deanne Loper, *Kabbalah Secrets Christians Need to Know: An In Depth Study of the Kosher Pig and the Gods of Jewish Mysticism* (n.p.: Amazon Services, 2019), 130.
40. Loper, *Kabbalah Secrets Christians Need to Know*, 130, citing Michael Higger, *The Jewish Utopia* (Baltimore: Lord Baltimore Press, 1932), 41.
41. Higger, *The Jewish Utopia*, 20.
42. Higger, *The Jewish Utopia*, 22.
43. Higger, *The Jewish Utopia*, 23.
44. Higger, *The Jewish Utopia*, 29.
45. Higger, *The Jewish Utopia*, 42.
46. Higger, *The Jewish Utopia*, 43.
47. Higger, *The Jewish Utopia*, 71.
48. Higger, *The Jewish Utopia*, 75.
49. Higger, *The Jewish Utopia*, 103.
50. Higger, *The Jewish Utopia*, 117.
51. See, for example, Michael Bachner, "Far-Right Rabbi Recorded Urging 'Strong Retaliatory Act' After Terror Attack," *Times of Israel*, January 24, 2018, https://www.timesofisrael.com/far-right-rabbi-recorded-urging-strong-retaliatory-acts-after-terror-attack/.
52. Yitzchak Ginsburgh, *Kabbalah and Meditation for the Nations* (n.p.: Gal Einai Institute, 2007), 42. In his view, there are threefold identities in the Godhead but Gentiles confuse these into three distinct persons.
53. Ginsburgh, *Kabbalah and Meditation for the Nations*, 179. These are the closing words of his book, hence representing the summary of his thought.

54. R. William Beaulieu, "A Review of the Book: The Jewish Utopia by Rabbi Michael Higger," Omega Countdown Ministries, accessed June 30, 2020, http://omega77.tripod.com/bookreviewhigger.htm.
55. John Sides, "Why Most American Jews Vote for Democrats, Explained," *Washington Post*, March 24, 2015, https://www.washingtonpost.com/news/monkey-cage/wp/2015/03/24/why-most-american-jews-vote-for-democrats-explained/. See also Mitchell Rocklin, "Are American Jews Shifting Their Political Affiliation?," Mosaic, January 18, 2017, https://mosaicmagazine.com/observation/politics-current-affairs/2017/01/are-american-jews-shifting-their-political-affiliation/.

CHAPTER 8

1. David Pawson, *Defending Christian Zionism* (Ashford, UK: Anchor Recordings, 2013), 7.
2. On the term Palestinians, see Robert Spencer, The Palestinian Delusion: The Catastrophic History of the Middle East Peace Process (Brentwood, TN: Bombardier Books, 2019).
3. See Brown and Keener, Not Afraid of the Antichrist.
4. Posted in a comment on the "ASKDrBrown" YouTube channel that has since been removed.
5. For further details, see Brown, Our Hands Are Stained With Blood, 35–45. For the positive contribution of John Nelson Darby, the founder of dispensationalism, see Paul Wilkinson, For Zion's Sake: Christian Zionism and the Role of John Nelson Darby (London, UK: Paternoster, 2008).
6. Dennis M. Swanson, "Charles H. Spurgeon and the Nation of Israel: A Non-Dispensational Perspective on a Literal National Restoration," The Spurgeon Archive, 2000, http://archive.spurgeon.org/misc/eschat2.php. See also C. H. Spurgeon, "The Church of Christ," sermon, New Park Street Chapel, Southwark, June 3, 1855, https://archive.spurgeon.org/sermons/0028.php.
7. Although some of these comments have been removed from our YouTube channel because of content (some of which has not been reproduced here because of vulgarity or other issues), we do have screen shots of each and every comment cited in this book, including, in most cases, the video to which the comments were posted.
8. This comment was posted to my mini-debate with Sizer, originally carried on Moody Radio but posted on my YouTube channel at "How Christian Is Christian Zionism? (Brown and Sizer Debate)," YouTube video, 54:02, posted by "ASKDrBrown," November 9, 2013, https://www.youtube.com/watch?v=22jgGE4hELI. The comment was eventually removed, though I still have the screenshot.
9. "Momentum Group Pulls Invite to 'Zionists Behind 9/11' Vicar for Gaza Fundraiser," Jewish News, September 19, 2019, https://jewishnews.timesofisrael.com/momentum-group-pulls-invite-to-jews-behind-9-11-vicar-for-gaza-fundraiser/.

10. Stephen R. Sizer, "The Promised Land: A Critical Investigation of Evangelical Christian Zionism in Britain and the United States of America Since 1800" (PhD thesis, Middlesex University and Oak Hill Theological College, 2002), https://eprints.mdx.ac.uk/6403/1/Sizer-promised_land.phd.pdf.
11. Stephen Sizer, *Christian Zionism: Road-Map to Armageddon?* (Downers Grove, IL: IVP Academic, 2006); and Stephen Sizer, *Zion's Christian Soldiers? The Bible, Israel, and the Church* (Nottingham, UK: InterVarsity Press, 2007). For a useful summary of Christian responses to Sizer's books, see Wikipedia, s.v. "Stephen Sizer," last modified May 18, 2020, https://en.wikipedia.org/wiki/Stephen_Sizer.
12. Steven Sizer, "What Is the Relationship Between Israel and the Church? Seven Biblical Answers," 5th ed., May 2019, https://stephensizer.com/wp-content/uploads/2019/04/7-Biblical-Answers-Israel-and-the-Church-2019.pdf.
13. David Pawson's book *Defending Christian Zionism* does a great job of setting the record straight while also pointing out some of the negative results of dispensational thinking, which include 1) seeking to "comfort" Jewish people rather than convert them ("convert" in the sense of bringing them to saving faith in their own Messiah, rather than incorporating them into Gentile Christianity); 2) supporting Israel right or wrong, or even to think Israel can do no wrong; 3) seeing the Middle East conflict solely in religious terms; and 4) ignoring believers in the region, both Israeli and Arab, or even being completely unaware of their existence. See Pawson, *Defending Christian Zionism*, 27–29. For his list of the positive contributions of dispensationalism, see Pawson, *Defending Christian Zionism*, 23.
14. Gev, "British Vicar Calls Israeli Messianic Jews an Abomination," Rosh Pina Project, October 14, 2011, https://web.archive.org/web/20111114154826/http://roshpinaproject.com/2011/10/14/british-vicar-calls-israeli-messianic-jews-an-abomination/.
15. "Momentum Group Pulls Invite to 'Zionists Behind 9/11' Vicar for Gaza Fundraiser." See also Rosie Gray, "Antiwar Activists, 9/11 Truthers Gather in Tehran for Anti-Zionist Conference," BuzzFeed News, October 1, 2014, https://www.buzzfeednews.com/article/rosiegray/antiwar-activists-911-truthers-gather-in-tehran-for-anti-zio.
16. Cited in Wikipedia, s.v. "Stephen Sizer"; Stephen Sizer, "A Critique of Christian Zionism: Tony Higton," March 11, 2009, https://www.stephensizer.com/2009/03/a-critique-of-christian-zionism-tony-higton/.
17. Scott Volk with Robert J. Gladstone, *Jesus Was Not a Christian* (n.p.: Burning Ones Publishing, 2019).
18. In the words of Pawson, "I believe we shall find, as in so many cases, that [Sizer] is right in what he affirms but wrong in what he denies, sound in many of his positive statements, but unsound in his negative inferences. His scriptural data is accurate, but the conclusions he draws not necessarily so"; Pawson, *Defending Christian Zionism*, 59.

19. Melanie Phillips, "Beware the New Axis of Evangelicals and Islamists," *The Spectator*, March 4, 2009, https://web.archive.org/web/20090309210305/http://www.spectator.co.uk/the-magazine/features/3409686/beware-the-new-axis-of-evangelicals-and-islamists.thtml.
20. "'Marching to Zion' Official Full Film—Youtube," YouTube video, 1:48:27, posted by "framingtheworld," May 14, 2015, https://www.youtube.com/watch?v=typ2pl2L47k; for Anderson's duplicity in recruiting rabbis for his film, see Stephen Lemons, "Steven Anderson, Wacko Tempe Pastor, Now in Anti-Semitism Business," *Phoenix New Times*, December 1, 2014, https://www.phoenixnewtimes.com/news/steven-anderson-wacko-tempe-pastor-now-in-anti-semitism-business-6651793. A less dangerous (but still very misleading) documentary is *With God On Our Side*, which I characterized as an "antisemitic hit piece"; see "Dr. Brown Critiques the 'With God On Our Side,' Anti-Christian Zionist Video (With Input From Israel)," *The Line of Fire* (podcast), July 14, 2011, https://thelineoffire.org/2011/07/14/dr-brown-critiques-the-with-god-on-our-side-anti-christian-zionist-video-with-input-from-israel/.
21. "ADL Deeply Troubled at Upcoming Documentary Film Denigrating Jews and Judaism," Anti-Defamation League, November 24, 2014, https://www.adl.org/news/press-releases/adl-deeply-troubled-at-upcoming-documentary-film-denigrating-jews-and-judaism.
22. Stephen Lemons, "Tempe Pastor Hails Orlando Massacre for Leaving '50 Less Pedophiles in This World': Video," *Phoenix New Times*, June 13, 2016, https://www.phoenixnewtimes.com/news/tempe-pastor-hails-orlando-massacre-for-leaving-50-less-pedophiles-in-this-world-video-8372346.
23. "Pastor Steven L Anderson Pisseth Against the Wall," YouTube video, 4:36, posted by "PastorMajor," April 20, 2009, https://www.youtube.com/watch?v=qo3o4nfiG7A.
24. Again, see Brown, *Our Hands Are Stained With Blood*.
25. "Marching to Zion [New 2016 Edition DVD]," Framing the World, archived June 29, 2016, https://web.archive.org/web/20160629061410/https://store.framingtheworld.com/products/m2zdvd.
26. "'Marching to Zion' Official Full Film—Youtube."
27. Anderson specifically claims that Jews do not believe in the circumcision of adult male converts, replacing it instead with the drawing of blood by a pinprick. Once again, he has used the views of liberal rabbis rather than the views of Orthodox rabbis, who require circumcision. As explained on a secular website in 2011, "If you're a man converting to Judaism and you're not circumcised, most rabbis—and probably all Conservative and Orthodox rabbis—would require circumcision;" Answer Fella, "If You Convert to Judaism as an Adult, Do You Have to Be Circumcised?," *Esquire*, April 18, 2011, https://www.esquire.com/news-politics/q-and-a/a5753/adult-circumcision-0509/. Anderson does not tell his viewers

the truth, either because he doesn't know it or because the truth would damage his antisemitic propaganda campaign.

28. "'Marching to Zion' Official Full Film—Youtube."
29. See Brown, *Answering Jewish Objections to Jesus, Volume 5*; more forcefully, see Eitan Bar and Golan Brosh, *Rabbinic Judaism Debunked: Debunking the Myth of Rabbinic Oral Law* (n.p.: One for Israel Ministry, 2019).
30. "'Marching to Zion' Official Full Film—Youtube." See also Peter Schäfer, *Jesus in the Talmud* (Princeton, NJ: Princeton University Press, 2009).
31. See Brown, *Answering Jewish Objections to Jesus, Volume 1: General and Historical Objections* (Grand Rapids, MI: Baker, 2000), 134–35, with references. For a specific, modern example, see George W. Cornell, "Founder's Slurs on Jews Renounced by Lutherans: History: The Denomination Is Officially Repudiating Martin Luther's Virulent Anti-Semitic Attacks. The Action Will Deplore the Impact His Tirades May Have Had on Nazism," *Los Angeles Times*, October 2, 1993, https://www.latimes.com/archives/la-xpm-1993-10-02-me-41383-story.html.
32. "'Marching to Zion' Official Full Film—Youtube."
33. "'Marching to Zion' Official Full Film—Youtube."
34. "'Marching to Zion' Official Full Film—Youtube."
35. Michael J. Vlach, *Has the Church Replaced Israel?* (Nashville: B&H Publishing, 2010), 42.
36. Vlach, *Has the Church Replaced Israel?*, 43, quoting Tertullian, *On Modesty*, 8, http://www.newadvent.org/fathers/0407.htm.
37. Origen, *The Song of Songs: Commentary and Homilies*, Ancient Christian Writers Series, vol. 26 (New York: The Newman Press, 1957), 103.
38. Vlach, *Has the Church Replaced Israel?*, 43, quoting Origen, *The Songs of Songs*, 44.
39. Denis Fahey, *The Kingship of Christ and the Conversion of the Jewish Nation* (Fitzwilliam, NH: Loreto Publications, 2018), 98.
40. Vlach, *Has the Church Replaced Israel?*, 46–47, quoting Augustine, *Sermons on New Testament Lessons*, Sermon 72.
41. "'Marching to Zion' Official Full Film—Youtube."
42. "'Marching to Zion' Official Full Film—Youtube."
43. *The Old Scofield Study Bible, KJV, Classic Edition*, Amazon, accessed June 30, 2020, https://www.amazon.com/Old-Scofield%C2%AE-Study-Bible-Classic/dp/0195274601.
44. Zechariah 2:8, NET, Bn.
45. See Michael L. Brown, "The Seed as Christ in Galatians 3:16," forthcoming in Stanley Porter and Alan Kurschman, eds., *The Future Restoration of Israel* (Eugene, OR: Wipf & Stock).
46. For a detailed argument that God still blesses those who bless Israel and curses those who curse Israel, see William R. Koenig, *Eye to Eye: Facing the Consequences of Dividing Israel*, rev. ed. (McLean, VA: Christian Publications, 2017).
47. "'Marching to Zion' Official Full Film—Youtube."

48. Numbers 24:1, 9.
49. "'Marching to Zion' Official Full Film—Youtube."
50. "'Marching to Zion' Official Full Film—Youtube."
51. "'Marching to Zion' Official Full Film—Youtube."
52. See further "How the Anti-Semitic Conspiracy Theories About the Rothschilds Began," *Retropod* (podcast), *Washington Post*, August 12, 2019, https://www.washingtonpost.com/podcasts/retropod/how-the-antisemitic-conspiracy-theories-about-the-rothschilds-began-1/; for an academic study, see R. W. Davis, "Disraeli, the Rothschilds, and Anti-Semitism." *Jewish History* 10, no. 2 (Fall 1996), 9–19.
53. "'Marching to Zion' Official Full Film—Youtube."
54. Azzam Pasha, Secretary-General of the Arab League, in Mustafa Amin, "A War of Extermination," *Akhbar al-Yom*, October 11, 1947, as quoted in David Barnett and Efraim Karsh, "Azzam's Genocidal Threat," *Middle East Quarterly* 18, no. 4 (Fall 2011): 85–88, https://www.meforum.org/3082/azzam-genocide-threat.
55. As quoted in Efraim Karsh, *Palestine Betrayed* (New Haven, CT: Yale University Press, 2010), Introduction.
56. As quoted in Efraim Karsh, *Palestine Betrayed*, chapter 5.
57. Daniel Pipes, "The Original Sin," *National Review*, April 29, 2010, https://www.nationalreview.com/magazine/2010/05/17/original-sin/.
58. Pipes, "The Original Sin."
59. For the record, under the Sinai covenant, the requirement for returning to the land was repentance leading to obedience to the Torah, not specifically belief in Jesus. I certainly believe that true repentance for a Jewish person today includes belief in Jesus, but I am simply pointing out another error of statement in the video.
60. "'Marching to Zion' Official Full Film—Youtube."
61. "'Marching to Zion' Official Full Film—Youtube."
62. Anderson's comment on 2 John 9–11 is "If we bless those who deny the Son of God, we are a partaker of their evil deeds."
63. Samuel A. Meier, "Rephan (Deity)," ed. David Noel Freedman, *The Anchor Yale Bible Dictionary* (New York: Doubleday, 1992), 677.
64. See "Testing the Star of David—119 Ministries," YouTube video, 15:14, posted by "119 Ministries," July 19, 2016, https://www.youtube.com/watch?v=-d7q2hzkG3s.
65. Ronen Shnidman, "The Star of David: More Than Just a Symbol of the Jewish People or Nazi Persecution," *Haaretz*, May 1, 2019, https://www.haaretz.com/jewish/holocaust-remembrance-day/the-star-of-david-isn-t-just-jewish-1.5323219.
66. "What Is the Star of David?," My Jewish Learning, accessed June 30, 2020, https://www.myjewishlearning.com/article/star-of-david-hot-topic/.
67. For positive explanations based on Jewish mysticism, see Naftali Silberberg, "Star of David: The Mystical Significance," Chabad.org, accessed June 30, 2020, https://www.chabad.org/library/article_cdo/

aid/788679/jewish/Star-of-David-The-Mystical-Significance.htm; for satanic explanations, see "Testing the Star of David—119 Ministries."
68. "'Marching to Zion' Official Full Film—Youtube."
69. "'Marching to Zion' Official Full Film—Youtube."
70. "'Marching to Zion' Official Full Film—Youtube."
71. Bradley Artson, "God of Jews, God of Humanity," My Jewish Learning, accessed June 30, 2020, https://www.myjewishlearning.com/article/god-of-jews-god-of-humanity/.
72. "'Marching to Zion' Official Full Film—Youtube."
73. "'Marching to Zion' Official Full Film—Youtube."
74. Michael L. Brown, "Did Jesus Come to Be the Messiah? A Response to John Hagee's New Book, *In Defense of Israel*," True Light Ministries, June 2, 2008, https://truelightministries.org/2008/06/02/dr-michael-brown-and-john-hagee/.
75. John Hagee, *In Defense of Israel*, rev. ed. (Lake Mary, FL: FrontLine, 2007), 179.
76. "'Marching to Zion' Official Full Film—Youtube."
77. "'Marching to Zion' Official Full Film—Youtube."
78. See, for example, "Incredible!! A Messianic Jew on Israeli Reality Show Talks Abo...," Facebook video post, 8:00, posted by "ONE FOR ISRAEL Ministry," November 15, 2017, https://www.facebook.com/watch/?v=2024891930862089.
79. Gil Hoffman, "From Praising Jesus to Tweeting Bibi, PM's New Recruit Has Colorful Past," *Jerusalem Post*, April 24, 2018, https://www.jpost.com/Israel-News/Politics-And-Diplomacy/From-praising-Jesus-to-tweeting-Bibi-PMs-new-recruit-has-colorful-past-552612.
80. "'Marching to Zion' Official Full Film—Youtube."
81. See Harry *Ostrer, Legacy: A Genetic History of the Jewish People* (Oxford, UK: Oxford University Press, 2012); for a cautious assessment, see David B. Goldstein, *Jacob's Legacy: A Genetic View of Jewish History* (New Haven, CT: Yale University Press, 2008); see also Jon Entine, *Abraham's Children: Race, Identity, and the DNA of the Chosen People* (New York: Grand Central Publishing, 2007).
82. For a five-minute, animated video making this argument, see "Is God a Zionist?," YouTube video, 5:02, posted by "ASKDrBrown," December 13, 2019, https://www.youtube.com/watch?v=EnxE417ZNkg&.

Chapter 9

1. Vince Dhimos, "Jesus' Message to 'Christian' Zionists," New Silk Strategies, December 24, 2017, http://www.newsilkstrategies.com/news--analysis/jesus-message-to-christian-zionists.
2. See further Brown, *Answering Jewish Objections to Jesus, Volume 1*, 145–75; Brown, *Our Hands Are Stained With Blood*, 159–205; Brown, "The Seed as Christ in Galatians 3:16"; more broadly, see Michael L. Brown, *Answering Jewish Objections to Jesus, Volume 4: New Testament Objections* (Grand Rapids, MI: Baker Books, 2006).

3. For hundreds of years, the English-speaking church has wrongly called the letter of Jacob the letter of James, as James in Greek is actually Jacob. I believe it is high time to correct this error and attribute this epistle to the apostle Jacob instead of the apostle James. For more information on how Jacob became James, see Michael Brown, "Recovering the Lost Letter of Jacob," Charisma News, March 11, 2013, https://www.charismanews.com/opinion/38591-recovering-the-lost-letter-of-jacob.%20Note%20also%20that%20Jude%20is%20really%20Judah. Note also that Jude is really Judah.
4. Note also that the word *synagogue* in the Greek refers primarily to a place of assembly. And while it is used almost exclusively in the New Testament for Jewish gathering places, the Greek does not require that it be used only in reference to Jewish places of assembly.
5. The closest he comes to this is Philippians 3:1–3, in the context of warning these Gentile believers against Jewish believers who wanted them to be circumcised physically, calling these misguided Jewish believers dogs. Paul then writes with a strong rebuke, "For we are the circumcision, who worship by the Spirit of God and glory in Christ Jesus and put no confidence in the flesh" (v. 3). So he is saying that the circumcision that really matters is the spiritual circumcision, as in Romans 2:28–29. But once again, we do well to remember what Paul then said about physical circumcision in Romans 3:1. It matters in every way! This was even more true in Paul's day, when only the Jews had the Scriptures and the rest of the world lived in darkness because the gospel hadn't spread to the nations.
6. The ESV uses the term "them" in Romans 10:1, but many other translations of that verse, including the NIV, KJV, NKJV, and NLT, use the terms "Israelites" or "people of Israel."
7. C. K. Barrett, *The Epistle to the Romans*, Black's New Testament Commentary Series (Grand Rapids, MI: Baker Academic, 1991), 200.
8. Gordon D. Fee, *The First and Second Letters to the Thessalonians*, The New International Commentary on the New Testament Series (Grand Rapids, MI: Wm. B. Eerdmans Publishing Co., 2009), 95–96.
9. Brown, "The Seed as Christ in Galatians 3:16."

CHAPTER 10

1. William I. Brustein, *Roots of Hate: Anti-Semitism in Europe Before the Holocaust* (New York: Cambridge University Press, 2003).
2. Brustein, *Roots of Hate*, 49.
3. Brustein, *Roots of Hate*, 49.
4. For a useful discussion of the dating question, see Wikipedia, s.v. "Claudius' Expulsion of Jews From Rome," last modified November 10, 2019, https://en.wikipedia.org/wiki/Claudius%27_expulsion_of_Jews_from_Rome.
5. Barrett, *The Epistle to the Romans*, 197. For a discussion of the passages cited by Barrett, namely Matthew 21:43 and 27:25, see chapter 9.

6. Charles Hodge, *Commentary on the Epistle to the Romans*, rev. ed. (Philadelphia: Alfred Martien, 1873), 578.
7. On this last question, which may not have been directly on the minds of these Gentile Christians, see chapter 7.
8. Vlach, *Has the Church Replaced Israel?*, 1.
9. Vlach, *Has the Church Replaced Israel?*, 11. See also Walter C. Kaiser Jr., "An Assessment of 'Replacement Theology': The Relationship Between the Israel of the Abrahamic-Davidic Covenant and the Christian Church," *Mishkan* 71 (2013): 41, http://www.caspari.com/wp-content/uploads/2016/04/mishkan71.pdf; and Ronald E. Diprose, *Israel in the Development of Christian Thought* (Rome: Instituto Biblico Evangelico Italiano, 1998), 2.
10. This concept even comes up in the work of a respected New Testament scholar like Gary M. Burge in his book *Whose Land? Whose Promise? What Christians Are Not Being Told About Israel and the Palestinians*, rev. ed. (Cleveland, OH: Pilgrim Press, 2013).
11. See Brown, "The Seed as Christ in Galatians 3:16."
12. Kenneth L. Gentry, Jr., *He Shall Have Dominion: A Postmillennial Eschatology* (Tyler, TX: Institute for Christian Economics, 1992), 159, as quoted by Randall Price, "AD 70: Preterism's Prophetic Dead End," *Israel My Glory*, January/February 2005, https://israelmyglory.org/article/a-d-70-preterisms-prophetic-dead-end/.
13. David Chilton, *The Days of Vengeance* (Fort Worth, TX: Dominion Press, 1987), 43, https://archive.org/stream/DaysOfVengeance-DavidChilton/Days_of_Vengeance_David_Chilton_djvu.txt. See also Price, "AD 70." Price's article provides a useful refutation of these errors. Dr. Gary DeMar, another preterist cited by Price, was one of those who told me in a public dialogue that while God literally and physically scattered Israel, the promises to regather Israel would be fulfilled spiritually. For our dialogue, see "Dr. Brown Debates Dr. Gary DeMar on Israel and the Church," YouTube video, 2:09:52, June 25, 2015, posted by "ASKDrBrown," https://www.youtube.com/watch?time_continue=3&v=uKJwH7_5QqU&. Note that neither DeMar nor Gentry are full preterists. Price notes that David Chilton, before his passing, switched from partial preterism to full preterism.
14. David Chilton, *Paradise Restored: A Biblical Theology of Dominion* (Tyler, TX: Reconstruction Press, 1985), 224, as quoted by Price, "AD 70."
15. Vlach, *Has the Church Replaced Israel?*
16. Ronald E. Diprose, *Israel and the Church: The Origins and Effects of Replacement Theology* (Waynesboro, GA: Authentic Media, 2000).
17. Andrew D. Robinson, *Israel Betrayed, Volume 1: The History of Replacement Theology* (San Antonio, TX: Ariel Ministries, 2018); Paul R. Wilkinson, *Israel Betrayed, Volume 2: The Rise of Christian Palestinianism* (San Antonio, TX: Ariel Ministries, 2018).

18. Gerald R. McDermott, ed., *The New Christian Zionism: Fresh Perspectives on Israel and the Land* (Downers Grove, IL: InterVarsity Press, 2016).
19. Barry E. Horner, *Future Israel: Why Christian Anti-Judaism Must Be Challenged* (Nashville: B&H Academic, 2007); Barry E. Horner, *Eternal Israel: Biblical, Theological, and Historical Studies That Uphold the Eternal Distinctive Destiny of Israel* (Nashville: Wordsearch Academic, 2018).
20. Both comments were posted on December 12, 2019, on the "TRUNEWS and Rick Wiles EXPOSED!!" video on my YouTube channel.
21. See especially chapter 9.
22. These are all cited in Pawson, *Defending Christian Zionism*, 82.
23. See further Karsh, *Palestine Betrayed*; and Spencer, *The Palestinian Delusion*; for an enlightening, older perspective, see Samuel Katz, *Battleground: Fact and Fantasy in Palestine* (Toronto: Bantam Books, 1973).
24. Yotam Berger and Jack Khoury, "How Many Palestinians Live in Gaza and the West Bank? It's Complicated," *Haaretz*, March 28, 2018, https://www.haaretz.com/israel-news/how-many-palestinians-live-in-gaza-and-the-west-bank-it-s-complicated-1.5956630.
25. For more on the glorious future of this city, see chapter 11.
26. For discussion of Acts 1:6–8, again see chapter 11.
27. See the discussion of the Abrahamic covenant in Pawson, *Defending Christian Zionism*, chapter 2.
28. See "Hebrew Insights Into the Hardening of Pharaoh's Heart," YouTube video, 17:03, posted by "ASKDrBrown," February 2, 2016, https://www.youtube.com/watch?v=pdgJrx1MM6I.
29. Email sent April 19, 2019, and quoted here with his permission.
30. Mark Mietkiewicz, "Nobel Prize and the Jews," Canadian Jewish News, December 10, 2018, https://www.cjnews.com/living-jewish/nobel-prize-and-the-jews.
31. Mietkiewicz, "Nobel Prize and the Jews."
32. See, for example, Noah Efron, "The Real Reason Why Jews Win So Many Nobel Prizes," *Haaretz*, October 21, 2013, https://www.haaretz.com/opinion/.premium-the-real-reason-jews-win-so-many-nobels-1.5276705; and Mark Creeger, "Five Reasons Jews Win So Many Nobel Prizes," Tribe, accessed March 28, 2020, https://www.tribeuk.com/sites/default/files/tribe%20Spark5%20reasons%20Jews%20win%20so%20many%20Nobel%20prizes%20(2).pdf.
33. David Masci, "How Income Varies Among US Religious Groups," Pew Research Center, October 11, 2016, https://www.pewresearch.org/fact-tank/2016/10/11/how-income-varies-among-u-s-religious-groups/.
34. Masci, "How Income Varies Among US Religious Groups."

Chapter 11

1. Pawson, *Defending Christian Zionism*, 100. See further Mark S. Kinzer, *Jerusalem Crucified, Jerusalem Risen: The Resurrected Messiah, the Jewish People, and the Land of Promise* (Eugene, OR: Cascade Books, 2018).
2. Pawson, *Defending Christian Zionism*, 100.
3. "TruNews' Rick Wiles: A Christian Response to Michael Brown's Neo-Nazi Accusations."
4. Loper, *Kabbalah Secrets Christians Need to Know*, 127.
5. Chris Wright, "A Christian Approach to Old Testament Prophecy," in P. W. L. Walker, ed., *Jerusalem Past and Present in the Purposes of God* (Cambridge, UK: Tyndale House, 1992), 19, https://www.theologicalstudies.org.uk/pdf/jerusalem_wright.pdf.
6. Peter Wyns, *Understanding God's Great Plan: A Jewish, Christian, Bible Perspective* (n.p.: First Great Reward Publishing, 2020), chapter 2.
7. The word *Jerusalem* is found ten times in the Hebrew text but eleven times in some English translations.
8. This is clearly demonstrated by Samuel Whitefield, "Was Zechariah 14 Fulfilled in AD 70?," SamuelWhitefield.com, March 17, 2016, https://web.archive.org/web/20190325075403/https://samuelwhitefield.com/1630/was-zechariah-14-fulfilled-in-ad-70.
9. See "Is Jerusalem Babylon the Great?," YouTube video, 6:02, posted by "ASKDrBrown," September 1, 2016, https://www.youtube.com/watch?time_continue=1&v=iY4Zbs_H7Do&.
10. Pesach Wolicki, "A New Christian Antisemitism," *Jerusalem Post*, November 28, 2019, https://www.jpost.com/Opinion/A-new-Christian-antisemitism-609334. Used with permission.
11. Wolicki, "A New Christian Antisemitism."
12. Wolicki, "A New Christian Antisemitism."
13. Wolicki, "A New Christian Antisemitism."
14. Wolicki, "A New Christian Antisemitism."
15. Wolicki, "A New Christian Antisemitism."

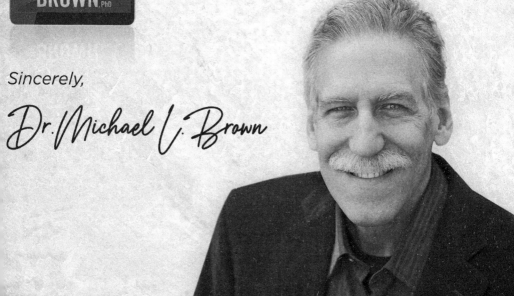